Learner-Centered Teaching

Learner-Centered Teaching

Five Key Changes to Practice

Maryellen Weimer

JOSSEY-BASS
A Wiley Company
San Francisco

Library of Congress Cataloging-in-Publication Data

Weimer, Maryellen, date.
    Learner-centered teaching: five key changes to practice/Maryellen Weimer.—1st ed.
        p. cm.—(The Jossey-Bass higher and adult education series)
Includes bibliographical references and index.
    ISBN 0-7879-5646-5 (alk. paper)
    1. College teaching. 2. Learning, Psychology of. I. Title II. Series.
    LB2331 .W39 2002
    378.1'2—dc21   2002005662

Printed in the United States of America
FIRST EDITION
HB Printing   10 9 8

The Jossey-Bass
Higher and Adult Education Series

Contents

For my aunt Barbara R. Friz,
in celebration of our splendid friendship
and in honor of her ninth decade

Preface

With more books on instruction than most faculty members have time to read and few professional incentives that encourage faculty to read pedagogical material, it seems prudent to begin by asking why. Why do we need yet another book on learning and teaching? It may be that authors lack some objectivity when it comes to answering the question, but it seems to me that there are five reasons that might be offered in support of this particular book. I did not have them this clearly in mind when I started, but as I now see the book in its entirety, I believe they justify yet another book on pedagogy, specifically one that explores how teaching might facilitate more and better learning.

This particular book is needed because after many years, the higher education community has finally discovered learning, and we need resources that further cultivate and capitalize on that interest. That we have so long ignored learning is somewhat difficult to explain. It seems more a case of benign neglect than willful rejection. Most of us just assumed that learning was an automatic, inevitable outcome of good teaching, and so we focused on developing our teaching skills. That we all but exclusively focused on them is a fact documented by even a cursory content review of the pedagogical literature. Its books, journals, magazines, and other publications address every aspect of how to teach, beginning with planning and ending with evaluation. No corresponding cadre of volumes describes learning at this level of detail.

As a result, practicing pedagogues know considerably less about learning than they do about teaching. We need resources that direct attention to learning in the same way they have focused attention on teaching. However, we do need to understand that the previous disconnect between teaching and learning has proved counterproductive. The learning outcomes of teaching cannot be assumed or taken for granted. This book aims to cultivate our understanding of learning, and it does so by connecting that knowledge to instructional practice. It addresses a simple question—the same question we should have been asking as we considered teaching: What do we know about learning that implicates teaching? That makes this book about learning also a book about teaching.

Second, despite the widespread interest in learning, few resources translate the talk into concrete policies and practices. Few identify the things a teacher should do if instruction is to promote learning. I am regularly perplexed and dismayed at how ideas and issues in higher education become trendy and faddish. Conferences feature them as themes, periodical publications prepare special issues on the topic, and blue ribbon committees write reports on their state within institutions. But does all this attention generate change in instructional practice? I am doubtful, in part because most of the talk occurs at such a high level of abstraction. The discourse advocates for learning, but seldom gets down to the level of detail. We are now all in favor of learning, just as we all aspire to be thin, but we have not changed what we cook and serve students.

To produce change at the level of practice, we need to translate what we know about learning into concrete instructional policies and practices. We need resources that set out to teachers who want to promote learning what to do about attendance, assignments, tests, papers, lecturing, group work, classroom management, content, and grades. I believe that most faculty care about learning and would like to teach in ways that promote it. If resources would deal with the nuts and bolts of instructional practice, I think most faculty would attend and start making some of those changes.

It would be presumptuous and inappropriate to present a definitive set of policies and practices that promote learning, but faculty need ideas and examples, and that is what this book aims to provide. It seeks to answer this question: What should teachers *do* in order to maximize learning outcomes for their students? It aspires to move the talk about learning down to the level of details and to make it more nourishing. I am concerned that if we continue to feed the interest in learning with nothing more than rhetoric, it will not flourish and grow into better instructional practice.

Third, we need resources that propose learner-centered strategies based on what is known about learning. The need to connect practice to what has been discovered empirically is obvious. Behind all the policies, practices, and behaviors used to facilitate learning ought to be some theoretical or empirical rationale. The justification ought to be more substantive than doing something because it has always been done that way. And yet many of us have taught for years, operating from an eclectic, idiosyncratic knowledge base grounded almost exclusively on personal experience. It is as if the two closely related territories of research and practice are separate planets, unknown and seemingly inaccessible to one another.

Who should build the bridges necessary to connect research and practice? Those who do the research tend not to be faculty who daily face passive students who are taking required courses. I once worked with a well-known researcher who studies college students and has multiple books and publications to show for it. We were working on a project in which we conducted focus group interviews with students. My colleague was very excited; I was amazed and appalled when I discovered why. "This is the first time I've done a research project where we actually talked with students," this researcher told me.

After that experience, I thought differently about the propriety of researchers' drawing implications from their findings. But if not researchers, should the task be left to practitioners untrained in the relevant disciplines? As it stands now, the task is the responsibility of no one, and so few in the academy try to connect research and practice. Those of us who do build the bridges with no blueprints to follow and few rewards to honor our work. But we keep building because it seems so clear to us that these territories are beneficially connected in theory and practice.

Looking toward practice from the research side, it is clear that teaching needs to change in some fundamental ways. I have confessed to some of my colleagues that I am glad I am writing this book now and not at the beginning of my career when my skin was thin and optimism unrelenting. Many will find the changes I propose disturbing. They challenge long-held assumptions and traditional ways of thinking about instructional roles and responsibilities. I expect they will spark controversy. My hope is that this disagreement will motivate others to review the research, study the theory, reflect on practice, and then build better and stronger bridges between research and practice. Much more of what we do in the classroom needs to be based on what we know.

In addition, but in some ways in contrast to resources that build on the empirical knowledge base, we also need books on teaching and learning that treat the wisdom or practice with more intellectual robustness. What little scholarship that practicing pedagogues complete is almost exclusively experientially based. And what we have learned in the school of hard knocks and by the seat of our pants is definitely worth knowing and worth passing on. However, much of that knowledge is idiosyncratic, isolated, unreflective, nonanalytical, and sometimes even anti-intellectual, and it gets lost in the great undifferentiated mass of anecdotal evidence about teaching. This great repository of experiential knowledge—what is justifiably called the wisdom of practice—remains unknown and devalued. Until it becomes characterized by the kind of intellectual rigor that faculty associate with scholarship, it will ineffectively advance instructional causes.

We need books on teaching and learning that treat experiential knowledge more analytically and more objectively. I have aspired to write such a book, one that deeply and honestly traces my own growth and development as a teacher and positions my experience against that of many other pedagogues who are working to make teaching more learner-centered. My efforts do not stand-alone; they need to be reported in the context of what is known and what others have experienced.

I have aspired to write a book that is more than just another technique-based, how-to treatment of teaching skills. It includes many techniques, because faculty find instructional details of great interest. But techniques need to be presented in ways that reflect the dynamic, complicated milieu in which they will be used. Having instructional techniques is one thing; being able to manage a repertoire of them is something quite else. Techniques need to be presented cognizant of the process by and through which they can be transformed to fit the content configurations of different disciplines. Techniques should not be presented as isolated ideas but as working parts of a coherent, integrated approach to teaching.

And finally, I have aspired to write a book on teaching and learning that is intellectually robust—one that makes us think, challenges unexamined assumptions, asks hard questions, and does not offer facile answers. I wanted to write a book that makes us appreciate what hard, mentally stimulating work teaching and learning can be. That kind of book values, indeed honors, the wisdom of practice. We need many more books of that caliber.

Finally, we need this book because it offers a positive way to improve teaching. Despite efforts during the past twenty-five years, instructional improvement has been slow in coming. Little documentation can be summoned that supports overall improvement in the level of instructional quality. Faculty development continues to operate at the margins, thriving in times of supportive administrations and withering when the institutional commitment to the teaching "excellence" center culminates in being able to say that we have one.

Faculty development has taught us some important lessons, one of the clearest being that efforts to improve instruction cannot be based on premises of remediation and deficiency. If faculty must admit they have a problem before they get help, most never seek assistance. Ask faculty members if they are interested in improving their teaching, and the response is almost always defensive. "Why? Did somebody tell you I need to?" Or, "Why should I? Teaching doesn't matter around here anyway."

But asking the learning question changes the paradigm completely. What self-respecting, even curmudgeonly, faculty member can respond any way other than positively if asked, "Are you interested in how much and how well your students learn?" And once they have said yes, what we know about learning easily and clearly links to teaching. But now we talk about ways of changing teaching that promote more and better learning. It is no longer about what is wrong and ineffective; it is about what best achieves a goal that faculty endorse. This book makes a contribution by basing instructional improvement on a positive and productive paradigm.

Distinctions Worth Noting

A couple of distinctions about this book are worth noting. First, this book is about being learner-centered. Some may associate that with being student-centered and use the two terms interchangeably. I make a number of significant distinctions between the two phrases and have chosen not to use the student-centered descriptor.

Being student-centered implies a focus on student needs. It is an orientation that gives rise to the idea of education as a product, with the student as the customer and the role of the faculty as one of serving and satisfying the customer. Faculty resist the student-as-customer metaphor for some very good reasons. When the product is education, the customer cannot always be right, there is no money-back guarantee, and tuition dollars do not "buy" the desired grades.

Being learner-centered focuses attention squarely on learning: what the student is learning, how the student is learning, the conditions under which the student is learning, whether the student is retaining and applying the learning, and how current learning positions the student for future learning. The student is still an important part of the equation. In fact, we make the distinction between learner-centered instruction and teacher-centered instruction as a way of indicating that the spotlight has moved from teacher to student. When instruction is learner-centered, the action focuses on what students (not teachers) are doing.

Because the instructional action now features students, this learner-centered orientation accepts, cultivates, and builds on the ultimate responsibility students have for learning. Teachers cannot do it for students. They may set the stage, so to speak, and help out during rehearsals, but then it is up to students to perform, and when they do learn, it is the student, not the teacher, who should receive accolades.

One of this book's reviewers recommended changing *learner-centered* to *learning-centered*. I opted not to make this change because I want to keep the focus on learners, on students, not as customers to be satisfied but as the direct recipients of efforts aimed at promoting learning. Learning is an abstraction, and much like content, for an audience that by its culture tends to gravitate toward that which is theoretical and abstract, I want to keep us firmly rooted and fixed on the direct object of our teaching: students. We do not want more and better learning at some abstract level; we need it specifically and concretely for the students we face in class. We do not need teaching connected to learning on some conceptual plane; we need instructional policies and practices with a direct impact on how much and how well students learn.

Finally, in addition to focusing on learning *and* students (as opposed to an exclusive student- or learning-centered focus), the learner-centered approach orients to the idea of "product quality" constructively. Being learner-centered is not about cowering in the competitive academic marketplace. It is not about kowtowing to student demands for easy options and is not about an ethically irresponsible diminution of academic standards in an attempt to placate "shoppers" who may opt to purchase educational products elsewhere. It is about creating climates in classes and on campus that advance learning outcomes. It is an orientation that advocates for more, not less, learning. It is about offering a better product.

Overview of the Contents

Chapter One recounts the story of how this book came to be and introduces the literature on learning on which it is based. Out of the experiences and literature described there, I have come to believe that in order to be learner-centered, instructional practice needs to change in five areas. Each of those changes is introduced and described in detail in Chapters Two through Six, with each change the focus of one chapter. These chapters are the heart of the book. The last three chapters are devoted to implementation details. Thus, this book is not just about what teachers need to do; it also addresses how they should go about implementing what has been proposed.

Chapter Two explores changes associated with the balance of power in the classrooms. It documents the extent to which faculty control learning processes and how those authoritarian, directive actions diminish student motivation and ultimately result in dependent learners, unwilling and unable to assume responsibility for their own learning. The solution is not an abrogation of legitimate faculty power—that born of content expertise and long experience as learners and teachers. Rather, it outlines some policies and practices with the potential to redress the power imbalance, ways that responsibly share power with students in the interest of positively influencing their motivation and learning.

Chapter Three tackles the function of content when the goal is instruction that promotes more and better learning. Here the problem is "coverage" and all that metaphor has come to imply about the amount and complexity of content necessary to gain credibility for a course and its instructor. But content coverage does not develop the learning skills needed to function effectively on the job and in society. When teaching is learner-centered, content is *used,* not *covered,* and it is used to establish a knowledge foundation, just as it has been. In addition, and just as important, content is used to develop learning skills. These learning skills are not only or mostly basic study skills, even though these are needed; they are the sophisticated skills necessary to sustain learning across a career and a lifetime. And finally, when teaching is learner-centered, it uses encounters with content to create an awareness of the self as a unique, individual learner. The function of content is enlarged and diversified, and this has implications for how much content can be covered in a course.

When teaching is learner-centered, the role of the teacher changes, as detailed in Chapter Four. Learner-centered teachers are guides, facilitators, and designers of learning experiences. They are no longer the main performer, the one with the most lines, or the one working harder than everyone else to make it all happen. The action in the learner-centered classroom features the students. Teaching action expedites learning. This includes the careful design of experiences, activities, and assignments through which the students encounter the content. It also includes being there during the encounter to offer guidance, explanations, wise counsel, critique, and encouragement. It means being there afterward with praise and with the kind of constructive critique that motivates an even better performance next time. It is a very different role for teachers who have sought to improve their teaching by cultivating effective presentation skills and one we are finding difficult to execute, even though we may understand and accept the intellectual rationale on which it rests.

Chapter Five's contents are inextricably linked to those of Chapter Two. Faculty share power so that students can make more decisions about the terms and conditions of their learning, but with increased freedom comes more responsibility. The responsibility for learning changes when the environment is learner-centered.

Beset with poorly prepared, passive learners who are neither confident nor empowered, faculty have compensated by setting all the rules and conditions for learning. Learner-centered environments are not rule-bound, token economies but places where learners understand and accept the responsibilities that belong to them. They come to class not because an attendance policy requires them but because they see the activities and events of class time as making important contributions to their learning. They see themselves as growing into ever more responsible learners. To develop these kinds of students, faculty must use policies and practices that start students down the road to intellectual maturity.

And finally for the changes, Chapter Six describes how the purpose and processes of evaluation change when teaching is learner-centered. As evaluation activities have come to be used to generate grades, faculty have lost sight of how powerfully these activities can promote learning. Learner-centered teachers still give grades, but they do so in the course of a series of events carefully orchestrated to realize as much of the learning potential as possible. And evaluation processes change as well. No longer do faculty do all the evaluation, although they continue to do the final grading; peers and the learners themselves are involved in evaluation activities. The ability to self-assess accurately and constructively judge the work of peers is an essential learning skill that teachers have the responsibility to develop during their students' college years.

Chapters Seven through Nine deal with implementation issues. Successful implementation of learner-centered teaching depends to no small degree on the faculty members' ability to handle issues in three areas. Chapter Seven addresses a common response to learner-centered teaching: resistance from students and colleagues. Once faculty move to an approach to teaching that emphasizes learning, they tend to do so with considerable enthusiasm and are often surprised and dismayed when the reaction of others is quite the opposite. Students make clear, sometimes passively and sometimes openly, their preference for the way things used to be. Colleagues ask pointed questions and make comments about lowering standards and pandering to students. The chapter explores the sources of that resistance, what it looks like when it is expressed, and ways that teachers can respond so that students and colleagues can be helped to move beyond this initial response.

Along with resistance, a second key implementation issue involves the developmental processes associated with the movement of students from being passive, dependent learners to becoming autonomous, intrinsically motivated, and self-regulating. It is a growth process that does not happen automatically or all at once. Faculty who aspire to be learner-centered teachers must be able to intervene productively in the process. Chapter Eight discusses what is known about the development of students as learners and proposes ways to sequence and organize learning experiences so that they positively influence the developmental process.

And finally, for a variety of reasons, faculty often assume instructional improvement tasks alone and unaided. Imagining that this book is the colleague alongside a faculty member's efforts to become learner-centered, Chapter Nine offers general advice on instructional improvement and specific counsel when the change agenda is learner-centered teaching.

Structure of the Change Chapters

Chapters Two through Six, each devoted to one of the five changes proposed to make teaching learner-centered, use the same organizational structure. This content is the heart of the book, and considering each area of change in terms of a shared set of chapter sections makes it easier to see how they are different but very much interdependent.

All begin by making the case against current instructional practice. The tone in these sections tends to be argumentative in order to make clear those aspects of current practice that I believe research has shown negatively affect learning outcomes. These sections then provide the rationale for change. I also use them for comparative purposes. The change can be seen and understood more clearly when it is benchmarked against current instructional practice.

The second section in these chapters defines, describes, and otherwise delineates the nature of the change. After exploring the change in detail, I identify what benefits it accrues. Sometimes these benefits turn out to be solutions to the problems identified in the first section. Other times the benefits accrue in areas unrelated to the problems. But in both cases, they are about improved learning outcomes.

The third section moves to the details, examples, and illustrations of the change operationalized as policies, practices, behaviors, assignments, and activities. For each of the changes, this is the section that answers the how-would-you-do-it question. It proposes a set of instructional practices that promote more and better learning. Not everything possible can be included in these sections, and certainly the examples themselves can be debated in terms of whether they effectively translate the relevant learning principles.

Each of these chapters ends with a section that raises the questions that have emerged out of my own efforts to implement learner-centered teaching. They are not questions I have found answered in the literature and yet seem central to the advancement of this approach to teaching. I deliberated at length about including a section like this. It seems risky to be writing a book before having all the answers. But I include them because I believe raising the hard, complicated questions and refusing to answer them in trite, simplistic ways demonstrates the intellectual richness that is part of critical reflective practice. Like many others, I am still in the process of learning to teach in this way. Moreover, as we tell students, sometimes we learn more from the questions than from the answers.

Although each of the five changes is discussed in a separate chapter, they are interconnected and overlapping. Some activities, assignments, and practices done to advance one may help to accomplish one of the others at the same time. Some of the changes are inseparably linked. For example, giving students more voice in the learning decisions that affect them (Chapter Two) should not occur unless those students accept the increased responsibility (Chapter Six) that is inherently a part of individual decision making.

Making teaching learner-centered requires nontrivial changes in instructional practices, even though all can (and probably should) be implemented incrementally. These changes are fundamental and far reaching. Most of us tend to improve our teaching by fussing around the edges, adding a new technique here and a different assignment there. Learner-centered teaching, in contrast, represents an entirely new way of thinking about teaching and learning tasks and responsibilities. It is transformational. As you start down this road, you need to realize that it will take you to a very different instructional place. Sometimes I hardly recognize the teacher I have become.

Yet as comprehensive as these changes are, they do not constitute some radical departure from instructional sanity. This is not about giving away all instructor authority. It is not about content-free courses. It is not about some greatly diminished instructional role for the teacher. It is not about giving students more responsibility than they are prepared to handle. And it is not about students' assigning grades. Learner-centered teaching is responsible instruction. Best of all, it is about teaching in ways that promote more and better learning.

Acknowledgments

No book happens without the support of many people. Among the people to thank are a number of colleagues at the campus where I teach: David Bender (who also reviewed the manuscript), Maureen Bokansky, Henry Patterson, Sheila Ridley, Ike Shibley, Lisa Shibley, and Blaine Steensland. I work with many wonderful people, but these folks have supported me in some very special ways. I am indebted to my friend and the former dean and CEO of the Berks Lehigh Valley College, Fred Gaige, who supported my request for a leave, when I wrote most of this book. As the years of one's career stretch out, colleagues come and go, but some stay, and those productive professional associations grow into firm friendships. Those colleagues are special, and I am lucky to have Chris Knapper as one of mine.

My original book proposal benefited enormously from feedback offered by long-time Jossey-Bass higher education editor Gale Erlandson. The higher education literature, especially that on teaching and learning, is much richer because of the strong, consistent editorial leadership she provided for many years. The manuscript was strengthened by insights of three external reviewers, and I received wise editorial counsel from David Brightman at Jossey-Bass.

I am blessed to have had the love and support of my parents and brother, John and Margaret Robertson and Mark Robertson, throughout my career. I had four aunts, all extremely important persons in my life; two remain: Ellen P. Bump and Barbara R. Friz. I dedicated my first book to Ellen, and this one is for Barbara. And finally there is my husband, Michael. He lets me work on weekends. He fixes supper and feeds the pets. He builds boats, beds, and birdfeeders. He puts racing decals on my truck. He is the love of my life.

April 2002   MARYELLEN WEIMER
                                                                            Marsh Creek, Pennsylvania

The Author

In 1994, Maryellen Weimer returned to the classroom as a full-time faculty member after thirteen years in administrative and research positions. She teaches communication courses at the Berks Lehigh Valley College of The Pennsylvania State University and is an associate professor of teaching and learning. Between 1998 and 2000, she served as one of the college's academic officers on an interim appointment.

Previously she was an associate director of the National Center on Postsecondary Teaching, Learning and Assessment, a five-year U.S. Department of Education research and development center. This center was part of the Center for the Study of Higher Education at Penn State, where she was a senior research associate.

Weimer has a Ph.D. in speech communication from Penn State, which she received in 1981. For the next ten years, she directed Penn State's Instructional Development Program.

She has consulted with over 175 colleges and universities on instructional issues and has delivered keynote addresses at national meetings and regional conferences. Recently, she conducted faculty development work in Singapore and Hong Kong.

Weimer has published widely and has served on the editorial boards of four journals. Since 1987, she has edited *Teaching Professor*, a monthly newsletter on college teaching. She has edited or authored eight books, including one on faculty development, one on teaching for new faculty, and an anthology edited with Robert Menges, *Teaching on Solid Ground*. Most recently, she was primary author of *Teaching Tools*, a collection of collaborative, active, and inquiry-based approaches to be used in conjunction with *Biological Perspectives*, an introductory biology textbook funded by the National Science Foundation and created by Biological Sciences Curriculum Studies.

Learner-Centered Teaching

Chapter One

Lessons on Learning

What I have come to believe about learner-centered teaching grew out of a serendipitous confluence of events and experiences. I will highlight three of the most important, roughly in the order in which they occurred, although all three overlap and are so intertwined that a stream-of-consciousness recounting would more accurately reflect the nonorder of their occurrence.

In 1994, after almost fifteen years of working in faculty development, disseminating educational materials, a variety of administrative assignments, and teaching the occasional upper-division and graduate courses, I returned to the classroom to teach entry-level required courses to beginning students. It was a sort of a midlife career move. As I took stock in midcareer, I realized that the most important and personally satisfying work I had done, the work with the greatest chance of making a difference, was work I completed in the classroom. I decided to return, finishing out my career as it had started, by teaching undergraduates.

At that time, I was motivated not to teach as I had during the first years of my career. Students had changed, and much more was known about their learning needs. As I thought about the beginning communication course I was to teach, it seemed to me that what prevented students from doing well was a lack of confidence. They needed to find their way past self-doubt, awkwardness, and the fear of failure to a place where they could ask a question in class, make a contribution in a group, and speak coherently in front of peers. It came to me that I might address the problem by making the students feel more in control. Would it help if I

1

presented them with some choices and let them make some of the decisions about their learning?

That first semester back, I tried this approach. I designed a beginning public speaking course that had only one required assignment: students had to give one speech. The rest of the syllabus presented a cafeteria of assignment options: a learning log, group projects of various sorts, credit for participation and the analysis of it, critiques of peers, conducting an interview or being interviewed or both, and conventional multiple-choice exams. Each assignment had a designated point value and evaluation criteria. Students could opt for as many or as few assignments as they wished, given the course grade they desired. Each assignment had a due date, and once past, that assignment could not be completed.

Initially, students were totally confused. I remember arguing with one about whether the exams were required. Here is how the conversation went:

"They must be required," the student insisted. "If the test is optional, no one will take it."

"Sure they will," I replied. "Students need points to pass the class."

"But what if I don't take it?"

"Fine. Do other assignments, and get your points that way."

"But what do I do on exam day?"

"Don't come to class if you aren't taking the exam."

Several students asked me to identify the assignments they should do, and virtually everyone wanted some sort of approval once they finally decided.

But what happened the rest of that first semester took my breath away. I had no attendance policy, but better attendance than in any class I could remember. More (not all, but most) students started to work hard early in the course, and some students determinedly announced that they would do every assignment if that was what it took to get enough points for an A. I was stunned by how willing they were to work, and with no complaints. Less concrete but no less real was the change in atmosphere and energy in the class. These students were committed to the class; they appeared genuinely interested in the content. They asked more questions, sustained discussion longer, and in the end disagreed with me and other students far more than I remembered my former beginning students doing. It was not instructional nirvana, but it was a decided improvement, and I was motivated to continue refining this approach.

Early in my experimentation with the course, I was asked to review a manuscript under contract with Jossey-Bass and subsequently published as *Becoming a Critically Reflective Teacher* (Brookfield, 1995). Few other publications I read before or since have so dramatically influenced my pedagogical thinking. The book took me in two different directions. (I describe the second later in this chapter when I get to the third major event that motivated me to write this book.)

Through Brookfield's book, I discovered how much about teaching can be learned by and through critical reflective practice. Brookfield describes methods that allow one to take a common instructional practice and through a process of analysis see the assumptions about teachers, students, and learning embedded in that particular practice. It was as if someone had held a mirror up to my teaching. In that reflection, I saw a different, and not very flattering, instructional image: an authoritarian, controlling teacher who directed the action, often totally unaware of and blissfully oblivious to the impact of those policies, practices, and behaviors on student learning and motivation. Displays of instructor power were present everywhere. I came to realize that the classroom environment I created ended up being a place where *I* could succeed and do well. Student learning just happened, an assumed outcome of instructional action that featured me.

Before reading Brookfield's book, I had redesigned my course; afterward, I attempted to redesign the teacher. Getting the course reshaped turned out to be much easier than fixing my very teacher-centered instruction. Flachmann (1994, p. 2) captures exactly how I felt then and now:

> I'm a little embarrassed to tell you that I used to want credit for having all the intelligent insights in my classroom. I worked hard to learn these facts. . . . I secretly wanted my students to look at me with reverence. I now believe that the opposite effect should occur—that the oracle, the locus and ownership of knowledge, should reside in each student and our principal goal as teachers

must be to help our students discover the most important and enduring answers to life's problems within themselves. Only then can they truly possess the knowledge that we are paid to teach them [p. 2].

A second event strongly influenced my thinking about learning and ultimately became another reason for writing this book. For years, my husband, Michael, aspired to build a wooden boat. He collected books, bought plans, subscribed to *Wooden Boat* magazine, and faithfully watched "Classic Boat" on Speed Vision (a cable TV channel devoted to racing). Then we bought property on an island, and it was time to build the wooden boat. We planned to build a house on the island and needed a boat big enough to haul supplies to the site. Armed with a set of blueprints (selected after having reviewed hundreds), he started on the hull. First, it was the frame and battens. His vocabulary changed; he talked of chines, sheer clamps, the kellson, and garboard. Then it was covering the hull with marine plywood, not something easily obtained in land-locked central Pennsylvania. The whole neighborhood showed up to help turn the hull. Next came the floor, designing the cabin, and finally the motor. At every step, there was a whole new set of tasks to learn. In our video collection, we have several tapes demonstrating fiber-glassing techniques. We still get catalogues from more marine supply companies than I ever imagined existed.

From nothing but hours of work and an unwavering confidence that he could figure out what he needed to know emerged *Noah's Lark,* a twenty-four-foot, lobster-style, wooden boat. She has a sleek white hull and dashing yellow stripe and a beautifully finished ash cabin, and she's powered by a fully rebuilt but not terribly fuel-efficient Merc Cruiser. She sits gracefully in the water, rises to a stylish plane, and cuts steady and stable through whitecaps and waves. She reliably tows barge loads of micro lam beams, bags of concrete, and sheets of plywood. Dockside, *Noah's Lark* turns heads. The bold inquire, "Where did you get that boat?" "Built her," my husband replies, unable to hide the pride in his voice.

It takes much more time and money to build a wooden boat than I had imagined. But after dealing with those realities, what amazed me most was the confidence my husband brought to the task. Where did it come from? On what was it based? He had never built a boat before—houses yes, furniture yes, but not a boat. As the bills kept coming in, I felt it financially prudent to keep asking, "Do you know what you're doing? Is this really going to turn out?" His answer was always the same, "No, I don't know what I'm doing, but I'm learning. Of course, it will turn out. We need a boat, don't we?"

At some level, I was really asking myself if I would tackle a project this complicated, this expensive, and this time-consuming if I knew as little as he did about it. And at another level, I knew the answer: I would not. Furthermore, I could not imagine any of my students doing it. Neither they nor I had faith that we could figure out this or many other complicated learning tasks that came to mind once I started thinking about them.

There was an irony here that stuck in my craw: Michael's confidence as a learner did not come from his experience of obtaining a degree in industrial engineering. In fact, quite the opposite had occurred. He graduated from college feeling that he had just squeaked by, keenly disappointed with what he had learned, and stressed by the conditions under which he was expected to learn it. He credits experiences with his father for developing his confidence. It irritated me that rather than reinforcing his confidence, his college experience had undermined it.

College should be the time when and the place where students develop prowess as learners. I started thinking about what kind of college experiences would result in learning skills as sophisticated and confidence as heart-felt as his. I came to accept that one of my tasks as a teacher was developing lifelong learning skills and the confidence to use them. What kind of teaching, assignments, and classroom environment would accomplish that? How would those kinds of learning experiences be evaluated?

Having accepted that goal, I saw course content in a whole new light. It moved from being the end to being the means. It went from being something I covered to something I used to develop learning skills and an awareness of learning processes. I saw evaluation as something much more meaningful than the mechanism whereby grades are generated. It become a potent venue for promoting learning and developing self- and peer assessment skills.

Although both of these experiences were instrumental in my early and continuing development as a learner-centered teacher, they are by no means the only events of consequence. Across the years and lessons learned, I have been informed, inspired, provoked, and encouraged by the occasional article and book, most of them personally reflective, that describe the attempts of others to move teaching to a different and more learner-centered place. My favorites are in the reading lists in Appendix C. If you learn more about yourself as a teacher by reading thoughtful reflections of other teachers, I recommend that reading list.

The Literature on Learning

In addition to these firsthand experiences, there was a third significant force in my development as a learner-centered teacher. Brookfield's book took me in two directions. In addition to introducing me to critical reflective practice, it was the starting point for a lengthy and still not completed trip around and through the literature on learning. After reviewing that manuscript, I realized how little I knew of and about learning, and so I started reading some of the radical and critical pedagogy referenced in that book, which led me to work on constructivism. Next, I got into self-directed learning and from there into the work in cognitive and educational psychology on deep and surface learning, motivation, perceived control, help-seeking behavior, and a host of other topics. Somewhere along the way, I explored feminist scholarship on pedagogy. I could not believe the trove of literature on learning that exists.

Before I knew it, I was imagining summarizing all this work, condensing and integrating it, and writing about it with clarity. Then I would extrapolate instructional implications from the findings, finally closing the gap between theory and practice. Had I been twenty years younger, I can see myself pursuing this noble and needed objective. But being older and wiser, I saw the folly of trying to corral a literature this vast. Understanding even a bit about the nature of this literature makes it obvious why that task is not easily accomplished. Three features in particular show how difficult it is to summarize what we know about learning.

First, the literature is vast. Interest in learning may be recent, but the study of it is not. It spans decades, starting in modern times with the work of Dewey. It crosses disciplines with work being done in education and various subfields like educational psychology, higher education, and adult education. Other relevant work is underway in women's studies and psychology. Still more work has been completed in fields with content totally unrelated to learning, like engineering and math. And finally there are interdisciplinary initiatives, like practitioner-oriented work on active learning, group work and inquiry-based approaches, the writing across the curriculum movement, and multicultural curricular reforms. Besides occurring across the decades and in multiple disciplinary contexts, the research and theory on learning is literally being completed around the world. It is a body of literature that would take a lifetime to read and another one to summarize and integrate.

Second, add to the vastness of the literature on learning the fact that this body of knowledge remains largely unassembled. It resembles a giant jigsaw puzzle that has a whole community working on it. A few sections are more or less finished. Collections of related but not yet connected pieces lie close together in other sections. And there are still a lot of individual pieces, definitely part of the puzzle but currently just spread out on the table. I do not mean to convey the impression that what is known about learning exists in some exceptional state of disarray. Like all other puzzles, this one comes with the picture on the box: we know what learning looks like when it happens. And what is still not known about how it all fits together could be said of the state of knowledge in many other fields. We push forward the horizons of knowledge faster than we map the newly discovered lands. But the disparate state of this vast knowledge base makes it more difficult to say how findings in one field and on one topic relate to what has been discovered in other fields and on different topics.

Finally, the task of extrapolating principles from the learning literature is made difficult by the ongoing separation of research and practice. For the most part, research results are presented with implications identified for future research. You can read many research studies, even the theoretical postulations that inform research, and rarely encounter advice for the practitioner. Some books and articles are exceptions, but recommendations for applying in the classroom what is being advanced as knowledge about learning are not regularly offered.

Despite the difficulty of corralling and making applicable this unwieldy knowledge base, we have missed much by remaining ignorant of so much of it. I return to my own practice and see how much it has been influenced (and I hope improved) by even this not very systematic, decidedly eclectic, meandering journey through the literature on learning. If more faculty encountered the literature, it would not only nourish and sustain the current interest in learning; it would also change practice.

Five Key Changes to Practice

As a consequence of my review of the literature, I believe that in order to be learner-centered, instructional practice needs to change in the five ways introduced in the Preface and elaborated in the next five chapters. Those changes are consistent with and supported by the literature on learning.

The Balance of Power

The influences of power on the motivation to learn and on learning outcomes themselves are a major theme in the writings of the radical and critical (the terms are used interchangeably) pedagogues and in feminist pedagogy. Freire (1993) first and most definitively articulated what has become the central tenet of critical pedagogy: education can be a vehicle for social change. Stage, Muller, Kinzie, and Simmons (1998, p. 57) elaborate: "Education's role is to challenge inequality and dominant myths rather than socialize students into the status quo. Learning is directed toward social change and transforming the world, and 'true' learning empowers students to challenge oppression in their lives."

As an educator in Brazil, Freire developed his theories of education and social change as he taught illiterate peasants to read and empowered them to challenge corrupt political regimes. Many object to the political agenda attached to education by this philosophy, especially those who see the advance and acquisition of

knowledge as an objective, rational process. The critical pedagogues counter that all "forms of education are contextual and
political whether or not teachers and students are consciously
aware of these processes" (Stage, Muller, Kinzie, and Simmons
1998, p. 57). Tompkins (1991, p. 26) illustrates the thinking of critical pedagogy when she describes the classroom:

> We tell ourselves we need to teach our students to think critically
> so that they can detect the manipulations of advertising, analyze
> the fallacious rhetoric of politicians and expose the ideology
> of popular TV shows, resist the stereotypes of class, race and
> gender. . . . But I have come to think more and more that what
> really matters . . . is not so much what we talk about in class as
> what we do. . . . The classroom is a microcosm of the world; it is
> the chance we have to practice whatever ideals we cherish. The
> kind of classroom situation one creates is the acid test of what
> it is one really stands for [p. 26].

In the same vein, feminist bell hooks (1994, p. 12) characterizes
classrooms as "radical spaces of possibility."

In the classrooms of the critical pedagogues, teacher authority
figures do not dispense knowledge. My ideas about how to redistribute power in the classroom were most strongly influenced by a
masterfully edited conversation between Horton and Freire (1990;
Horton's theories of education emerged out of his work preparing
blacks to pass voting tests). Another scholar writing about Freire
(Aronowitz, 1993, pp. 8–9) operationalizes what Tompkins describes and what Freire did when he taught: "He means to offer a
system in which the locus of the learning process is shifted from
the teacher to the students. And this shift overtly signifies an
altered *power* relationship, not only in the classroom but in the
broader social canvas as well." Very persuasive to me was the fact
that both Freire and Horton shifted power and control to cohorts
of students most faculty would consider unprepared to assume
responsibility for learning.

With feminist pedagogy, the frame of reference is more focused and the issues gendered, but the critique of existing educational theory and practice is no less comprehensive. On issues
of power, feminist pedagogy finds that teaching is too authoritarian, power in the classroom is not equitably distributed, and the

imbalance negatively affects learning outcomes, especially for women. Higher education has long been male dominated, and the forms of patriarchy so entrenched in society have also found root in the academy and its classrooms. As a result, students (usually females, especially in male-dominated fields) are often treated differentially. Learning is limited and inhibited when power structures protect and preserve the powerful.

Also inherent in the work of feminist pedagogues is a critique of the competitive aspects of education. They believe that historically, education has done a good job of teaching students to be competitive. It has much less successfully taught the lessons of co-operation. (For an interesting and compelling case against the competitive aspects of various educational practices, see Kohn, 1986. Grading on a curve does not make much sense from the evidence presented in this book.)

Because the messages of both radical and feminist pedagogy are confrontational and the agenda political, discussion of this work is often cantankerous. Moreover, the work done by radical pedagogues uses highly specialized jargon that makes it difficult to read. Although I have treated work done by radical and feminist pedagogues together in this brief discussion, there are distinctions and disagreements despite the fact that both deal with many of the same issues. This work calls into question traditional power structures and the role of authority in the classroom. Alternatively, it proposes more democratic and egalitarian views of education that open it to the possibility of different kinds of learning. These shifts have dramatic effects on student motivation and engagement.

The Function of Content

What content contributes to and in the learning process is addressed in empirical work carried out in cognitive and educational psychology. Some of the most important was launched with a seminal study by Marton and Saljo (1976, updated and analyzed in Marton, Hounsell, and Entwistle, 1997), who had students read material from an academic textbook and then asked them to describe what they had been reading. Ramsden (1988, p. 18), another important scholar working in this area, has succinctly summarized their findings: "They found evidence of *qualitative* differences in the outcome of students' reading. The differences were not about how much the students could remember, but about the meaning the author had tried to convey. Some students fully understood the argument being advanced and could relate it to the evidence being used to support it; others partly understood the author's message; others could only mention some of the remembered details."

When students concentrated on memorizing the facts, focused on the discrete elements of the reading, failed to differentiate between evidence and information, were unreflective, and saw the task as an external imposition, Marton and Saljo characterized their approach as surface learning. When students focused on what the author meant, related new information to what they already knew and had experienced, worked to organize and structure the content, and saw the reading as an important source of learning, Marton and Saljo characterized the approach as deep. Ramsden says of students using surface approaches, "Texts were a flat landscape of facts to be remembered, rather than an area dotted with salient features representing principles or arguments around which stretched plains of evidence" (p. 23). Findings like these challenge the conventional push to "cover" and otherwise convey ever more content. Ramsden notes that "learning should be seen as a qualitative change in a person's way of seeing, experiencing, understanding, conceptualizing something in the real world— rather than as a quantitative change in the amount of knowledge someone possesses" (p. 271). In order to facilitate learning that changes how students think and understand, teachers must begin by discovering students' existing conceptions and then design instruction that changes those conceptions. That most certainly has implications for how much content can be covered.

Some work in cognitive psychology is directly tied to constructivism, a currently prominent educational theory. At its core, this theory is about the relationship between learners and content: "Constructivist approaches emphasize learners' actively constructing their own knowledge rather than passively receiving information transmitted to them from teachers and textbooks. From a constructivist perspective, knowledge cannot simply be given to students: Students must construct their own meanings" (Stage, Muller, Kinzie, and Simmons, 1998, p. 35). This view of education and learning rests on the work of a variety of psychologists and philosophers, most notably Jean Piaget, Jerome Bruner, Ernst von Glaserfeld, and Lev Vygotsky.

Constructivism has had an impact on instructional practice. For example, that learning occurs in social contexts like communities and builds on the experiences, background, and cultures of community members finds voice in the seminal work of Bruffee (1993), whose notions of group work from the constructivist perspective helped to spawn the collaborative learning movement. In this approach to group work, the teacher functions as a master learner and resource. Group members function as a community and jointly create their own unique solutions to problems. Sometimes these learning communities become formalized structures that tackle the integration of content across disciplines and around themes.

These ideas of the collective construction of knowledge fit in humanities fields where content supports more tentative and less definitive conclusions. It is more difficult to see how knowledge can be socially constructed in science, math, and engineering fields where there are more "right" answers and much less disagreement about the status of knowledge. Although this view of knowledge and learning has been resisted, there are some notable exceptions. The idea that students need to be told less and to discover more is realized in another collection of strategies that we might loosely group here as problem-based learning. Students start with a problem, usually a scenario or case, and must find the content in the fields that explains, answers, or resolves the problem. Typically, they do this work in groups. Some attempts have been made to realign whole curricula, course sequences, and individual courses based on the assumptions and principles of constructivism. For example, Ege, Coppola, and Lawton (1996) used constructivist theories to redesign the introductory organic chemistry taken by all chemistry, biology, and pre-med majors at the University of Michigan.

Constructivism prescribes a whole new level of student involvement with content. It makes content much more the means to knowledge than the end of it. It and the empirical work in psychology change the function of content so it is less about covering it and more about using it to develop unique and individual ways of understanding. Consider how Fosnot (1996) describes the interaction between content and students from the constructivist perspective. Learning, she notes, "requires invention and self-organization on the part of the learner. Thus teachers need to allow learners to raise their own questions, generate their own hypotheses and models as possibilities and test them for validity" (p. 29). A bit later she writes, "Challenging, open-ended investigations in realistic, meaningful contexts need to be offered, thus allowing learners to explore and generate many possibilities, both affirming and contradictory" (p. 29).

The Role of the Teacher

Work in all three of these areas (critical and feminist pedagogy, cognitive and educational psychology, and constructivist theory) has large implications for the role of the teacher. Critical and feminist pedagogy challenge long-standing assumptions about power, authority, and teachers. The critique is damning, asserting that the exercise of power in the classroom often benefits teachers more than it promotes student learning.

Constructivism challenges faculty expertise, not so much arguing against its validity as objecting to its exclusivity, opening and legitimizing students' interaction with the content. According to constructivist theories, students need not wait until they have developed expertise before they interact with content. They are encouraged to explore it, handle it, relate it to their own experience, and challenge it whatever their level of expertise. Obviously, less knowledgeable and experienced learners will interact with content in less intellectually robust ways, but the goal is to involve students in the process of acquiring and retaining information.

Feminist pedagogy builds on constructivist theory when it raises questions about the nature of knowing and identifies different ways of knowing, as it did most notably in the now-classic, *Women's Ways of Knowing* (Belenky, Clinchy, Goldberger, and Tarule, 1986). Challenging the nature of knowledge and raising questions about the role of expertise require that faculty revisit and reassess long-held traditional views of the teacher as the exclusive content and classroom authority.

Work in educational psychology most clearly shifts our focus from the teacher to the learner. What teachers do is important only in terms of how those actions address learning. The action always features students and what they are doing. This view deemphasizes teaching techniques and methods if they are considered separate from the subject matter and learning structures of the discipline. How faculty teach is intrinsically a function of what they teach and how students learn in that discipline.

Like learners, teachers move through developmental stages that reflect how much they focus on students and learning. Biggs (1999a, 1999b) outlines this developmental "route map," which is discussed in detail in Chapter Eight, where a variety of developmental issues are considered. At this juncture, it is worth mentioning work like that of Kember and Gow (1994), who developed a questionnaire for faculty that measures orientation toward one of two approaches to teaching: knowledge transmission or learning facilitation. They tabulated the data for both individual faculty and departments and then, using an instrument developed by Biggs (and recently updated by Biggs, Kember, and Leung, 2001) to measure the extent to which students report using surface or deep approaches to learning, correlated the teaching and learning approaches. Kember and Gow's (1994) results suggest that

> the methods of teaching adopted, the learning tasks set, the assessment demands made, and the workload specified are strongly influenced by the orientation to teaching. In departments where the knowledge transmission orientation predominates, the curriculum design and teaching methods are more likely to have undesirable influences on the learning approaches of students. . . .
>
> . . . Meaningful approaches to learning are discouraged when lecturers believe that their role is restricted to transferring the accumulated knowledge of their discipline to the minds of their students [pp. 69, 71].

If the goal of teaching is to promote learning, then the role the teacher takes to accomplish that goal changes considerably. Teachers no longer function as exclusive content expert or authoritarian classroom managers and no long work to improve teaching by developing sophisticated presentation skills. They will lecture less and be much more around the classroom than in front of it. There is no sense in any of the literature that I read that this is a diminished, less essential role. Learner-centered teachers make essential contributions to the learning process. However, they are significantly different from those contributions most teachers currently make.

The Responsibility for Learning

Some years before my current interest in learning I encountered the ideas of self-regulated, self-monitored, independent learners in the work of Boud (1981), whose edited anthology describes how education makes students dependent learners. They depend on the teacher to identify what needs to be learned, to prescribe the learning methods, and finally to assess what and how well they have learned. In recent years, work on self-regulated learning has advanced, with Boud and others now proposing that the goal of education ought to be the creation of independent, autonomous learners who assume responsibility for their own learning. Learners take this stance during formal educational encounters and on their own as learning occurs across their lifetimes.

Because we so seldom see independent, autonomous learners and function in mostly teacher-centered environments, we forget how effectively some individuals assume responsibility for their own learning. Most of us can summon an example—the self-taught gardener, trekker, knitter, or my spouse's boat-building adventure—where the learner takes an avocation to high levels of knowledge and skill. But we often disconnect these examples of informal learning from the formal experiences that happen in school. Researchers who study self-directed learners do not. They often start with these models of independence, self-motivation, and individual responsibility.

The book that most effectively summarizes work in this area is Candy's *Self-Direction for Lifelong Learning* (1991). His "Profile of the Autonomous Learner" is an apt summary of his book and the research in this area. In it he lists over one hundred of the "attributes, characteristics, qualities, and competencies" (p. 459) used by and in research to describe the autonomous learner. I think of it as a description of the "perfect" student, the one I dream of teaching. But this work on self-directed learning challenges us to do more than dream. It establishes that students can and should be made responsible for their own learning. This work provides the justification for that approach.

Learning skills as sophisticated as those needed by autonomous self-regulating learners do not develop simply through exposure to the content of disciplines. They must be taught, and so it is this literature on self-directed learning that makes the strongest case for skill instruction, especially for students who arrive in college without even the most basic skills. The point is made almost relentlessly: our students will be lifelong learners. The skills they acquire and the awareness of themselves as learners that they develop during their formal educational experiences will be used throughout the course of their professional and personal lives.

This literature is very good at describing where students should end up. The authors delineate all that characterizes independent, autonomous learners. They address much less frequently how it is one begins with students who are at the other end of the continuum (dependent, passive, and not self-confident) and starts moving them in the direction of intellectual maturity and autonomy. This is a nontrivial omission; development as an independent learner is not the inevitable outcome of formal educational experiences.

Evaluation Purpose and Processes

Work in educational psychology extensively documents a finding we all know but do not always act on: What do students learn in a course? They learn whatever it is they are tested or evaluated on. Tests and assignments are a course's most potent impetus to learning. Nights before a test in my courses, I savor knowing that a significant percentage of my students are having what I hope is an extended encounter with the course's content. They are finally getting around to learning all this important stuff.

Assessment promotes learning, but the question is, What kind of learning does it promote? If you examine honestly and reflectively what most faculty test students on and the assessment mechanisms they employ, the results create dissonance. And there is a simple way to make that clear. Think about how you would respond to this query: You're at the mall and run into a student who took your course five years ago. As the student looks at you and remembers the course, what would you like to have running through the student's mind at that moment? Now examine your tests and assignments, and see what you can find there that contributes to those desired learning outcomes. The point cannot be made more clearly than Biggs (1999a) did: "What and how students learn depends to a major extent on how they think they will be assessed. Assessment practices must send the right signals" (p. 141).

The literature on assessing learning does not deal with the instructional realities of large classes, heavy teaching loads, no clerical support for teachers, pressure to publish, and required service to the institution. Those realities necessitate some compromises, but all of us need to reconnect with the fundamental fact reiterated over and over in this literature: what students are most likely to learn in a course is directly related to what they are evaluated on. Evaluation is not just something used to generate grades; it is the most effective tool a teacher has to promote learning. So how can it be used to its maximum potential, given instructional realities and the strong motivation students have to get grades?

The literature on self-directed learning also underscores the importance of assessment, only in this case it is the ability of students to self-assess accurately. Sophisticated learners know when they do or do not understand something. They can review a performance and identify what needs improvement. They know when their lack of objectivity necessitates their soliciting external feedback. They have mechanisms for its collections and methods for evaluating it and acting on it. Do today's college students have these skills? More incriminatingly, do we teach them?

Good Literature on the Lessons

The literature highlighted in this chapter is only some of what is referenced throughout the book. What I have focused on here are the large streams of work that support the changes proposed and explored in the next five chapters. I will support the changes with specific studies and narrower lines of work that belong to these larger streams.

The reading list on learning in Appendix C is by no means comprehensive, but includes the sources that have been most instrumental in developing the approach I advocate in this book.

Particularly "good," that is, informative, easy-to-read, and well-documented, sources are noted in annotations that accompany each reference. This list is organized around five major areas of work highlighted in this opening review: autonomy and self-directed learning, critical and radical pedagogy, feminist pedagogy, constructivism, and cognitive and educational psychology.

Finally, what I am advocating here as the ways and means of promoting more and better learning is consistent with any number of other reports and articles. The same problems with current instructional approaches keep being identified, and solutions not unlike what ends up being proposed here are advocated. Let me mention four such sources, drawn from a larger pool.

The Wingspread Group on Higher Education (1993) began with the current problems in American higher education, focusing mainly on the mismatch between the needs of society and the preparation of undergraduates. This report documents student failures on many fronts and proposes a solution: put learning at the heart of the educational enterprise. The group sees this as a profound change. Making it a central mission "will mean overhauling the conceptual, procedural, curricular and other architecture of postsecondary education on most campuses" (p. 14).

Widely quoted and perhaps more influential than any other article in setting the current learning agenda, Barr and Tagg (1995) outline the comprehensive changes involved when institutions move from a teaching to a learning paradigm. They identify teaching and learning structures that create climates for learning. They describe learning theory that shapes knowledge individually as mediated by personal experience, makes learning student-centered and controlled, and teaches students how to learn as much as it teaches what to learn. They describe faculty as instructional designers who put together challenging and complex learning experiences and then create environments that empower students to accomplish the goals.

O'Banion (1997), president of the League for Innovation in the Community College, a professional organization for two-year institutions, authored a monograph on creating more learner-centered community colleges. He proposes that "learning colleges" will exemplify six principles:

1) the learning college creates substantive change in individual learners; 2) the learning college engages learners in the learning process as full partners assuming primary responsibility for their own choices; 3) the learning college creates and offers as many options for learning as possible; 4) the learning college assists learners to form and participate in collaborative learning activities; 5) the learning college defines the roles of learning facilitators by the needs of the learners; and 6) the learning college and its learning facilitators succeed only when improved and expanded learning can be documented for its learners [p. 15].

Finally, Gardiner (1998) summons the research evidence that mandates change in educational practice:

> In this article, I hope to acquaint readers with important research that has been done over the past three decades on how students learn and what constitutes effective educational experience. . . .
> The studies reviewed here, taken together, consistently show that the college experience for most students comprises a loosely organized, unfocused curriculum, with undefined outcomes, classes that emphasize passive listening, lectures that transmit low-level information, and assessments of learning that frequently demand only the recall of memorized material or low-level comprehension of concepts [pp. 71–72].

However, he ends by pointing out that what is known about student development, learning, teaching, and academic organization does lead to methods and approaches that can help students develop to a very high level.

The changes necessary to make teaching learner-centered are not trivial. They get to the bedrock of instructional practice. They have encouraged me to revisit long-held assumptions and widely used approaches. However, it is not possible to sample even a modest amount of the literature on learning and continue teaching as most of us were taught. Very little there justifies traditional approaches, especially given the learning needs of students and society today. At some level, most of us already know this. We have embraced the methods of active learning, cooperative and collaborative learning, and writing across the curriculum, to name but a few of the initiatives that put students in new relationships with content, their fellow learners, and their teachers. Almost all institutions now offer learning skills instruction. We all know we are teaching too much content and emphasize grades to the detriment of learning. Most faculty do not connect these changes in instructional practice and attitude with the knowledge base on learning, but they do pave the way for the more comprehensive and integrated approach I call learner-centered teaching.

Last week, one of my students told me that he recommended my entry-level communication course to a friend. When I asked why, he said, "It changes the way you think in some really good ways." I wished for a bit more specificity but then decided that I will hope my experiences, the changes I propose in this book, and the literature summoned in support of them will have exactly the same effect on you.

Part One

What Changes When Teaching Is Learner-Centered?

| The Balance of Power

How would you characterize today's college students? Empowered, confident, self-motivated learners? That is not how I would describe mine. The ones in my classes are hopeful but generally anxious and tentative. They want all classes to be easy but expect that most will be hard. They wish their major (whatever it might be) did not require math, science, or English courses. A good number will not speak in class unless called on. Most like, want, indeed need, teachers who tell them exactly what to do. Education is something done unto them. It frequently involves stress, anxiety, and other forms of discomfort.

When my colleagues and I discuss our students, we always end up asking the same question: How can we overcome these kind of attitudes that often compromise students' ability to learn? But we should be asking a more fundamental question: What makes learners like this? Why are so many students anxious, indecisive, and unsure of themselves as learners? And even more pointed, is there something about the way we teach that discourages students' development as learners?

According to theories of radical and feminist pedagogy, and theories and research related to self-regulated learners, students' motivation, confidence, and enthusiasm for learning are all adversely affected when teachers control the processes through and by which they learn. Do we control those processes? Yes, but teacher authority is so taken for granted that most of us are no longer aware of the extent to which we direct student learning.

See if honest answers to the following set of questions provide insight. Who decides what (content) students learn in the course?

Who controls the pace (calendar) at which content is covered? Who determines the structures (assignments, tests) through which the material will be mastered? Who sets the conditions for learning (things like attendance policies and assignment deadlines)? Who evaluates (grades) the quantity and quality of the learning that has occurred? In the classroom itself, who controls and regulates the flow of communication, deciding who gets the opportunity to speak, when, and for how long? Overall, who makes all (or even most) of the important decisions about learning for students?

If that set of questions fails to convince, consider more tangible evidence of our propensity to control. Look at the number and tone of the directives contained in most syllabi. Even comparatively mild-mannered, normally gentle faculty resort to edicts, demands, and otherwise definitive directives as they set down the law for students: "No late papers accepted, ever, under any circumstances." "Failure to meet participation expectations will result in lower grades." "Do not talk in class. Keep quiet. You are here to listen and to learn." "You must do the reading before you come to class. Your uninformed opinion does not add to the discussion." We do need to clarify expectations for students. They frequently arrive in college and class with any number of inaccurate ones, but must those messages always be communicated with heavy-handed language? Language like this has a subtext that relates to power and control.

Baecker (1998, p. 60) writes of the syllabus, "All of these issues of power and authority come together in this document, the creation of which, it is important to note, is a right reserved for the instructor. Our students certainly don't come to us on the first day with a written list of their demands and expectations." She continues to explore, using an analysis of fifteen syllabi, how we establish control, often using language that appears inclusive and collaborative but really is not. She concludes, "If the syllabi I examined in this study are any indication, we do a very poor job of negotiating power in the classroom" (p. 61).

Still more concrete evidence can be summoned from other instructional arenas. Consider any number of faculty policies directed at student behaviors, and then inquire honestly as to the connection between those behaviors and learning. There are faculty who will not teach if students wear baseball caps in the classroom. Others specify all the logistical parameters of papers: font size and style, paper weight, margin width, and whether it should be stapled or clipped. Still others prohibit gum chewing in class. I know a faculty member who expects students to clean his overhead transparencies. Faculty are good at justifying these kinds of policies and practices; we always have our reasons, and maybe some are legitimate, but sometimes the links between the policies and power issues are more obvious than their connections to learning.

You may be ready to accept that we do exercise considerable power over student learning but believe we do so for good reasons. Consider three of those reasons, and then assess their validity. The reason that faculty name first involves the students themselves: they cannot be trusted to make decisions about learning because they lack intellectual maturity, do not have good study skills, are not well prepared, do not like the content area, take courses to get grades, and do not care about learning.

These characteristics do describe many college students and must be addressed if students are to make more decisions about their own learning. Much of the content in this chapter and subsequent ones deals with developing student capabilities as learners and with preparing them to take more responsibility for learning. But the fact that students need to be prepared to handle learner-centered approaches is not an endemic reason that justifies our making all the decisions about their learning for them. Mallinger (1998, p. 473) points out, "The argument for instructor-directed leadership assumes that students are not *capable* [emphasis added] of expanding their maturity level." He believes, as I do, that faculty can reduce the amount they control at the same time they use structures that promote student growth and provide quality education.

Second, faculty make the decisions about student learning because we always have. It is an assumed, unquestioned part of what it means to be the teacher. Braye (1995, p. 1), writing about teacher control, describes the traditional view: "A 'good' teacher dominates the classroom and its elements. She prepares lesson plans for efficient use of class time, prescribes course objectives, and disseminates information clearly and effectively so that students may learn it quickly, remember it well, and reproduce it upon demand." We assume that making all these decisions and being indisputably in charge benefits students, but we have never really thought about it or carefully analyzed how learning might be affected by our actions.

Should you decide to embark on this kind of analysis, be prepared for some surprises. For years in my own teaching, I made decisions motivated by what I thought was the best interests of my students. I never recognized that those decisions sometimes benefited me more than my students. I began to see that as I made my way through Brookfield's *Becoming a Critical Reflective Teacher* (1995), which encourages critical reflection, the in-depth analysis that begins with the details of instructional practice and uses them to uncover the assumptions and premises on which they rest. Brookfield says that reflection is critical when it aims to accomplish two purposes: "The first is to understand how considerations of power undergird, frame and distort educational processes and interactions. The second is to question assumptions and practices that seem to make our teaching lives easier but actually work against our own best long-term interests" (p. 8). The process of critical reflection creates a rationale for classroom policies and practices, grounding them on something other than tacit, uncritical acceptance of what has always been.

Finally, we are motivated to control because teaching makes us vulnerable. Teachers almost never mention this reason, probably because their understanding of it is more intuitive than explicit. An anecdote shared by a colleague illustrates the complex interplay of variables related to control and vulnerability. My colleague is an experienced, poised, confident, and highly effective teacher who has a recurring bad dream about teaching. It is the first day of his large entry-level business class. He is going through his usual introduction, pointing out that he is a full professor and no longer required to teach beginning classes, but he chooses to do so. Somewhere in the middle of these promotional messages, a student whose face he can never quite make out stands up, interrupts, and loudly declares that the instructor is bogus, a great big fake, and he ought to be removed. Students have paid for and deserve better. As this student interlocutor energizes the class, they surge toward the front of the room. My colleague awakes kicking and screaming as he is bodily removed from class.

The dream is funny, but something about it makes us nervous. It might trigger a flashback to that day we added an extra assignment or moved up the test date. We were not bodily removed from class, but we nevertheless felt vulnerable even there behind the podium and fully in charge. On that day, we stood our ground, and students went along with the decision. However, for a fleeting moment, there was a question, and we realized that students can refuse to accept our authority and can challenge our position in the classroom.

Despite all that we can control, students do make some important decisions on their own. One example makes the point: students themselves decide whether to learn at all. If they decide not to, that puts faculty in a bind. Although learning can and does regularly occur in the absence of teacher-based instruction, if teaching regularly occurs and no learning results, that becomes a serious indictment of the teaching—one that ultimately challenges its purpose and existence.

Most faculty do not feel vulnerable in the classroom because students are not learning. We tend to think that is their fault anyway. The threats we respond to in the classroom are much more immediate and visceral. We think someone is challenging our authority. Then we really make it clear who is in charge. Ironically, overreacting nets the opposite result. The iron-clad syllabus with its completely specified policies effectively handcuffs students to the course and sets up an adversarial relationship that all but dares students to challenge the authority. Kearney and Plax's research (1992) documents that student resistance to faculty efforts to control is common and widespread. They estimate that about 21 percent of students engage in some form of resistance. Their work makes clear that although most students resist passively, some do confront the teacher openly and aggressively.

Our understanding and response to the power dynamics of the classroom bespeak our naiveté and failure to understand the complicated continuum of control that exists between teacher and learner. We feel the need to be in control and assert our position and authority over students, but we fail to understand that the need results from our own vulnerabilities and desire to manage an ambiguous and unpredictable situation successfully. The idea of giving up control, of involving students in decisions faculty have traditionally made, frightens many teachers. Won't students take advantage of diminished teacher control? They could orchestrate some sort of coup and overthrow the teacher! How can we possibly give up control when our hold is already so tenuous?

We are about to address those questions, but I move to them having asserted that faculty exercise broad and deep control over the learning processes that affect students. I have argued that we exercise that kind of power for a variety of not very carefully thought out or convincing reasons. But our vested self-interests may make it difficult for us to understand and accept, at least initially, the negative role power has played in learning. May I encourage your continued contemplation of the role of power in your classes as we now explore how the decision-making dynamic changes when teaching is learner-centered.

How the Balance of Power Changes

Radical and feminist pedagogues and those who study self-directed learners posit that to be truly learner-centered, we must begin with greater insight into the role of power in our classrooms: who exerts it, why, and with what effects and what benefits. With a more explicit understanding of the power dynamic, we are ready to explore how the balance of power changes in a learner-centered environment. And then we can ascertain whether involvement in the decision making associated with learning has a positive impact on students' educational experiences. Do the benefits justify their involvement?

Power Is Shared

When teaching is learner-centered, power is shared rather than transferred wholesale. Faculty still make key decisions about learning, but they no longer make all decisions and not always without student input. But even so, this change immediately raises ethical issues for faculty. It gets to the heart of what it means to be a teacher and what teachers are supposed to do.

Many who object to the ideas of radical pedagogy do so on the ground that if faculty relinquish control, they abrogate legitimate instructional responsibility. Students, they say, end up running the class and teaching themselves, leaving the teacher no viable role in the educational process. It is true that this educational philosophy ultimately dispenses with the teacher. The goal is to equip students with learning skills so sophisticated that they can teach themselves. However, both conceptually and pragmatically, this is a gradual process, not an all-or-none proposition. Power is redistributed in amounts proportional to students' ability to handle it. As explored at length in Chapter Five, with more freedom to make learning choices comes more responsibility to accept the consequences of those choices. Although I suspect that some of the radical pedagogues would object to an implementation process as gradual as that proposed in this book, to transfer decision making too quickly does seem to me an ethical violation of legitimate instructional responsibility.

An example will help differentiate between an unethical transfer of power and an appropriate sharing of the decision-making process. A teacher violates his legitimate power and authority if he allows entry-level students in his required survey of sociology course to select the textbook. These students do not have experience in or knowledge of the discipline to make a good textbook decision. Alternatively, imagine if the teacher surveyed a variety of textbooks in the light of his goals and objectives for the course and his understanding of students' learning needs and then selected five books that would accomplish his aims and meet student needs. He could then create a student textbook review committee and as a group project let them make and justify a textbook recommendation. I have a colleague who routinely uses this method for textbook selection. He reports two surprising results: students almost never select the textbook he predicts they will, and he never gets low scores on the student rating question that inquires as to the quality and appropriateness of the textbook.

In addition to the ethical ramifications of power sharing, faculty also fear giving up too much control, especially in the light of their students' abilities to handle more responsibility. But there are ways of limiting decision making as students learn to make good decisions and assume responsibility for them. For example, giving students the chance to offer input or make recommendations is not the same as letting them make those decisions. Letting students make decisions in one or two areas is not the same as giving them discretion over the whole range of decisions about learning. Student decisions can be constrained by limiting the scope of their decisions. In my course, I let students decide which assignments they will complete in the course (one is required), but I set the parameters of those assignments. Although students select a particular assignment, they do not decide what that assignment entails or when it is due.

Although I am advocating for a gradual transfer of power and control, make no mistake that the power sharing described in this chapter constitutes a major change. It is premised on theories of teaching and learning radically different from those that ground current instructional practice. These theories propose that faculty, willingly and responsibly, begin to give up some of their control in the interest of creating motivated, confident, responsible learners.

The Benefits of Power Sharing

Power sharing benefits students and learning. It also benefits teachers and the learning environment in a class and at an institution. Consider the advantages in each of these areas in more detail.

The biggest and most important beneficiary of the power transfer is students and, subsequently, their learning. The impact on students and their learning is so interconnected that it is not possible to discuss them separately. But students benefit first, although initially efforts to share power meet resistance. When I introduce learner-centered approaches, my students are confused. They do not understand it, and once they do, they try to give the power back. They do not (in my experience and the experience of others) take the power given, grab more, and run off with the course. They actually prefer teacher-centered classrooms, but not for reasons that benefit their learning.

When it becomes clear that I will not make the decisions I have given them, they begin to exercise their power tentatively and anxiously. They want feedback and need reinforcement. Then they move forward with a bit more confidence. It is difficult to say precisely when it happens, but one day, quite unexpectedly, the students are engaged and involved with the course and its content. There is an energy about the class, a kind of enthusiasm. Instructional nirvana does not descend. Not everybody is involved and engaged, and some activities and assignments still bomb. But student response to my efforts to share power has been the most eloquent evidence to me that learner-centered teaching is a powerful pedagogy.

If students are engaged, involved, and connected with a course, they are motivated to work harder in that course, and we know from so many studies that time on task results in more learning. In addition to how much students learn, how well they learn it is important. In my case, they become able to apply the content to their own communication. They learn not just about how communication works from a theoretical and conceptual basis; they come to understand themselves as communicators and suddenly see communication happening all around them. Knowledge is power, and it brings my students confidence. They now exercise their power with purpose and sometimes with poise.

Power sharing also benefits teachers. You no longer struggle with passive, uninterested, disconnected students. Their energy motivates and drives you to prepare more, risk more, and be rewarded more by the sheer pleasure of teaching. Power sharing avoids the adversarial relationship that too often comes to characterize the teacher-class relationship. The you-versus-them distinction blurs. Because they no longer feel powerless, they are much less likely to resist your requirements. I have often felt more in control in these classes than I ever did before. Someone once said, Give power away and get more back!

Power sharing affects the environment in the classroom too. Here, the benefits have to do with ownership and comfort. There is a much stronger sense that the class belongs to everyone. When something is ineffective, students are much more willing than in the past to help me fix it. My classes are louder and sometimes seem chaotic. People work in groups, others mill about, and sometimes a pair works something out on the board. I worry more when faculty peers come to observe. One of my students once accosted a peer reviewer, asking what he was doing in the class. He then proceeded to tell my colleague that this class was "unconventional" but that I should not "get in trouble" because it was an excellent class. I listened, simultaneously feeling thrill and horror.

In the Trenches: Policies and Practices That Redistribute Power

How do you design a course, a set of assignments, and day-by-day classroom activities in ways that give students more control over learning processes? The examples in this section are organized around four areas of potential decision making for learners: course activities and assignments, classroom policies, course content, and evaluation activities.

Activities and Assignment Decisions

Students can be involved in decision making about course activities and assignments in a number of ways and at different levels of decision making. In my entry-level public speaking course, students decide what assignments they will complete. I have restructured the course so that there are no required assignments save one: students must give one speech. It is, after all, a skills-based course, and although many of my students would aspire to try, public speaking is not a skill developed in theory. But in place of the formerly required assignments is now an array of options from which students pick and choose. (Appendix A contains the syllabus.)

In their first log entry (see the syllabus for details on this assignment; a list of log entry prompts is provided in Appendix A), students make some initial assignment choices and share reactions to the course's structure. Their responses are not very encouraging. They say they plan to do the easy assignments (although they disagree as to which ones those are). They also pick assignments they "like" with little insight as to how these choices might reflect learning preferences. They believe a teacher might design a course this way because "you like students and want to give us a chance," or "you don't want any student blaming you for a bad grade."

However, when I ask, "How do you think this strategy will affect your performance in the class?" I hit pay dirt. "I think this structure will really help me. It puts me in charge." "With this class it's up to me and although that scares me, I really think that's the way it should be." "I'll have to see but I think I'm really going to work hard in this class. I feel like I have a chance."

The design challenge is to give students an authentic role in making decisions about their assignments but to create a context or framework that positively influences the kinds of decisions they make. Given the level of most students' skills, making all the decisions about assignments (not just selecting which ones) could be the pedagogical equivalent of giving a sixteen year old the keys on Friday night and saying, "See you Monday morning." I put student decision making about assignments in the context of a detailed course calendar that we follow religiously. Every assignment has a due date, and once a deadline is past, the assignment cannot be completed. This prevents students from finally getting motivated in week 13 of the semester and in a flurry of activity completing a number of assignments at a questionable quality level. Each assignment itself is highly structured; none allows students much in the way of choice. Letting students make the decision as to what and how many assignments happens in the context of deadlines and structure that my beginning students need.

Assignment decision making has a significant impact on who works in the course and how hard they are willing to work. I have lots of B-level and C-level students—ones the old method never motivated very well—who seem particularly empowered by the fact that in this class, maybe they can get an A, and they are willing to complete a great number of assignments. The assignments are not mastery based, in the sense that those who complete them get the credit. Each assignment is graded against specific criteria, and to have any assignment count, the student must earn at least 50 percent of the points.

Consider a second and quite different example of how students can be involved in decision making about course assignments and activities. One faculty member lets students set all the due dates and deadlines for a major group project in a 300-level business course. After making the assignment (a detailed report that attempts to entice a business to locate a new factory in the county), he asks the group for a memo in which *they* identify the major steps necessary to complete the assignment and when they need to be done in order to meet the final due date, which they propose. They also list assignment parts for which they would like his formative feedback and when they will have those to him. In an especially interesting twist, he has students identify appropriate penalties should they miss any of the deadlines. He says that frequently, student penalties for missed deadlines are more severe than those he would use and that overall they miss deadlines much less often under this scheme. This approach does result in assignments being submitted at different dates, but this sequencing actually eases the grading task because there is no imposing stack of papers to be graded all at once.

Course Policy Decisions

Students can also be involved in decision making about course policies. Here I will illustrate with an extended example of how students set the participation policy in my beginning public speaking course, including how their policies compare with mine, how the experience has affected all of us, and what learning outcomes I have observed.

Before I involved students in the process of establishing the policy, I was already convinced that my assessment of student participation needed to be much less subjective and summative. I needed criteria that were more explicit and a design that included a feedback opportunity through which students might learn how to make more constructive contributions. (Lyons, 1989, persuasively illustrates the kind of criteria we ought to be using.) Building on this, I use a round-robin technique to start the class working on the policy. Students are placed in groups of four, and each student is given a different question about participation (for example, "What behaviors should count positively toward participation credit? Should some participation behaviors count more—which ones?" "Should students lose participation credit for engaging in some kinds of behaviors—what behaviors and how much credit should they lose?"). Each student asks every other person in the group his or her question, takes notes on the answers, and responds to the questions that have been given to others.

Next, all persons with the same question form a new group in which they share the responses collected and look for common themes and differences. Their task is to construct a group answer, which they turn in at the end of the period. I respond by the next period with a memo to each group that raises questions and asks for elaborations. Students work on the issues raised in the memo and by the middle of the period have posted their group's answer to the question. We spend the rest of the time comparing and contrasting the responses and trying to work out areas of disagreement. From their answers and our discussion, I put together a draft of the participation policy. We review it the following period, occasionally revise it further, and then vote on whether to accept it.

In general, students come up with policies that closely parallel the ones I am comfortable using, but not always. I was somewhat taken back when one class proposed that right and wrong answers should count equally. I did not know how to respond. Should I go with what I had promised (implement the policy they proposed), or point out that this was not a realistic or right answer? The next day, I went to class still undecided and honestly shared my quandary. Two student responses persuaded me that I could live with their plank: (1) "When you give a wrong answer and the teacher points that out in front of the entire class, it takes a good deal of courage to raise your hand next time," and (2) "Teachers always tell us we shouldn't be afraid to make mistakes, that we learn from them, so why shouldn't we get credit for making them?"

Student reaction to this activity is always interesting. In almost every class, at least a couple of students see this as some group exercise that has no bearing on reality. The light finally comes on about the time we are ready to vote. As one student blurted out, "Is this, like, for real?"

Much more telling are their repeated attempts to put the ball back in my court. Proposed planks will be decidedly vague—for example, "Students should get credit for trying." When I object, asking how I am supposed to know if students are trying, they promptly respond, "You decide. You're the teacher." I try to force the point by making it extreme: "I'll tell you what. I don't think engineering majors ever try. [I almost always have five or six per class.] I've had lots of them in class before, and I've never seen one try yet. I'm not giving any engineers credit for trying." Their typical response is decidedly naive: "You can't do that. You're the teacher. You have to be fair." "And what in the world can you do if I'm not?" I respond. The notion that a clear, explicit policy might protect them is a new idea.

Finally, every class (close to twenty sections now) has opted for a policy that students will volunteer rather than be called on. I am struck because the most common way faculty solve the nonparticipation problem is by calling on students. What do students learn when we call on them? We assume that they learn they can speak up and therefore speak up more. Recent research challenges that assumption, however.

A study by Howard, Short, and Clark (1996), based on observations in 231 class sessions, found that 28 percent of the students made 89 percent of the comments. Another study (Nunn, 1996) also involving classroom observation documented that on average, only 25 percent of the students in a given class participate. Other evidence documents the still small percentage of class time devoted to interaction and faculty behaviors that inhibit and facilitate student response (Fassinger, 1995, 1996; Auster and MacRone, 1994; these studies and others are summarized and their findings integrated in Weimer, 1996). The findings make clear that calling on students is not solving participation problems.

My answer to what students learn when we call on them has changed. I now think they learn how to speak up when somebody is there to call on them. In my professional life, I have been in many situations where nobody called on me, and had I not been able to speak up, my views and the views of those I represent would not have been heard. Students need to learn how to speak up on their own when they have something to say and when their views and positions need to be heard. How does calling on them teach that lesson?

I now see calling on students as one of those instructional policies that benefit faculty more than students. It is awkward when no one responds to a question we have asked. But we summarily dispense with the discomfort if we promptly call on a student. This policy takes care of our problem, but it creates another set for students—for example, the anxiety of not knowing if they're going to be called on; the pressure to say something when they don't know what to say; the fear of looking foolish because they've given a stupid answer.

Making class participation policy the object of such focused attention (in part justified in my class because it is a communication course) has had the benefit of making students much more aware of participation on a daily basis. Students see that various behaviors constitute participation: answering questions asked by the teacher and other students, asking questions of the teacher and other students, asking follow-up questions, commenting on the questions and answers of other students, asking questions about the reading or material presented previously, and offering examples or experiences to illustrate. Ironically, in my experience, using the student-developed participation policy has more effectively generated responses to questions than calling on students ever did. On average, about 75 percent of the students select this assignment option, regularly including a number who report that up to now, they have never contributed in class unless called on. Generally, they all participate, and by the end of the course, a significant number of those who have not selected the option have also contributed.

Woods (1996) reports student outcomes similar to what I have experienced in a senior-level engineering class where he had students design the instrument used to assess involvement in discussion. He also involved students in the assessment process. (His experiences are highlighted fully in Chapter Six.)

Course Content Decisions

Course content offers an especially challenging arena in which to involve students in decision making. The difference between what faculty and students know about the content is so dramatic and compelling that at first pass, it seems irresponsible to give students any voice in course content, to say nothing of impossible, given what we are required to "cover" in the course. We do then justifiably ask whether there are any ways student can be involved in content decisions.

The answer is yes. In fact, we can start with a set of content decisions we already allow students to make. We let them choose speech topics, select subjects for artwork, and write papers, even major research papers, on topics of their own choosing. And most of us can speak firsthand to the difficulties they have deciding on a topic. Often that decision seems motivated not by their interests, but by what they think we want them to choose. It is worth asking ourselves why that so concerns them.

It helps to think of content decision making as a continuum and how we can move further along from the kind of content decisions we are comfortable having students make. I had a teacher who let students determine the content of the review session. The week before the exam, he arrived in class and announced that next Tuesday he would spend the period reviewing for the exam and go over whatever material we identified. He gave us five minutes at the end of the period to write him a note that listed the topics and any specific questions we had about them. On review day, he posted the topics most often requested and proceeded to work with us on them. I must confess that when I started using the technique, it was because it makes the teacher look highly responsive to student needs, but I quickly discovered that it provided me with important feedback about the areas students thought were most important and those they understood least well. What I see now is a technique that responsibly gives students a decision about content.

Chapter Six discusses a variety of strategies faculty use to involve students in the creation of exam questions. The focus there is on enhancing the learning outcome of evaluation activities, but using some student-generated questions is another way of giving them a small but important role in deciding what course content is important. The previous example of entertaining student textbook recommendations provides yet another possibility. If you act on either of these activities, including some student-generated questions on the exam or selecting the textbook they recommend, you will find students take these activities very seriously.

Black (1993) inches still further along the continuum in an organic chemistry course he restructured. He uses the textbook to "cover" the content; he does not give lectures on topics that are explicated in the text, but lets students decide what content gets worked on during in a period. He explains how he gets students to work with text content before they come to class and then describes what happens in class: "Currently, the class is run much like a discussion section. . . . I generally query the students at the beginning of each class to determine what they are having trouble with, and what they want to talk about. From their suggestions we make a list of topics, and during the class I try to address the problems they are having with these topics, perhaps by clarifying and explaining, providing examples, or whatever else I can do to help"

(p. 142). His next comments pertain to what has occurred as a result of this approach: "Interestingly, the course does not collapse when I come in and ask what the students want to talk about, because it is always in the context of the current chapter, and the schedule for working on those chapters is in the syllabus. Going to class each day is a pleasure, and always somewhat different. I am relaxed, enjoy the time, and it shows to the students. I feel no pressure to enter a mad race to cover the material; rather, we work together on what is currently their work" (p. 144). Using a similar approach, Tichenor (1997) reports on student involvement in the design of labs in a physiology course.

Finally, we move forward by yards to the other end of the continuum. Are there any circumstances under which students could make content decisions for a significant portion of the entire course? What about a graduate course, say, on college teaching, one that serves as an elective in a variety of graduate programs? The instructor begins by generating a long list of possible topics for the course. She could at that time identify an appropriate set of readings on each of the topics. The students begin with a short, informal paper that sets out the reasons they are taking the course, what they hope to learn, and what content they think might help them accomplish those learning goals. After writing the paper and sharing it with a small group of fellow students, the group gets the instructor-created list of potential topics. Together, the group uses that list and their papers to construct a prioritized list of course topics. These are submitted, and from them, the teacher selects the topics that will be covered in the course, creates a calendar, and assembles a collection of readings. If the majority interests have ruled out a topic of interest to a particular individual, that person could be encouraged to use an assignment to explore that content area.

Evaluation Activities

Assessment, long the exclusive purview of faculty, offers yet another challenging arena for involving students in making decisions. (Chapter Six is devoted to the various ways and means of getting students involved in evaluation processes.) The summary example here is of a single activity that gives students the opportunity to make recommendations about all aspects of the course. Johnson (2000, p. 1) involves students in the development of the entire course syllabus. He explains his motivation: "One principle of learning which has always been important to me as a learner, and as a teacher has application here. Students are very much turned on when they are involved in making the decisions that affect them. The converse is especially poignant. They are turned off when someone else makes their decisions for them." He does prepare a syllabus before class, but the copies he takes to class have *draft* written on the top of the first page. He begins class by having students interview each other as to what they most want to learn from the course. They share what others have told them, and Johnson writes what he hears on newsprint. Next, he distributes the draft syllabus and charges small groups to answer this question, "Building on your own needs, the results of our interviews, and my commitment to include your input, how would you revise the course?" Students may propose revisions to any part of the syllabus, the goals and objectives, the content, teaching methods, assignments, and proposed evaluation procedures. Johnson reports they make a variety of suggestions, many of them excellent: "I cannot recall a case where the students tried to find the easy way out, or to water down the course" (p. 1). He carefully considers their input and then revises the syllabus to include as many of their recommendations as he feels he justifiably can. He ends up with a syllabus jointly created and owned with the class. This example and others in this section are illustrations of how students can responsibly be given some control over the learning processes that affect them.

Questions That Emerge When the Balance of Power Changes

Out of this exploration of power sharing come a number of significant and important questions. We have already asked the most fundamental one: Can you design a set of course activities and assignments that responsibly give students more control over the decisions that affect their learning? I let the variety of examples offered stand as my answer to that question. Out of experience and the examples in the previous section emerge three other questions, and within each of them is a subset of related questions. For all these questions, I have much less concrete answers. However, if we have interest in moving forward our understanding and the effective use of learner-centered instruction, then these questions merit consideration.

How Much Power Is Enough?

If having power (some voice in decision making) motivates learners, how much does it take? Individual instructors can answer that question for themselves by sharing some power with students and seeing when their motivation and involvement in the course change. But we need more than individual answers. We need principles and guidelines that will help to establish professional norms and standards.

The question of how much power is enough leads to some related questions. First is how much decision making might be required to motivate one student versus how much it takes to motivate the class. In my own practice, I believe I have redistributed enough to motivate most students, but I am not reaching all students. I still have students who fail. They choose not to work or do such a minuscule amount of work that they do not learn enough to pass the class. I regularly wonder how much of their failure is a function of the way I have structured the course.

Students whose motivation and involvement are affected differently by this kind of decision making raise the final question related to power sharing. Can we give decision making differentially? That is, what are the implications of giving more to some students and less to others? Does that violate the principle of fair and equitable treatment for all students? Is it pragmatically possible, especially if the class is large?

How Much Freedom Can They Handle?

The answer to this question closely links to the previous one. The amount of decision making it takes to motivate students must be weighed against their intellectual maturity and ability to operate in conditions that give more freedom at the same time they also require more responsibility. Most students arrive in college classrooms having made almost no decisions about learning. We have an educational system that successfully creates very dependent learners (this is explored much more in Chapter Five). They turn to us for all manner of decision making. "How many pages should the paper be?" "How many homework problems do you think I need to do?" "Is it okay if I include more than five sources?" The questions annoy us, but we need to recognize that part of their need to know arises from an inability to decide for themselves.

In addition, many students are missing the solid study skills that would inform good learning decisions. In one of my log entries, I have students develop a plan for studying for an upcoming exam. It involves a time line and list of activities they will do to prepare for the exam. I am always amazed by the number who report that this is the first time they have developed a review plan. I am further dismayed after the exam by an equal number who report that the plan had no influence on their behavior. As usual, they waited until the night before the exam and crammed.

With little experience making learning decisions and lacking the sophisticated study skills that characterize effective learners, the chance that students (especially beginning ones) will make poor learning choices is high. What then is the teacher's responsibility? Should we intervene or let them live with the consequences of their decisions and hope they will learn from their mistakes? I routinely have students who participate regularly in class, doing everything the class participation policy requires for points, but they did not select this assignment option. I query them and point out how their contributions are precisely the ones called for by the policy. Most readily admit they made a mistake. I do not let them add the option after the fact, but I wonder if that is the right decision.

Clearly, there are developmental issues in moving students along the continuum from being dependent to independent learners. In Chapter Eight, I address those issues in detail, but the conclusion there is relevant here. Many details of the development process remain unclear. For example, we know very little about how to sequence assignments and learning experiences so they move students forward, always constructively pushing them but not so much that their decision making ends up being compromised. But figuring that out is not easy or obvious.

Finally, the issue of the class and the individual arises again with the question of how much freedom they can handle. Not all students in a class are at the same level of intellectual maturity, so some may be able to handle more responsibility than others. The goal is to find about the right level for the majority of the class—what most students can handle. But that still leaves the question of individuals unable to function at that level. I had one student who failed because he had about twenty-five fewer points than he needed to pass. He came to see me the next semester surprised and dismayed that he had failed. "How many points did you have?" I asked. "I don't know. I never added them up. But if I had known I was short, I would have done more work." I pondered this situation for quite a while after he left. Should I be distributing point totals to students throughout the semester? I give them a grid on which to record their points. Every time I return an assignment, I remind them that it is their responsibility to keep track of where they stand in the class. I have all their points recorded, but I add them up only at the end of course. What responsibility does the teacher have to an individual student when his or her capacity to handle learner-centered approaches is at a different level from the rest of the class?

When Do Teachers Compromise Professional Responsibilities?

The question of the teacher's responsibility for the individual student leads directly to the issue of how much control and decision making can be shared with students before compromising the responsibilities associated with being the teacher. How do you know when you have crossed the line?

Those who write about self-directed, autonomous learners see teachers ultimately phased out of the learning process. Nevertheless, most students are years, if not decades, away from having the skills and intellectual maturity necessary to assume responsibility for their own learning. But the point of that literature is that ultimately there are no responsibilities currently assigned the teacher that cannot at some point be relinquished to learners. So we compromise professional responsibility not by what we hand over but when we make that transfer.

However, given our discussion of where we start with most students, there are areas where teachers need to retain some control, perhaps significant control. I have already alluded to some of these. As long as grades are used as gatekeepers to subsequent educational experiences, like graduate and professional schools, teachers must not lose control of the major components of the assessment process. Given the way the curriculum (especially the undergraduate curriculum) is organized, including sequencing courses and using courses in a major to accomplish designated purposes, teachers cannot let students be completely (or perhaps even significantly) in charge of course content. And given our discussion of student preparedness to deal with more decision making and its incumbent responsibility, teachers need to retain control over the design and structure of course activities and assignments.

The question of knowing when the line has been crossed is easy in extreme cases. I once had to find a replacement for an ill faculty member. Students strongly objected to the newcomer. They wanted the policies of the previous teacher continued. "We get to grade our own group work," they said. I did not understand and asked, "You mean you assess what the other groups do and then the teacher reviews that when group grades are assigned?" "No, we grade the other groups, and those are the grades." "What do you use for criteria?" I wondered. "We just give them the grade they deserve." "Do you ever give groups less than C's?" "No, we only give A's and B's." Clearly this teacher inappropriately transferred decision making.

In the less extreme cases, it is more difficult to see where the line is, and so it helps to keep questioning ourselves about our ethical responsibilities. I must be honest, though, and confess that this part of the issue I do not find particularly worrisome. Most faculty control decision making about learning so completely that the possibility that they will transfer too much power too quickly seems remote. It reminds me of those faculty members forever fearful that if they tell a joke, they will cross the line and "entertain" students, thereby totally compromising their credibility as educators. Most faculty can only dream of careers in entertainment, regardless of how many jokes they might tell in class.

That all of these questions are related is clear; much less clear are definitive answers to them. At best, I have hinted at some answers and encourage their continued exploration in the context of individual practice and empirical inquiry. What I have illustrated is how this change in instructional practice raises important and intriguing questions that if answered first individually and then collectively can take our understanding of learner-centered teaching to a new and deeper level.

To Finish Up

Learner-centered instruction involves a reallocation of power in the classroom. It requires that faculty give students some control over those learning processes that directly affect them. And this reallocation does require a change. In most college classrooms, power, authority, and control remain firmly and almost exclusively in the hands of teachers. It is part of what continues to make instruction very teacher centered and what makes many students disinterested in learning. We have explored ways of involving students in these decisions, ways that responsibly deal with students' lack of experience and preparedness to make learning decisions, and ways that allow faculty to meet their professional obligations. The power issues involved in teaching are pervasive, subtle, and intriguing. They merit careful analysis as we seek to use power to affect learning outcomes more positively.

Chapter Three

The Function of Content

Strong allegiance to content blocks the road to more learner-centered teaching. Unlike power, where the influence is largely unrecognized, the content barrier explicitly impedes faculty. Most of us have no trouble acknowledging that the need to cover content strongly influences, if not dictates, most instructional decisions. Our thinking about content has long been dominated by one assumption: more is better. The time has come to challenge that assumption—not with content-free courses but with new thinking about the function of content. Learner-centered objectives allow us to do just that.

Our strong content orientation is reflected in the metaphor used to describe the action we take with respect to content: we "cover" it. But what exactly does that metaphor mean? We "cover" content—like leaves cover the forest floor? Like a bedspread covers the bed? Is that the relationship that ought to exist between the teacher and content when the goal is learning? I rather prefer one I have seen illustrated in a cartoon. A faculty person (usually male and rotund) is standing squarely in front of a blackboard with pieces of a problem appearing on either side of him. The caption proclaims: "Aim not to cover the content but to uncover part of it."

At the end of a course, most of us readily admit that we have way too much jammed into the ten or fifteen weeks, but when the time comes to get the syllabus ready for next semester, it is only after great agony that we decide to leave anything out. We know we have a problem but are paralyzed to do anything about it. Perhaps if we traced the origins of our commitment to content, we might better understand why we orient so strongly to it.

The allegiance to content begins in graduate school, where long years of course work develop content expertise. We begin and many of us continue our academic careers knowing a great deal about the disciplines we teach. Most of us begin and continue knowing nothing or very little about teaching and learning. We may participate in a few workshops that aim to "train" us, but what we know of pedagogy pales in comparison to all we end up knowing about content.

We are comfortable with and gravitate toward content knowledge. This natural allegiance is further cemented by links made between course reputation and content. The more content there is and the more complicated that content is, the more rigorous and therefore the better that course and its instructor are. At most research universities, and some other types of institutions as well, faculty can commit many pedagogical sins and find forgiveness so long as their courses have rigor and standards. Easy is never good when it comes to a college course. The easy course, it is assumed, has less or lightweight content, never mind how much or how well students may learn the material in either course.

Many of the consequences of this allegiance to content are counterproductive. Let us begin with faculty. The perceived value of covering content has taken away the discretion of some to teach less. A math faculty member, for example, cannot leave out the last three chapters in the textbook even if there is not enough time to cover them because the next course in the sequence depends on that material having been taught. The nursing or accounting professor cannot substitute a project for content if that material is likely to show up on the licensing exam. Even the decision making of the tenure-track faculty member is constrained by what colleagues might conclude about courses with anything less than a massive amount of material.

Have we ever stopped and asked ourselves how much content is enough? How much is enough in the major courses? In the entry-level ones? This is a question we ought to put to ourselves every time we make a content decision. We also need to ask it collectively in professional contexts where curriculum requirements have precluded individual decision making. But in either context, individual or professional, we will find few, if any, criteria that might be useful in guiding decisions as to the amount of material. Take away the more-is-better assumption, and we have no idea how much content is needed in an entry-level course, major course, elective course, or senior or first-year seminar.

The race to cover content has equally negative consequences for students. It reinforces learning strategies that focus on memorizing, regurgitating, and forgetting (recall the differentiations between deep and surface learning highlighted in Chapter One). For a while, a graphic metaphor circulated on many campuses: comprehensive finals were dubbed academic bulimia for the way they encourage students to binge and purge knowledge. That students retain little understanding of course content has been documented so many times and in so many different contexts that it is impossible to list all the research—not that we need research evidence. We see it all too clearly when we teach the next course in the sequence. Sitting before us are students who received A's and B's in the prerequisite course, and yet when asked a question that draws on prior knowledge, they look perplexed and confused; most do not venture even a guess.

Finally, in terms of impact on students, our strong allegiance to content prevents us from using methods and activities that strengthen learning outcomes and develop learning skills. Many times at the end of a faculty workshop on active learning, a participant will say to me, "I know you're right. I really should get students doing more, but I just can't. In this particular [as if it were special, unique and unlike most every other] course, I just have too much material to cover." Notice the dichotomous thinking: either content is being covered or active learning is happening, as if the two were isolated, independent, and unrelated activities.

Ramsden (1988) has summarized the negative consequences of our fixed focus on covering content:

> The message of scores of studies on student learning is unambiguous: many students are highly adept at very complex skills in science, humanities and mathematics. They can reproduce large amounts of factual information on demand; they have

appropriated enormous quantities of detailed knowledge: they pass examinations successfully. But they are unable to show that they *understand* what they have learned. They harbor profound misconceptions about mathematical, physical and social [phenomena]. They have hazy notions of the accepted form of expression in the subjects they have studied [pp. 13–14].

If these negative outcomes are not reason enough to revisit the assumptions made about the role of content in the college experience, then add to them another set of reasons that relate to the changing nature of knowledge and what we are learning about the acquisition of it. First, so much knowledge exists now that it is impossible to teach students everything they need to know about anything. They must be able to continue learning after their formal educational experience ends. A metaphor made this clear to me. I was interviewing Chris Knapper (Weimer, 1988b) about *Lifelong Learning and Higher Education* (Knapper and Cropley, 1985), and in discussing the need for students to learn from and throughout life, he pointed to how much this differed from our traditional notion of "education by inoculation," where we give students a "dose" of content and hope that it will be enough to carry them through their working lives. That may have been the case in previous centuries but no longer. Learning will be a lifelong occupation for our students.

Second, as students face a lifetime of learning, they will not be learning new information, they will be relearning old information. Not only is knowledge growing explosively, but old understandings are constantly being replaced by new ones, so what students may have learned in college, they will need to relearn. The net effect of the expansion and evolution of knowledge is that learning will be a much more important aspect of professional life than in the past. Students need to graduate from college knowing as much about learning content as they know about the content itself. Jarvis, Holford, and Griffin (1998), who identify thirteen societal shifts that have contributed to the emergence of lifelong learning as an educational reality for students today, arrive at this conclusion too. So do Knapper and Cropley (2000) in the third edition of *Lifelong Learning and Higher Education*. With each edition, they make the case more strongly: in college, students must develop sophisticated learning skills because they will need them throughout life.

Third, faculty have assumed (often tacitly) that learning skills develop by osmosis—that by solving problems, students learn problem-solving skills, for example. Research does not verify that outcome. One of many illustrative studies (Woods, 1987) found that in a four-year engineering program, students observed professors working more than one thousand problems. The students themselves solved more than three thousand homework problems and worked problems on the board. "Yet despite all this activity, they showed negligible improvements in problem solving skills. . . . What they did acquire was a set of memorized procedures for about 3,000 problem situations that they could, with varying degrees of success, recall" (p. 59). It may be that student understanding of problem solving, critical thinking, or whatever else the learning skill might be develops intuitively, that they really do know how to solve problems but cannot articulate the process. That assumption merits testing, but until knowledge is explicit, it masters the learner rather than the learner's mastering it.

Finally, the electronic environment has changed the role of content in learning by fiat. It has rendered the teaching-as-transfer-of-information model pretty much obsolete. Most of us understand that, but higher education is responding slowly and tentatively. *Dancing with the Devil* (Katz and others, 1999) contains a strong and scathing critique of higher education's response to the electronic environment. We have not quite figured out how to respond to technological devices that literally put a world of information at our fingertips. A lot of what used to have to be stored in brains, plus a good deal more than could be placed in most brains, is now only a few clicks away. Information management skills are now as important as information acquisition skills. Today's learners must be able to access information, find resources, organize them, and, perhaps most important, evaluate the ocean of information that now exists in that electronic sea.

As it currently stands, content, not teachers or learners, centers the instructional universe. If we aim to be learner-centered, content still needs to be a focal point of the universe, but it can no longer be the exclusive center, the only or even most important variable when it comes to instructional decision making.

How the Function of Content Changes

The content change in learner-centered environments involves a dual function for content: establishing a knowledge base and promoting learning. In learner-centered teaching, content functions as a means as well as an end of instruction. It becomes the means whereby learning outcomes are explicitly advanced. This section explicates the new relationship in more detail, outlines the benefits that accrue from it, and tackles some existing attitudes that prevent faculty from using content to accomplish more than knowledge base building.

Understanding the New Content-Learning Relationship

An understanding of this relationship requires an understanding of what learning means when content functions to promote it. Certainly, students are "learning" the content now. And that is the purpose for which we use content: students "learn" a body of knowledge. When content functions to accomplish two purposes, students still learn the body of knowledge, but they also learn about learning. Content can teach students about learning in three ways.

First, we "use" content (not "cover" it, a point made clear to me by Finkel, 2000) as a vehicle to develop learning skills. This means that we help students acquire a repertoire of strategies, approaches, and techniques that they can use when they need to learn material like that of the discipline. These may be basic skills like time management, communication and computational skills, and study skills, important to learning almost any sort of material, or they may be much more sophisticated skills, ones uniquely associated with the acquisition of a particular kind of content.

Second, we use content to promote self-awareness of learning. Students need to be made aware of themselves as learners and develop confidence in their ability to tackle learning tasks on their own. They need to understand how they learn, including their natural proclivities and preferences as learners. They also need to develop an accurate assessment of their strengths and weaknesses as learners and then acquire strategies that help them build on strengths and compensate for weaknesses. Self-awareness is the foundation on which further development as a confident, self-directed, and self-regulated learner grows. Drawing from work in many areas, Rawson (2000) builds a strong and well-documented case for this personal development, arguing that learning must be thought of as more than just a basic skill set.

Finally, content promotes learning when we let students use content so that they learn and experience it firsthand. In a learner-centered classroom, students do more than hear from the teacher about the work that biologists do; they do the work themselves. That does not mean that they are in sophisticated labs pushing back the horizons of knowledge, but rather than having the teacher tell them how biologists collect observational data, they collect data; rather than having the teacher tell them the outcome of a classic experiment, they are given the data and challenged to hypothesize about the results. Using content to promote the development of learners means using active learning strategies every day.

These three features differentiate this new content-learning relationship from what currently happens. First, content is not covered; it is used to develop a knowledge base. Second, content is used to develop learning skills, and finally, it is used to create learner awareness. These changes are accomplished through active learning strategies that allow students firsthand experience with the content.

The Benefits of the Content-Learning Link

Using content to develop a knowledge base and prowess as a learner makes for a more complex and connected relationship between content and learning. A kind of synergy makes the two together more than each was separately. Currently, we tend to think of the relationship dichotomously; either we are covering content, or we are doing things that promote learning. In a learner-centered environment, content and learning are thought of as mutually reinforcing. Two examples will illustrate how this synergy can work.

The first is active learning, that large repertoire of strategies and techniques designed to involve and engage students. Active learning is not a set of tricks to use with basically bored students. It is a powerful learning tool with well-established results. Those results, however, accrue only when active learning strategies involve

content. Whatever it is that students are doing should involve legitimate, bona-fide course content. When it does, there is a better
chance that students will learn the content, and it is learned
through mechanisms with the potential to teach them important
lessons about learning in the process.

This melding of active learning and content is not always (or
usually) done smoothly. When students "do" the content, they end
up "covering" it much less efficiently than faculty can. Given our
experience and expertise, this is not surprising. But what is lost in
efficiency is offset by gains in motivation and learning skill development. Moreover, the efficiency loss may be temporary. As students develop more sophisticated learning skills, their ability to
"cover" and use content increases. The example illustrates how
content and learning benefit when they are combined in active
learning strategies.

The benefit of linking content and learning can be seen in a
second arena as well. One of the findings emerging out of extensive experience with remedial course work is that students do not
develop basic learning skills or more sophisticated ones nearly as
well absent a disciplinary context. The best place to teach learning
skills is not the remedial course but the regular course. This is not
a surprising conclusion. There is not much motivation to think critically when there is no legitimate content to think about. There is
not much motivation to work on skills that prepare for future
encounters with content. We teach learning skills more effectively
when that instruction occurs in the context of a course with disciplinary content.

Adjusting Attitudes

Regrettably, a number of attitudes prevent faculty from experiencing the benefits possible when content and learning outcomes
are connected. Consider three; they may relate to your own beliefs
and instructional practice.

The first hearkens back to our attachment to content and sense
that keeping lots of complicated material in a course is a matter of
maintaining standards. The attitude that needs adjustment is the
belief that teaching learning skills dilutes the intellectual currency
of the course, partly because the course will include less content

but also because learning skills are viewed as less intellectually robust. Candy's profile of the autonomous learner (1991) lists over one hundred research-identified competencies related to successful independent learning. These competencies involve an explicit understanding of complicated learning skills like the ability to be methodical and systematic, to have well-developed information-seeking and retrieval skills, and to have the ability to be flexible and creative.

Within the contexts of our disciplines, learning skills involve understanding the unique configuration of content within a field and how that particular organization differs from the way knowledge is structured in other fields. It involves the ability to apply theoretical information to complex practical problems. It involves the ability to integrate information from different areas creatively in order to explain particular phenomena better. This is not watered-down content but complex understandings that go to the heart of what we know and how we know it.

The second attitude that prevents us from using content to promote learning is the rather high-minded belief that college faculty should not have to teach basic skills. In some ways, it is a moot point. We can say that we should not have to, that basic education has failed us, that it is our students' fault and therefore not our responsibility. But when our students graduate still missing those basic skills, we have already seen whom society (and specifically legislatures) holds accountable. We need to move beyond an existential consideration of what we should and should not have to do and face the reality of today's college students. Gardiner (1998) reports that in a sample of 745 undergraduates, only 14 percent said that they had been taught how to study. Kiewra and others (2001, p. 4) ask an obvious question: "How can strategy instruction be remedial if strategy instruction never occurred in the first place? The truth is strategy instruction is not remedial; it is enriching." Moreover, it is possible to teach basic and more sophisticated learning skills in ways that do not gut the content or intellectual potency of the course. Consider the examples that follow in the next section.

Finally, there is the "add-on" attitude—the belief that you can just add on learning skill instruction and fit it in rather than cut course content. In fact, some content must go. We cannot continue to teach as much as we are teaching, always jamming in more and then teaching learning skills on top of that. Not all or even most content must be eliminated, but we need to make room to include material, activities, and assignments that focus on the learning of this content. And we need to release that content, understanding that for many, the decision has political ramifications and must be made carefully, but still accepting and acting on the strong reasons that justify, indeed demand, that we teach less content.

Content in a learning-centered environment functions to accomplish two purposes: it establishes the foundation of knowledge on which subsequent learning rests, and it becomes the vehicle whereby and through which learning skills and awareness are developed. Students need to leave college knowing content *and* knowing how to learn more. If we need to adjust our attitudes in order to act on this second goal for content, let us make those adjustments and move on to implementation.

In the Trenches: Policies and Practices That Connect Content and Learning

The examples that follow illustrate the guidelines for teaching learning skills and developing learner awareness. They also show how content can be used to accomplish learning objectives without robbing the course of its content integrity.

Because a great deal has already been written on active learning and its many strategies that allow students to use, experience, and otherwise work with content, I will not "cover" or summarize this voluminous and comparatively well-known literature. If you have not sampled this work, by all means avail yourself of it. I have listed and described a few of my favorite books in Appendix C. I do so with the caveat that as many good sources are missing from the list as are included.

Developing Learner Skill and Awareness: Some Guidelines

The decision to teach less content in the interest of doing more to develop students as learners is a political one. Faculty need to make that decision in the light of potential consequences. Most of us are not going to find ourselves in positions where we can release as much content as we might like or need to in order to develop the kind of skills outlined here. For the time being, we have to cut here and there and work around the edges of our courses. The guidelines assume a large, continuing presence of content, but it is now present in courses that are being taught by faculty with a commitment to do what they can to develop learning skills and learner awareness. Much that is worth doing can be accomplished in small spaces and times carved out during courses.

For most faculty, teaching students to be better learners marks a foray into a new area. However, there are many ways to develop learning skills and learner awareness, and most of them are not difficult. The guidelines offer how-to advice. They do so assuming teachers may not have much previous experience or expertise in the area.

Given these two realities, the guidelines and examples that follow address skill development and learner self-awareness at basic levels. These are not guidelines and examples that develop sophisticated learning skills or learner awareness. Those are omitted because this is basically a book for beginners: faculty new to learner-centered teaching and students in need of stronger basic skills and first insights into themselves as learners.

Think Developmentally

The process of developing learning skills and awareness starts with students at one place and through a variety of content learning experiences moves them to a place of greater intellectual maturity, responsibility, and learning competence. It is a gradual process. Activities and assignments build on the previous ones, and these current experiences become the platform that supports subsequent ones. (Chapter Eight is devoted to a consideration of a variety of developmental issues that relate to learner-centered teaching.)

Make Short Activities Routine

Do not underestimate what can be accomplished in five minutes. And if you regularly devote short time intervals to learning issues, that creates the expectation that the course is about content *and* about learning skills and self-awareness. Both of these help students successfully master the material in this course (and probably other courses as well).

Target Skill and Awareness Development

No one course can do everything that needs to be done for learners. Given the skill and awareness level of most students, it is easy to come up with a lengthy list of skills they need and self-awareness they lack. Coming up with a long list is fine, but prioritize the list. What do your students most need to succeed with the content of this course? And how many learning issues can you realistically tackle in the course? Without clear answers to both questions, you are likely to end up working on too many different skills. When efforts are spread too thin, you lose the more powerful impact that can be achieved by a set of integrated activities designed to target one or two critical learning areas. Do not take it upon yourself to do everything that needs to be done with students. (More discussion of this guideline occurs in Chapter Nine on implementation issues.)

Take Advantage of the Need-to-Know and Ready-to-Learn Moments

There are times in the process of doing or having completed an activity or assignment when students need to know or are ready to learn. Take advantage of those moments. Use them to underscore the importance of a skill or insight, offer material or resources relevant to skill development, or guide students to an important insight about themselves as learners.

Partner Positively with Learning Center Professional

Professionals in your local learning center are allies in efforts to develop learning skills and awareness. Too often, we undermine what they can contribute by making the learning center a place where nobody wants to go. "Anybody with a score less than 60 on the exam, you need to go to the learning center and get help." "You go to the learning center, get those writing problems fixed, and then I'll talk with you about the content ideas in this paper." True, the learning center is a place to go for help with problems, but for a lot of students who lack confidence in themselves as learners, having to admit they have a problem prevents many of those most in need of help from taking advantage of it.

Help-seeking behavior has been studied in a variety of contexts, including the academic one. Some of the most widely referenced work has been done by Karabenick (for example, Karabenick and

Knapp, 1988, 1991; Karabenick, 1998). In a very useful nontechnical summary of his research that includes instructional implications, Karabenick (1990) differentiates between two different goals of help seekers: the "executive" help seeker who wants answers to the math homework so he will not have to do it and the "instrumental" help seeker who wants to learn how to do the work himself.

The work of Karabenick and others looks at help seeking as a process and studies what influences decisions at each step of the process. First, students must determine that a problem exists and that help will alleviate the problem. Next is the complicated decision of deciding to seek help—not an easy one for students or anyone else in a culture that prizes the ability to figure it out for yourself, where the request for help undermines the sense of personal adequacy and is cause for embarrassment, and where getting the help itself may cause performance anxiety. And finally, students must seek help. Here, Karabenick has studied both the formal sources of help such as that provided by a learning center as compared with and to informal sources like other students, friends, or family. Students find the informal sources less threatening and more convenient. After encountering the work of Karabenick, I thought differently about my role connecting students to and with the help they need.

Use Supplementary Materials

Supplementary materials are the most common way faculty work on skill and awareness development. They are favorites because they can be assigned for working on out of class and thereby do not take class time away from content. I advocate using supplementary materials because good supplementary materials can support your work on developing learning skills and awareness by underscoring what is already an in-class priority and by helping make students responsible for their own development. (Chapter Five addresses learner-centered instruction that develops student responsibility.)

We need to think much more creatively and innovatively about supplementary materials. We tend to favor strongly worded, authoritarian directives, typically including them in the syllabus, where they are not likely to be read, at least according to results reported by Becker and Calhoon (1999). Appendix B contains some samples of supplementary materials that demonstrate the kind of creative formats, tone, and content we need to aspire to with supplementary materials—for example:

- Learning strategy material on note taking formatted as a matrix
- Material that puts the ball in student courts, like a handout describing how students (on their own) can form and get credit for study groups and a "bill of rights" outlining what those groups owe their members
- A research summary that describes the impact of four different note-taking strategies
- Advice delivered with style and without condescension

Besides supplementary materials you might develop on your own and borrow from colleagues, do not neglect professionally developed resources. There are many. For starters, consider an instrument developed by Biggs and recently updated by Biggs, Kember, and Leung (2001) that helps students (and their teachers) ascertain the extent to which students are using the deep or surface approaches to learning. I recommend inventories like the Learning and Study Skills Inventory (LASSI; Weinstein, Schulte, and Palmer, 1987), which gives students a comprehensive and constructive overview of study skills, and the Perceptions, Expectations, Emotions and Knowledge About College inventory (PEEK; Weinstein, Palmer, and Hanson, 1995), which helps students assess their thoughts, beliefs, and expectations about personal, social, and academic changes likely to occur in college. PEEK is a great tool for helping students develop accurate expectations about what it takes to succeed in college. Better known are the various learning style inventories that develop awareness by giving students feedback on the approaches they take to learning. A very short inventory (Fleming and Mills, 1992; also available and scorable on-line at www.active-learning-site.com/inventory1.html) gives feedback on preferred approaches to learning and offers study strategy advice based on the approaches. The learning center undoubtedly will have a variety of learning resources available and recommendations on others too.

Learning Skill Development: Examples

The examples that follow for developing learning skills connect content and learning and illustrate the guidelines in action. They can be adapted for use with a variety of kinds of content and in a range of instructional settings. Lists like these also can stimulate individual thinking about other possibilities. How might you develop learning skills, given your students, your content, and your instructional setting?

Teaching Reading Skills Developmentally

Imagine that it is the first day of class in an entry-level course where most students do not have strong textbook reading skills. You make a reading assignment, and tell students to come to the next class session with their books and having done the reading. The next day you arrive, knowing in your heart how many books and prepared students will be in class, but still positive and with your book. You start the discussion by opening the book to page 3. "See, here on page 3, I have the second sentence in this first paragraph underlined." Turn the book toward the class, and show the underline. "How many of you have underlined this sentence?" The students respond. The few books that are in class are opened. The rest find their pencils. "What page was that? What sentence?" They write it down. You know that by tomorrow, that sentence will be underlined in most books—not an especially encouraging response but still a start.

The next day in class, along with the students, many more books and markers come to class. Perhaps this is the class of every student's dream: the one where the teacher tells you exactly what to underline. But it is not that kind of class. Today, the teacher does not tell students what she has underlined, but has the whole class turn to the discussion of Plato's political influence on pages 36 through 39. "What do you have underlined on these pages? . . . You have all of page 36 underlined? . . . It is all equally important? Let's talk a few minutes about how you decide what to underline. . . . Are there other things you might do with important text besides underlining it? . . . Now, let's talk further about what you do with the material you've underlined."

The third day in class, there might be a short lecture, followed by the question: "How does the material I've just presented relate to what you read last night? Let's see if we can articulate that relationship. . . . Does what I've said contradict what's in the book? Does it agree? Have I provided examples to illustrate concepts presented in the book? Did I repeat what's in the book? Why might it be important to understand the relationship between the material I present and the material contained in the book?"

This example illustrates a targeted effort to work on developing reading skills using the course textbook. I would schedule it early in the course so that students acquire some skills with text reading at the beginning of the course. Obviously, no teacher can develop sophisticated reading skills with three short sequences, but you begin the process and if you follow up with events that regularly confront students with how they are doing the reading as well as what they are getting out of it, they will read more efficiently during the course and leave it with better textbook reading skills.

Letting Students Learn How to Summarize

The last five minutes of a period are the most difficult instructional time of a class. One of my colleagues describes what he called the "book bag levitation factor": as the period moves into its final minutes, book bags start being picked and packed up. Once a critical mass is off the floor, the period is effectively over regardless of how hard the teacher tries to keep control of those last few minutes.

Consider alternative approaches that work on summarizing skills and may keep book bags on the floor as well:

Let the students summarize during those last five minutes. You can do that in a variety of different ways—for example, give them two minutes to review their notes and underline what they think are the key ideas. Have them trade notes with a person sitting nearby and discuss what they do and do not both have underlined. Finish by having a couple of pairs share their conclusions.

Ask a student to take notes on an overhead transparency. During the last five minutes, put those notes on the overhead, and have the class propose what should be underlined; perhaps elaborations or revisions are needed as well.

Have students write two- or three-sentence summaries of the material presented. Ask to have those submitted, and use a couple of good examples to tie content from the previous period to this new one.

Ask students to summarize by suggesting what material in their notes they think they are most likely to see on the exam. Have them do the summary by writing possible test questions.

The last suggestion is one of my favorite strategies because sometimes I get a question or something close to one that I can use on the exam. Once students see questions from this summary activity on the exam, I have had classes ask me if they can propose possible questions during the last five minutes. Sometimes their motivation is not the same as mine, but I still use it because reviewing notes, selecting a piece of key content, and framing it as a test question is an excellent way to learn how to summarize and check for understanding.

I do a lot of instructional observation and almost always see faculty summarizing the content. Why don't we let students summarize—not just at the end of the period but at the conclusion of discussions and at the end of units? I think it is because they do not do it especially well and/or efficiently. As we wait and then work with them on what they propose, we start feeling anxious about how much time this is taking. Soon we jump in, doing it for them or finishing up whatever they have started. Perhaps students learn how to summarize from our good examples. Because I am old and cynical, I think it is more likely that students learn that if they wait and make a few feeble attempts, the teacher will bail them out. But they will learn to summarize if we regularly devote those last five minutes to student summaries, working to help them pull together the key content elements of the period.

Learning About Learning from Each Other

A physics professor I once observed had students who had done well on exams in class the previous semester write a set of study suggestions for students in the next class. He distributed these the week before the exam, on a handout, with the students from the previous semester identified, along with their course grades (he had their permission, of course). I happened to be observing on a day when he distributed them and was amazed at the attention students directed toward that handout. Everyone was reading it; lots of students were underlining parts of it; and it went into everybody's notebook. And guess what sort of advice students offered? You could all but hear faculty speaking:

"Be sure you do the homework problems every night. They really help you with the exam."

"Do practice problems to prepare for the exam."

"Don't skip this class; the more times you see, hear, and encounter these problems, the better."

"Ask him questions in class. He can answer them then. It's too late during the exam."

A number of faculty have students from one class write letters to students the following semester telling them how to do well in the course. A lot of faculty use these letters to give themselves feedback about the course (which they do very effectively), but a compilation of excerpts from several makes an excellent handout for distribution early in the course. Another faculty member invites three or four students who received A's in the course to come to class and discuss how they approached the work. After introducing the panelists, the instructor leaves so that students can have an open and honest exchange. It takes a certain amount of faith to let this discussion happen unmonitored, but doing so adds an extra level of authenticity that motivates students to participate and take the advice much more seriously.

The Learning Center Comes to Class

A colleague in history invites a learning center professional to class. He presents the material, and the students and learning center representative take notes. Students then give their notes to the learning center professional, who returns to class during the next session with some general responses to how students are taking notes and some specific examples from notes taken in class. The learning center presentation takes twenty minutes. This strategy illustrates the powerful connection between content and learning when the two are married in an activity that promotes both. This example could exist in other iterations. For example, have students write a couple of paragraphs describing how they prepared and studied for an exam. Share those with the learning center person along with your sense of common problems and errors on the exam. Have that person come to class when you debrief the exam, and make specific preparation and study recommendations based on how students say they studied and you say they performed.

Developing Learners' Self-Awareness: Examples

As you consider the options that follow and use them to generate ideas of your own, bear in mind that activities and assignments that develop learning skills and those that cultivate awareness of the self as a learner are often related and can be linked. When you work on textbook discussion skills generically, incorporate a component that encourages students to confront and analyze their individual skills in this area. Taking this approach allows you to tackle development efficiently. Moreover, the impact of one activity increases when it connects with other learning experiences in the course.

Students' lack of confidence is another important consideration when developing activities that promote self-awareness. So many students now arrive in math and writing courses convinced that they "can't do" math and writing that the biggest instructional challenge ends up being trying to dislodge those convictions. When confronted with new material or learning tasks, these students give up quickly and easily. They run out of alternative approaches to try just about the same time they decide that for inherited or genetic reasons, they probably will never be able to figure it out anyway. For these reasons, it is important to use activities that help students build confidence in their ability to learn as they develop self-awareness.

How Do You Learn?

I routinely ask my students (graduate students too) to write a short paper identifying their favorite and most effective learning strategies as they relate to the content in this course. From the undergraduates, I get short, tortured paragraphs about using flash cards and recopying (*not* rewriting) their class notes. From the graduate students, I get paragraphs less tortured but no more insightful. What would we get if we asked faculty to write the same paper?

More substantially, you might have students track their learning using a learning log. Students not experienced in writing about learning may need some prompts to stimulate careful, in-depth analysis. But putting on paper what you have learned effectively reinforces that learning and directs attention to the learning processes themselves. For faculty in disciplines that do not rely as much on writing or for faculty who might need a concrete example, I recommend Maharaj and Banta (2000). Although their context is engineering, their delineation of different types of entries is helpful in learning log assignment design.

What Can You Learn from Exam Results?

When I debrief the first exam in my entry-level course, I do the standard discussion of most missed items, but I also have every student do a simple item analysis in three categories. They make a list of the number of each question missed. Then they go back through their notes and identify how many of those questions were from days they were not in class. In the process, I raise for verification the widely held student assumption that they can miss class so long as they get notes from somebody else.

For the second point, students return to the list of questions missed, and I read the numbers of the questions that came from the reading. Then I have students determine whether they are missing more questions from the reading or from class notes. Most miss more from the reading, which provides another opportunity to work on reading skill development, but I do not offer advice on how to do it. I ask students who missed none or few of those questions to share with the rest of the class how they study the reading. I ask how many in that group did not do the reading. I ask how many waited until the night before the exam to do the reading. Few hands raise in response to either question, on a good day.

Finally, I have students return to their exam and look for the number of questions where they changed answers and how many times they missed or got the answer correct when they changed it. I talk with them a bit about the mixed research results on this point and encourage students to make an individual assessment on this exam, subsequent ones in this class, and exams in other classes so that they know whether it pays to change their answers.

Following this analysis, I have students write freely for five to seven minutes. They address the note to themselves and in it jot down some things they have learned from taking this exam that they would like to remember when preparing for the second exam. I collect these. I do not read or grade them but return them to students the week before the second exam. I begin that review session for the second exam by giving them three minutes to read what they wrote. The majority of the class does so with considerable interest.

How Can I Make Group Work Better?

Most students function in groups unaware that individuals in groups fulfill different roles and equally unaware of how they function in groups. To prepare students for participation in group work, I use the two-page Classroom Work Style Inventory (Kinsella and Sherack, 1995; this is one of several excellent surveys developed by Kinsella, some with colleagues), which gives students some feedback on the attitudes they have about working with others. I have them write in their logs about the results and assess whether those results mesh with their own perceptions of how they work with others and contribute in groups.

Later in the group activity (this is a study group and shared exam experience I write more about in Chapter Six), I have them do a paper analyzing how the group work is progressing. They comment on the roles of others as well as their own contributions. If a student's self-assessment differs wildly from how the rest of the group characterizes the role, I share that feedback with the student—not in an evaluative context but simply as information to consider and explain as the student analyzes how he or she functions in groups.

Sometimes the needed personal insight can come from a specific but generic discussion. Borrowing and adapting from what a colleague does, I frequently have students in study groups begin their group interaction by discussing the best and worst studying experiences they have had with other students. They conclude that exchange by writing a memo that outlines how they plan to work together constructively. They address the memo to me, and every student in the group signs it.

In these examples of how learning skills and learner self-awareness can be developed, content plays a central role. These activities and assignments stand to make students more effective learners in this course and other courses to come. When teaching is learner-centered, this larger and more productive relationship exists between content and learning.

Questions That Emerge When the Function of Content Changes

Trying to get a handle on the amount of content in courses and trying to use it in ways that promote learning skill development and self-awareness has raised several difficult and perplexing questions for me. They are difficult because the questions address problems that transcend the practice of one individual. They are questions best answered in the context of our institutions and professional associations and by instructional improvement experts. Minus their answers, we need to continue to ask, challenging ourselves for answers and pressing others with these issues central to student learning.

How Much Content Is Enough?

The decision to cut content has political ramifications. Although content may be cut to promote the development of students as learners, the decision is still a political one.

As long as the amount of content and course credibility remain linked, caution must be urged. If you are on a tenure track, think carefully before you change the amount of content in your courses significantly. If you teach a course in a sequence, consider how students will fare in the next course without what that course instructor considers prerequisite knowledge. If you teach in a program where the content you are deleting may appear on an accrediting exam, understand the consequences for your students and the program.

Still, every faculty member can delete some content. There is always room to advance the learning agenda even in courses that need to remain crammed with content. And if there is room to cut, the question of what and how much merits consideration. In my own course planning, I am often helped when I focus on a related question: What is it my students need to know and be able to do during their professional lives? What skills and knowledge will stand the test of time, given the dynamic nature of knowledge and information?

But in my own practice, I remain unable to answer the how-much-is-enough-content question when I think of it in a broad philosophical sense. If we take away the more-content-is-always-better assumption as the measure of course quality, what should replace it? How will we know a "good" course now? In contrast, we know a lot about instructor competence. The ingredients or components of effective instruction have been identified in the extensive work on student ratings. But we know much less about course effectiveness and assess the impact of courses much less often as well. Granted, current empirical methodologies make it tough to tie gains in learning directly to particular aspects of a course. However, if we want faculty to abandon the more-content-always-makes-a-better-course criterion, then we need alternative standards more in line with how content functions when the goals are learner-centered.

How Do We Change Attitudes About the Role of Content?

The decision to use content differently (including the decision to delete some of it) would be simple if there was support within our departments, colleges, and professional associations. But not only is there no support, there is virtually no discussion of the content-learning relationship despite the current interest in learning. There is some ongoing discussion of the ways and means to promote learning, but no one is proposing that learning skills be developed in lieu of some content. There is plenty of complaining about how much content we have to cover and a woe-is-us kind of response to the learning needs of students, but rarely have I heard colleagues (even tenured ones) venture out on the limb and propose that we pull back on content.

The question that has emerged out of my attempts to implement learner-centered teaching is this one: How do we encourage departmental, institutional, and disciplinary dialogue about the amount and purpose of content in courses? I am not sure I have much to offer in terms of an answer. I have had some luck pressing colleagues with the how-much-content-is-enough question. It raises the issues, and the ensuing discussion generally makes it clear that we do not have very good answers and that their absence does incriminate us. Perhaps this book will help start the dialogue. Certainly senior faculty have less to lose in the conversation than those in the process of getting tenure. And those of us who are fussing with the amount and purpose for which we use content and liking the results must describe accurately what happens when we start using content in the ways proposed. Finally, we can certainly hope that students who have experienced learner-centered environments will stand as eloquent evidence of the positive consequences that accrue when content is used to develop the knowledge base and the skills of learning.

What About Students at Different Skill Levels?

This is a repeat of the question raised in the previous chapter with respect to varying levels of student maturity. Students also vary in their level of learning skills and self-awareness. Many need basic skill development. For those who do not, what should we do for and about those with sophisticated reading skills when we need to take time to develop the much more basic skills of the majority? Is it ethical to let some students do one thing with skill development while others do something quite different? Is it pragmatically possible, given class size and teaching load?

Most skills (and reading skills are a good example) exist along a continuum, and so it is not too difficult to have students responding to text at different levels. If you are working with them on marginal notes (an interesting technique that seeks to encourage written response in the text as a way fostering interaction with text content; Moulds, 1997), it is reasonable to expect the more sophisticated readers to respond at a deeper and more insightful level. I find the same is true when I work with students on participation. Some are poised and confident about making contributions in class. My challenge to them is to take those skills to a new level. If they can ask and answer teacher questions, they should work on asking and answering fellow students' questions. If they like to express their opinion, let them do that not in response to what is happening in class at that moment, but in response to what they have read in the textbook. In this example, students who contribute in different ways enrich class discussion. However, most of the time, dealing with different skill levels is not this easy or obvious.

How Do I Adapt Generic Learning Activities to Fit the Content I Teach?

I believe that we greatly underestimate the complexity of the process involved in taking a generic active learning strategy and adapting it so that it fits the content, learning needs of students, instructor style, and instructional setting in which it will be used. The process is rarely addressed in active learning material or workshops. The focus there is on building a collection of techniques, an important objective, but real teaching skill shows itself in the management of that technique repertoire.

We know more intuitively than explicitly that the configuration of content directly shapes techniques. As a chemistry colleague pointed out to me early in my career as a workshop presenter, the periodic table is not "discussed" in the same way as themes in a novel are "discussed." That seems obvious, but what precisely is different about those two discussions? How do you take a strategy like learning logs that effectively promotes and reinforces content acquisition as it develops learner self-awareness and adapt it for use with different kinds of content? What content do you have students write about? What prompts do you pose about it? Do assessment processes and criteria change with different kinds of content?

Fortunately, for some strategies and in some areas, we can point to helpful pedagogical scholarship. I have already referenced an article on using learning logs within an engineering curriculum (Maharaj and Banta, 2000). But even valuable scholarship like this is about the experience of faculty members who did it in the context of a given course, and although they describe all the details associated with how they used logs, they do not generally discuss the process of adaptation, how they came to decide to use logs in these ways. Moreover, they do not extrapolate from their individual experience any larger set of adaptation principles that could be used. And to these omissions must be added the absence of scholarship in other fields on using logs and the absence of almost any discussion of a host of less well-known techniques.

In the chapter on implementation (Chapter Nine), I revisit the adaptation issue and propose some ways of approaching the task, but it is relevant now to raise the fact that all learner-centered strategies must be adapted, shaped, and molded so that they fit the context in which they are being used. In my own practice, I have struggled to make those changes, sometimes getting something finally to work, but still not fully or clearly understanding the nature of the changes I needed to make. Much more often, getting it right resulted from making some lucky guesses.

To Finish Up

Although there are serious impediments to implementing the changes outlined in this chapter, there is much all of us can do that will help students develop as learners. Anyone who aspires to be learner-centered has the responsibility to try. Faculty are bright, curious, intrinsically motivated learners. If we cannot figure out how to organize our content more efficiently so that we have five minutes now and then to work on the developing our students as learners, then nobody can.

In this chapter, we have seen that there are reasons to teach less content. We have seen that there are reasons that justify, indeed obligate, a larger focus on the development of learning skills and learner self-awareness. And we have seen that there are reasons and ways to join content and learning in a dynamic relationship that benefits content acquisition and learner development. Let us resolve to stop "covering" content and start "using" it to accomplish learner-centered objectives. Perhaps we need to post this admonition of Vella (2000, p. 11) in a prominent place where we will encounter it every day: "A good teacher does not teach all that he knows. He teaches all that the learner needs to know at the time, and all that the learners can accountably learn in the time given."

Chapter Four

The Role of the Teacher

Learner-centered teaching requires significant changes. Chapter Two challenges faculty to redistribute the balance of power in the class so that teaching more effectively empowers and motivates students. Chapter Three pushes on long-standing assumptions as to the preeminence of content and proposes that faculty need to do more than teach it; they must use it to develop learning skills and learner self-awareness. This chapter tackles something no less sacred or central: the role of the faculty member in the classroom.

Widespread interest in active, collaborative, and cooperative learning and other inquiry-based approaches has raised indirectly the issue of the teacher's role. Indeed, the effectiveness of these more learner-centered methods depends on faculty being able to step aside and let students take the lead. However, having been at the center so long, we are finding it tough to leave that spot, even briefly. As a result, what happens in most college classrooms continues to be very teacher centered, despite the interest in, support for, and some use of these more learner-centered methods.

Not all faculty accept that instruction remains teacher centered. I seek to make the case by describing what is observed in most college classrooms, what the empirical evidence documents, what receives attention in the teaching literature, and what the responses of students reflect about faculty roles. Daily events in most classrooms feature faculty. We deliver the content, lead (often controlling and directing) the discussions, preview the material and then summarize it, and provide the examples and ask students the questions about them. We are there solving the problems, providing the diagrams, graphs, and matrices. We work diligently to lay before students the disciplinary landscape of our fields. When it comes to who is working the hardest most days in class, we win, hands down.

Empirical evidence also bears witness of the extent to which we continue to dominate the instructional action in the classroom. Nunn's observational study (1996), confirming earlier findings reported by Barnes (1983), found that only 5.86 percent of total class time involved student participation: one minute per forty minutes of class time. Although the actual percentage varied widely among individual instructors, the highest percentage of time was 23. And when asked how actively students are involved in discussion, faculty consistently say students are more involved than students report they are (Fassinger, 1996).

Researchers at Kansas State University (Hoyt and Perera, 2000), surveying faculty users of their IDEA student rating form, asked faculty to identify which of nine teaching methods were their primary and secondary approaches. Twenty-seven percent listed lecture as their primary approach and discussion as their secondary. Add to that another 9 percent who listed a lecture and lab combination, and another almost 9 percent identifying lecture and skill and activity; the result is that 45 percent of faculty in the sample list as their primary method the most teacher-centered instructional method of all: lecture.

Consider next the literature on pedagogy, specifically books on teaching. They typically begin with a chapter on the characteristics of effective instruction, follow with advice on developing teaching style, explain how to analyze and improve classroom performance, explore selecting and organizing course content, say what teachers must do to interest and motivate students, and conclude with advice on evaluation. The how-to-teach literature focuses attention almost exclusively on actions that teachers perform. That effective teaching results in learning is assumed but rarely discussed explicitly. The preoccupation of the pedagogical literature with teaching provides clear evidence of a profession tightly connected to teaching but only loosely linked to learning.

If we look to student behavior, what we see there also reflects the extent to which we dominate the instructional action. They rely on us to make all their decisions and push us when we do not. "What do *you* want in this essay?" they ask. If we decline to answer and tell them they are missing the point, often they refuse to believe and continue trying to figure out what we want. Why do they think we want something? Where does that question come from? Could their need to know be related to the fact that they are used to having teachers who dominate the action in the classroom?

Getting students involved and participating in class is such hard work. We blame them, and some of the blame rightfully belongs there. But are they so reluctant and seemingly lazy because they have gotten used to teachers who talk most of the time—to teachers who answer their own questions at the first sign of student hesitation. Do we honestly believe they came to education as passive as they now appear?

Behaviors in the classroom, the empirical evidence, the pedagogical literature, and the responses of students all bear witness to the continuing teacher centeredness of most instruction. How much do you dominate the action in your classroom? I taught for years without ever realizing how much everything in the classroom focused on me. To be very honest, stepping out of the spotlight has been the most difficult part of my quest to become learner-centered. And finding yourself in the spotlight is only the first step. Once you realize you are there, you must step aside and then perform different actions.

How the Role of the Teacher Changes

In learner-centered teaching, instructors guide and facilitate learning. The role is not new; it has been written about for years. The difference is that it has been proposed as an alternative, one among a number of roles a teacher might choose or rotate between. With learner-centered teaching, the role is not optional. Our continued insistence on always being at the center of classroom activities directly compromises attempts we make to be learner-centered. We must move aside, often and regularly.

Defining the Role

Most often, the role is described metaphorically. Deshler (1985, p. 22) says that metaphors are the "stuff with which we make sense of the world." We can begin to understand and define the role sampling a collection of metaphors, including a number that have been around for some time now. Fox (1983) proposed four "personal theories" of teaching that can be equated with roles. In the learner-centered model, he compares the teacher's role to that of the gardener—the one who prepares the ground, tills, and cultivates, but whose plants do the growing. And although the gardener may take some credit for a beautiful garden, the real accomplishment belongs to the plants. They grow, bloom, and bear fruit.

Learner-centered teachers have been described as midwives. Ayers (1986) writes,

> Good teachers, like good midwives, empower. Good teachers
> find ways to activate students, for they know that learning requires
> active engagement between the subject and "object matter."
> Learning requires discovery and invention. Good teachers know
> when to hang back and be silent, when to watch and wonder at
> what is taking place all around them. They can push and they can
> pull when necessary—just like midwives—but they know that they
> are not always called upon to perform. Sometimes the perfomance
> is and must be elsewhere [p. 50].

The learner-centered teaching role has also been compared to that of a guide. Hill (1980, p. 48) eloquently describes the shared vulnerabilities when teachers and students climb together: "The Teacher as Mountaineer learns to connect. The guide rope links mountain climbers together so that they may assist one another in the ascent. The teacher makes a 'rope' by using the oral and written contributions of the students, by forging interdisciplinary and intradisciplinary links where plausible, and by connecting the course material with the lives of students." More recently, Marini (2000) revisited this metaphor and drew other useful comparisons.

Like the guide metaphor, the comparison to a coach (Dunn, 1992) also reinforces the facilitative aspects of the role. Barr and Tagg (1995, p. 24) play with this metaphor on a less obvious level: "A coach not only instructs football players . . . but also designs football practices and the game plan; he participates in the game itself by sending in plays and making other decisions. The new faculty roles go a step further, however, in that faculty not only design the game plans but create new and better 'games,' ones that generate more and better learning."

Eisner (1983) compares the teacher to a maestro before an orchestra, offering insights on the role from yet another perspective. You stand on the podium, the content score laid out before you. In front of you is a collection of musicians who play different instruments, at different levels of ability, and who have practiced this score varying amounts. Under your direction, they make music. I love the grand possibilities this metaphor implies, but from the podium before my classes, the sounds that I hear lead to only one conclusion: I am working to make music with the local band, not the New York Philharmonic.

The metaphor most used in current discussions of the learner-centered teaching role originally appeared as an article title: "From Sage on the Stage to Guide on the Side" (King, 1993). This pithy depiction accurately relocates teachers to a learner-centered position.

The prevalence of metaphors used to describe teaching roles attests to faculty's affinity for these kind of characterizations. But none of them is a functional description when it comes to defining the role precisely. From the metaphors, we learn what learner-centered teachers are like as opposed to what they do. It is more useful to describe the role in terms of actions, like these, for example: Learner-centered teachers connect students and resources. They design activities and assignments that engage learners. They facilitate learning in individual and collective contexts. Their vast experience models for novice learners how difficult material can be accessed, explored and understood.

Black (1993, p. 142) explicates the guide and resource role with this functional description: "My role . . . is as a guide and resource to the students while they work to master the material in their text. I help by directing their work with the text, by helping them to learn how to solve problems, and by helping them develop their own understanding of the concepts."

Metaphors and more functional characterizations combine to outline a facilitative, guiding role for learner-centered teachers. They position themselves alongside the learner and keep the attention, focus, and spotlight aimed at and on the learning processes. That is the role in a nutshell.

Why This Role?

The reason this role works is simple and obvious: when the focus is less on teaching and more on learning, learning is not assumed or presumed to happen automatically. Faculty become much more aware of how teaching influences learning. What students do and do not learn starts driving the instructional decision-making process. Students "learn" content and develop as learners much less effectively and efficiently if they are never given the opportunity to "do" the learning tasks that facilitate acquisition of content. Most do not learn how to summarize by listening to our summaries or reading those in the textbook. Examples like these can be summoned from almost every area of instructional practice.

When you present a concept in class and need examples to illustrate it, do you tap the well of student experience or ask them to identify ones that appear in the textbook? If you tap students, you know that getting the examples takes time and produces few as rich as those drawn from the much deeper well of your own experience. And you justifiably give your examples if you know that students are always going to be in positions where someone else will supply the examples (summaries, hypotheses, or answers). But I suspect that most students will find themselves in professional situations that will require them to come up with examples (outlines, theories, or solutions) on their own. How then do we teach them how to find or generate examples (questions, problems, or critical analyses) when they need them?

The conclusion here is general and much larger than examples, summaries, hypotheses, questions, answers, outlines, theories, problems, solutions, or critical analyses. Perhaps it is best offered in the context of the guide metaphor. What is the role of the guide? Guides show people the way, and sometimes they even go along, but guides do not make the trek for the traveler. Guides point out the sites; they do not experience the excitement of seeing them for the first time. Guides offer advice, point out the pitfalls, and do their best to protect, but it is not within their power to prevent accidents. Learner-centered teachers are there every step of the way, but the real action features students and what they are doing.

What Makes It Hard to Move Over?

Despite intellectually understanding and accepting the need to move over, most of us, even those of us committed to learning, are still in the driver's seat. We might squeeze over closer to the door and let students sit next to us, maybe even hold onto the wheel, but for all intents and purposes, we are still doing the driving. Why has it turned out to be so hard for us to let the focus be on students and learning? Consider several possibilities as they relate to faculty generally and you specifically.

First, we like having the main role. In many of us, there is a bit of the ham, maybe some frustrated entertainer. With a captive audience, we simply cannot pass up the opportunity to show our stuff. I love to spin a tale, and as the years have accumulated, so have my stories. Some I have told enough that I have perfected the lines. On a good day, I can spin one of those yarns, and even virtually comatose students come to life with faint smiles and a repositioning of lead bottoms. I relish the challenge and feel a sense of accomplishment when raucous laughter sweeps the class. And students remember my stories. Years later when I meet them, they remind me of the "dishwasher" story. The problem, of course, is that they rarely have the point of the story then, and so all my rationalization about stories being nails on which I hang all sorts of conceptual stuff (Amstutz, 1988) is really just an excuse for me to flaunt my storytelling prowess.

I do not think learner-centered teachers are forever forbidden from telling stories or whatever else they enjoy and do well in the spotlight. Besides, on some occasions, my stories do enable students to understand more easily. Rather, it is about honestly analyzing my motives (more critical reflection) for telling a story and making sure that I am telling it for right reasons, not self-serving ones.

Second, in addition to liking being at the center of the action in the classroom, we see the role of standing alongside learners as inherently less important than the one we have standing in front of them. But we are engaging in a bit of reality reconstructing here: we are not as essential and central as we like to believe. Despite expansive involvement in all aspects of instruction and student learning, we cannot guarantee delivery of the product. A student cannot be forced to learn, and a teacher cannot learn anything for a student. Students completely control the most central and important part of the educational enterprise. This is an enterprise that centers on learning, no matter where we position ourselves.

We also need to reassess our notion that this role is somehow a lesser one. It depends very much on the perspective taken. Most women panic at the thought of giving birth without some sort of guide alongside. Only very foolish and daring hikers ascend treacherous peaks alone. No orchestra makes music very long without a conductor. Teams without coaches do not have winning seasons. True, facilitative roles do not offer as much personal performance thrill, but they do hold for teachers the promise of more intimate, obvious, and essential involvement with students' learning. We can take, and students are much more likely to give, credit for what made learning possible. They learned because of us, not in spite of us.

Another and darker reason sometimes prevents us from moving toward more facilitative teaching roles. Teacher-student relationships can become entangled with issues of codependency and all the psychological benefits that accrue to both parties when relationships are dependent. For the student, there is the freedom from responsibility. For faculty, there are more unpredictable teaching variables nailed down, fewer loose cannons, and less vulnerability, plus the feeling of importance associated with making decisions for others. But for both parties, dependent relationships are basically unhealthy, ultimately limiting the potential for personal growth.

More obvious is yet another reason related to students. They often resist our attempts to move into more facilitative roles, and for very good reasons. Think back to the example of students generating examples. It is work for students to come up with them. For them, it is easier, more efficient, and much more comfortable having teachers provide the examples. Besides, that is what other teachers do. (Chapter Seven is devoted to ways of dealing with and overcoming student resistance.)

We use still another student reason to justify staying in the limelight, usually phrased as follows: "My students just can't handle the level of responsibility you're proposing. They are so immature, so poorly prepared, so passive, so uncooperative that it just would never work with them." In most cases, this masquerades as a reason—one that quite effectively precludes the necessity of confronting any of the real and much more personal reasons. (If this is your objection, proceed to Chapter Eight, where I outline the developmental issues involved and the approaches that can be taken.) You can start with students wherever they might be. I have been using these learner-centered approaches with decidedly average beginning students in a required course that meets at 8:00 A.M. And do not forget that Freire used them with illiterate peasants.

One last reason bridges us to the next section: we do not know how to do the new role. When we try, we feel awkward and uncomfortable, not good feelings to experience in front of a crowd. Facilitative instructional roles require skills most of us have not had the opportunity to polish. And we are so vested in our performance in class that we are often not objective or insightful when it does not go well (sometimes even when it does). We just know that it did not feel right, did not happen the way we wanted it to, so we conclude that this way of teaching does not work or judge ourselves failures and move back to that familiar and comfortable role that features us in charge of everything.

The Role Is Difficult to Do

Besides not knowing how to teach in ways that facilitate learning, the role itself requires a complex interplay of skills. If we go back to the generating examples illustration and play it out a bit more, we can learn what the role entails and why we often underestimate how difficult it is to execute, especially for those who aspire to do it well.

You have presented the concept and decide to go to the students for the examples: "Can someone give me an example to illustrate this concept? Maybe it's something from your experience or something that you read in the textbook that might illustrate this concept." You wait. Then you ask again, trying to sound confident and patient. No response. You look at Frieda; she almost always comes through. Her nonverbal behavior is not negative and so you do call on her: "Frieda, we need an example." Frieda starts off slowly. Some days she does back into answers but usually gets there. But today, her example does not make much sense even after several follow-up questions and some minor massaging of the idea on your part. You put it on the board anyway. This process takes so much work, the quality is marginal, and the process is time-consuming. It is a role that requires enormous patience, persistence, and tenacity, to say nothing of an ability to make something happen when nothing is and then an ability to take something of marginal quality and work with the student to make it better.

In addition, you must be willing to tolerate the messiness of learning that is happening right in the classroom. Lecture content sometimes causes great confusion, but students are so good at faking attention and not asking questions that the problem remains hidden until it emerges on the exam. When students are engaged in group work and executing the task poorly, that feedback is tough to miss. And part of the challenge is knowing what to do when a mess occurs in class. Do you point it out? Do you clean it? Or do you make them clean it up?

Moreover, you cannot always predict when they will execute poorly, and when they do, you must respond. You have no time to collect your thoughts calmly, analyze what has happened, why it happened, and what you will do about it. If students do not come up with good examples, you have to get them, and when instruction is learner-centered, always bailing them out with your own good examples is not an option. Now you add to this scenario student resistance and the pressure to cover content, and you begin to understand that successful execution of the facilitative roles may well require more sophisticated skills than orchestrating the show when only you perform.

There are all sorts of reasons to make that commitment to facilitative roles and all sorts of approaches, strategies, and techniques that help make their execution successful. Chapter Nine tackles your skill development for learner-centered teaching generally. The next section looks at the details of doing more facilitative teaching.

In the Trenches: Guiding Learners

This section focuses on what teachers do (and in a couple of cases do not do) when instruction is learner-centered. Here, we need more than examples. In fact, before the examples and then backing them up, we need general principles that can ground the actions used to execute the role. I identify, discuss, and offer examples for seven of these principles. The examples are but a few of the many options possible when putting the principles and role into action.

Principle 1: Teachers Do Learning Tasks Less

Teachers must stop always doing the learning tasks of organizing the content, generating the examples, asking the questions, answering the questions, summarizing the discussion, solving problems, constructing the diagrams, and others. The key word in the sentence is *always*. On occasion (and in some classes, there may be lots of occasions), teachers need to do all of these things for students. The principle is about gradually doing them less frequently, until the point is reached when doing them is the exception and not the rule.

I have already offered a variety of approaches for getting students involved with end-of-class summaries. Another possibility is to have them summarize discussions whenever they occur. I once observed a colleague who used the following technique: the class was discussing part of a novel. They were seated in a **U**, and they contributed ideas without being recognized. As they spoke, the teacher noted their comments on the board. She did not speak but focused on getting the essence of the contributions noted. After about ten minutes, she said to the class, "Where are we? We need to think about this exchange and see if we can draw some general conclusions out of it. Please review the notes I have made on the board." After several minutes of silence, she said, "Anybody see any connections between these comments?" As people ventured connections, she drew lines and circles, added numbers, occasionally revised, and sometimes erased. Gradually, some general conclusions emerged, and she asked students to attempt to phrase them in their notes. She had three put their phrases on the board. The class proceeded to discuss the merits of each. The one they finally came up with integrated several of their individual ideas.

The powerful part of the demonstration was how effectively the recording role removed her as the focal point of the discussion. Students were directing their comments and responses to each other. On most days in my class, it does not seem to matter where

I position myself in the classroom; students direct their comments to me nevertheless, but then I am the one who most often responds to the comments they make.

Black (1993) avoids doing the problem-solving work in his organic chemistry class with the following strategy. He arrives in the room early and writes problems on all the available board space. As students arrive, pairs are randomly selected and assigned a problem on the board. By the time class begins, eight to ten students are working on problems, and they continue to do so for the first five or ten minutes of the class. Black circulates around the classroom talking with other students and checking with those doing the problems to see how the work is going. If they are stuck, he may give a hint or ask a leading question. "As work finishes," he writes, "students other than those at the board are called upon . . . to analyze or comment on a given problem and its answer. . . . I help by providing questions to direct their assessment of the answer. Is the solution correct? Could it be better? If they do not think it is right, then what is the problem and how can it be fixed? What is the central idea? What principle is involved? How would you have done it?" (p. 143). Notice how his questions focus on the problem-solving process, not just the right answer.

Principle 2: Teachers Do Less Telling; Students Do More Discovering

Teachers have a serious propensity to tell. We tell students everything. We do a demonstration, and we tell students what we are going to do; when we have done it, we tell them what happened. We tell students when and how they should study. We tell students to do the reading and what parts of it are most important. We tell them to come to class. We tell them how to write their papers and which homework problems to do. In labs, we tell students every step on the way to a predetermined result. And what is there left for students to figure out for themselves? Are all these messages necessary? Do we know for sure that they promote learning? Do we know how they affect student attitudes toward learning?

Let me illustrate just how vicious these "telling" circles have become. We prepare a syllabus that outlines the details of the course and individual class sessions. But we have to "go over" it in class because students do not read it. We may editorialize and elaborate a bit here and there, but mostly we are repeating the written text. And so now students do not have to read. Moreover, they will continue to ask questions ("When is that group project due?") that are answered in the syllabus. And how many of us continue to answer those questions?

I can describe an alternative approach. The syllabus for my entry-level speech communication course is long and complicated (see Appendix A). I pass it out as students walk in on the first day. I give them ten minutes to read the document and say that I will answer any questions they might have about it. Invariably there are none. Remember that this class is not structured like most others; it requires students to make choices about assignments and includes unfamiliar learning activities, yet still nobody has any questions.

The first year, having no backup plan, I caved in and went over the syllabus with them. Now I say, "No questions, fine. Understanding the syllabus and how this course works is really a very important part of being successful in the course, and because part of my job is to help you be successful, let's do a little quiz and see how well you do understand." I have no intention of grading the ten-question true-false quiz I distribute, but I do not divulge that just yet. Once they have finished the quiz, I have them partner with the person sitting next to them and compare answers, consulting the syllabus for any about which they disagree. I then put the quiz on the overhead, and the class votes on the answers. For any that are close or wrong, I have students look at the syllabus outside class, and we begin the next class session by seeing if we can determine from the syllabus which responses are correct.

Two outcomes regularly result from this approach: the process generates good discussion about the class and its structure, and students start the course having looked at the syllabus for course-related information. I build on this beginning by introducing every assignment by having students get out the syllabus, read the description there, and then ask questions. When a student asks a question that is answered in the syllabus, I do not answer but kindly refer him or her to the syllabus.

Collectively, these simple actions stop me from telling students everything they need to know about the course and begin to make it their responsibility to find out what they need to know. You can use this "let them discover" principle with a variety of issues. If someone asks a question that is answered in the text, refer that person to the text, but always with the proviso that after checking, he or she is welcome to consult with you. If you have already covered some aspect of the content that reemerges in a new context, let students find the previous information in their notes.

To help you break the "telling" habit, you might try the approach Shrock (1992, p. 8) uses:

> Students say that my office reminds them of granny's attic: books and papers share space with political posters, Depression-era advertisements, campaign buttons, and ERA pennants. . . . But the most important sign is not politely historical, but fiercely oriented to the present and future. It refers to the constant challenge of student-centered teaching; it is deliberately placed at the side of my office door (above the light switch) so that it is the last thing I see before I head for class. In my own plain writing, the sign silently but simply insists: "Why are you telling them this" [p. 8].

Principle 3: Teachers Do More Design Work

The instructional design aspects of the teacher's role are much more important in learner-centered environments. Activities and assignment become the vehicles by and through which learning occurs. The most effective ones aim to accomplish one or more of the following four goals. First, they take students from their current knowledge and skill level and move them to a new place of competence, and they do so without being too easy or too difficult. Key here is our ability to sequence a set of related learning experiences so that they build on each other. (Examples of how to do this are included in Chapter Eight.) Second, the assignment and learning activities need to motivate student involvement and participation. The goal is to construct tasks that draw students in, so that they are engaged and energized almost before they realize it. Third, the assignments and activities need to get students doing the authentic and legitimate work of the discipline. These are not fake, artificial, or otherwise contrived activities or activity for the sake of activity, but ones that allow students to do (at their level) what biologists, engineers, philosophers, political scientists, and sociologists do. And finally, related and possibly overlapping a bit with the third goal, the assignments and activities of the learner-centered classroom explicitly develop content knowledge and learning skills and awareness (see Chapter Three for more details).

These goals set high standards, and it is unrealistic to expect to achieve them all with every activity and assignment, but they can effectively benchmark our design efforts. I will share examples that relate to all four goals but focus on the two not addressed elsewhere in the book: designing learning experiences that draw students in and providing authentic experiences with the content.

The design work of drawing students in needs to be tackled with ingenuity and creativity. The goal is finding structures and formats that highlight and otherwise showcase the inherent interest and intrigue of the content. Case studies, especially on controversial topics of interest to students, can effectively get passive students involved. I have had success with some cases that Silverman and Pace (1992) developed to stimulate faculty dialogue and discussion. My favorite is about a student who charges a teacher with a racially motivated grade and says that a learning disabled student in the class got preferential treatment. I give students the case the period before and tell them to read it and to come to class prepared to take a side. I structure the discussion using Frederick's forced debate method (1981). I create a center aisle in the room and then face the chairs toward this open space. As students arrive, they sit on the side that corresponds with the position they have decided to take. They then talk to each other about the reasons they are on that side. If they change their minds at any time during the discussion, they move to the other side of the room.

I am the recorder, dividing the board in half, noting arguments for changing on one side and arguments against on the other. Once I stop hearing new arguments, I have groups convene to discuss which of the arguments on their side they think are strongest and how they would answer what they believe are the best arguments from the other side. Then I have a volunteer from the side that does not think the grade should be changed be the teacher and a volunteer from the other side be the student. They then role-play an exchange between the two.

The activity never fails to generate student involvement. Students get warmed up and start to speak with feeling. Ideas fly back and forth. They argue, refute, summon evidence, and confront each other. This gives students the opportunity to argue publicly, which beginning students are often reluctant to do. It provides a great source of examples once we begin exploring different kinds of arguments, the principles of logic, and the forms of proof that qualify as evidence. The activity is adaptable in a variety of contents. There have been some great debates in science and even great scientific discoveries where the experiment itself becomes the case and students use their knowledge to predict the outcome. Herreid (1994, 1999) has proposed a number of excellent strategies for using cases in science classes.

Principle 4: Faculty Do More Modeling

Here faculty assume the role of master learner and demonstrate for students how skillful learners approach learning tasks. The best way to do this is by doing some legitimate learning in the class, but with an entry-level course that you have taught from the dawn of time, this may not always be possible. A good second way is always making sure that we are learning new things and not just more content in our fields. For many years, I have made the radical proposal that the best way to improve college teaching would be to require faculty to take a credit course not in their field once every three years. (For how effectively this reconnects faculty with relevant aspects of the learning process, see Starling, 1987, and Barrineau, 2000.) We need to experience the learning process regularly if we expect to appreciate and understand our students' first encounters with content now so familiar it feels as if we have always known it. As I complete final manuscript revisions, I am taking (along with sixty first semester, beginning students) an astronomy course, my first science course in more than thirty years. I can attest firsthand that it is an exhilarating and humiliating experience.

In lieu of taking courses, you can model learning processes by doing simple things like talking through the problem-solving processes you use when confronted with a problem. What goes through your mind? Share with students the dialogue you have with yourself. A related approach that also helps students is to try to recall when you first learned the material. Can you remember what mystified you and how you finally figured it out? Share your reflections, including what did and did not help you.

Students need to see examples of how learning is hard, messy work even for experienced learners. A colleague once shared that her students were demotivated by the revising and rewriting process; they took it as yet another sign of what really poor writers they were. She solved the problem by making copies of a set of revisions on her most recent paper. The students were amazed at how many changes their teacher had to make.

Principle 5: Faculty Do More to Get Students Learning from and with Each Other

Faculty frequently underestimate the potential value of students working together. Much research establishes their ability to learn from and with each other (Qin, Johnson, and Johnson, 1995; Springer, Stanne, and Donovan, 1997). Recently, group work, most often under the collaborative or cooperative learning rubric, has gained considerable popularity and much wider use. But like every other instructional method, good group learning experiences do not happen automatically. This should not surprise us, given the experiences most of us have on faculty committees.

Good group learning experiences are more likely to result when faculty attend to two areas, group dynamics (a relevant topic well addressed by a collection of sources in Appendix C) and the design of group tasks and structures, so that they address the four goals identified in the section opening and demonstrate to students the value and necessity of learning how to work together. Consider one example.

I try to demonstrate the value of collaboration in a venue students take seriously: exams. In my entry-level course, they may choose to be assigned to a study group that prepares jointly for the second exam and then participates in a group exam experience. The study group part of the assignment is one of the few open-ended options in the course. I convene the groups and have members start by sharing some informal writing they have done on best and worst study group experiences. Beyond that, I do not prescribe how much time the groups should spend together or how they should study. Despite having spent considerable class time on the fundamentals of group process, some groups still fail to function very effectively. They have trouble finding time to meet, some members miss meetings, they go over material in a cursory sort of way, and they spend most of their time telling each other that they understand what they need to know. More efficient groups assign individuals to be content experts for particular chapters, prepare study guides for each other, and query each other during review sessions. If groups have not functioned well as study groups, they may have individuals who do well, but they usually do not do well collectively on the exam.

Because for most students this is a new experience involving an important course event, I keep the grading stakes low. Good group performance gets rewarded; poor group performance is not punished. The grading bonus works like this. All students take the forty-question multiple-choice exam individually first. After all have completed the exam, they convene as a group and do one exam for the group. I grade the individual exams first and calculate an average score for group members. Then I grade the group exam. If the group score is higher than the individual average, that difference (usually between four and fourteen points on this eighty-point exam) gets added to each individual score. In his engineering course, Mourtos (1997) raises the grading stakes by forcing greater interdependence among group members. His bonus accrues only if all students score at a certain level on the exam. Benvenuto (2001) uses a similar approach in chemistry on weekly quizzes.

Watching the groups do the exam is my favorite day of the class. They hunker together around it. Their discussion starts out with a quiet intensity, but then the disagreements begin and the debate starts. My students avoid conflict and disagreement like a plague; they are scared of it. But here it happens without their even noticing. And this intense debate is over course content. They never talk about content with this kind of passion on any other day.

For students in the groups, insights about the value of collaboration are expressed in an analysis paper written after the exams are returned. Those receiving bonuses have tangible evidence of how the group helped them. Those who did not get bonuses can generally identify the reasons. And there are insights for other students as well. Participation in the group exam experience is an option in the course. The group of students that usually select not to do the group exam are usually the best students. To help them see the benefits of collaboration, I list the five highest scores (with no bonuses added) and indicate which are individual and which are group scores. Typically, four out of five are group scores. I then list the average score for students in groups (bonuses added) and the average for individuals taking the exam. Usually, the group students' average is about ten points higher. Again, I try to let the facts speak for themselves, although sometimes I cannot refrain from asking one of those bright, independent operators what he or she makes of the exam results.

Principle 6: Faculty Work to Create Climates for Learning

Learner-centered teaching environments have climates known to affect learning outcomes positively. (This principle is explored fully in Chapter Five.) Teachers are much more involved in designing and implementing activities that first create and then maintain conditions conducive to learning. Very important here are activities and events, indeed a whole orientation to the class, that move students steadily toward a place of intellectual maturity and responsibility. Students need to find the motivation and learn how to take responsibility for their own learning. That motivation is not something a teacher can force or require, but research has shown that certain kinds of learning climates foster it.

Principle 7: Faculty Do More with Feedback

This principle does not say that faculty do less grading. Grading responsibilities remain intact in learner-centered environments, but what changes is the focus of those efforts. (See also Chapter Six.) Evaluation events are used in ways that maximize their learning potential. More time, energy, and creativity are devoted to finding and using mechanisms that allow the constructive delivery of feedback to students. It might be that a group gets a memo with feedback on a task or an individual student gets a letter with feedback on a paper. Assignments still generate grades, certifying mastery of content and skills, but they are used developmentally so that students get more out of the experience than just the grade.

These seven principles combine to form an approach to teaching that moves the teacher from the center of the classroom. If followed, these principles will help teachers serve as facilitator, resource person, mentor, instructional designer, and master learner.

Questions That Emerge When the Teaching Role Changes

The questions associated with implementing more facilitative approaches to teaching all became clear during one group activity. What transpired was simple and typical, and yet the questions that emerged are central to successful implementation of the learner-centered teaching role.

I was using an in-class, two-period, small group activity. Students had completed the first half of the task and now needed to take their work to the next level. To guide that process, I had written each group a memo; most were three or four faculty-length (long and complex) paragraphs. I handed the memo to someone in each group while I quickly reviewed the task. They had fifteen minutes to read the memo, discuss the issues it raised, and then revise their first draft proposal. All groups but one proceeded the same way: one member read the memo to the rest of the group.

Up front to my left sat a group populated with a very shy crowd. The person to whom I had given the memo proceeded to read it to herself while the rest of the group waited patiently. When she finished, she passed the memo without comment to the person sitting next to her, who also proceeded to read the memo silently. And so it continued until everyone had read the memo. The group now had less than five minutes to discuss and revise their work.

At first, I was amazed. What were they thinking? Well, clearly they were not thinking. Why weren't they looking around at the other groups? Usually students are good at aping what everyone else does. Why didn't somebody in the group say something? Could they all be that reticent? Didn't anybody care about the quality of their work? Next, I was perplexed. What should I do? Should I intervene? That seemed like another cave-in—back to the teacher's jumping in and fixing the problem every time students make a bad decision. But the quality of their work and their potential to learn from it were being compromised by their action (inaction in this case).

The dialogue in my head continued. What should I do if I intervened? How could I intervene without conveying how stupid I thought their approach was? Maybe they should know I thought they had made a poor decision and should have known better. More important, what should I say to them that was not just telling them they had a problem. I was afraid that if I asked, "How are you doing?" they would all nod and say "Fine." Maybe I could ask, "Do you understand the task?" "Yes." "Well, how much time do you have left, and what do you still have to do?" I would hope then that they would see the obvious conclusion.

I resolved the issue by doing nothing, and they did poor work. I do not know if they ever made the connection between the way they approached the task and their evaluation. If I had to guess, I would say not. I expect most of them had yet another experience that confirmed what they had long suspected about group work. But my inept response to this group and their conclusions about the experience are not really the issues of importance here. The example raises three fundamental questions about how to do this more facilitative kind of teaching. They are relevant in all kinds of instructional contexts. The first two are so linked it makes sense to consider them jointly.

Do You Intervene, and If So, When?

If the approach involves letting students discover and experience the consequences of their decisions, do you intervene? You could make the case that you do not—that every intervention compromises the potential of students to learn from their mistakes, and we can all list powerful lessons learned from our mistakes.

With my beginning students, I have to believe it is a matter of degree, not an absolute answer. Certainly, I can and should intervene much less than I do. (In other words, the nonresponse example I started with is not typical of my teaching.) But with beginning students (perhaps with all students), there are occasions that warrant intervention. The trick is deciding which occasions and when in the course of the event the intervention should occur. Some situations are more obvious than others. We intervene when a decision is about to hurt a student—for example, the student plans to take eighteen credits and work thirty-five hours a week. We intervene when the decision of one student jeopardizes a larger group—one group member rarely attends and never comes prepared, for example. We intervene when a group decision compromises the learning potential of another group—the students in the back row who routinely chat and disrupt class. We intervene when students' efforts to figure something out produce such enormous frustration and anxiety that the learning potential of the experience is compromised. But in other situations (like the opening example), the need for faculty action is less clear and the consequences of that intervention more mixed.

What we need but still do not have is a set of guidelines or principles that could help individual faculty put a larger frame around what are still very isolated, context-dependent, and frequently unclear decisions about if and when to intervene in the learning experiences of students.

What Do You Do When You Intervene?

If you decide that your ethical responsibilities as a teacher and the learning potential of the experience demand that intervention, what do you do when you intervene? Ask questions and hope that you lead them to the needed insight or understanding? Ask them to describe their process and explain why they are pursuing it on the chance that there is a reasonable method behind their apparent madness? Let them proceed, make the mistake, experience the consequence, and then intercede at the point when they are trying to figure out what went wrong?

Again, these are not questions I can answer or have seen addressed elsewhere. They are questions that emerge at the level of practice when one tries to operationalize metaphors and sometimes ambiguous descriptions. A guide leads the way and keeps everyone in the group safe. A midwife is there at the side with experience and advice that ease a painful process. The coach cannot stop the team from losing, but at the next practice, all their mistakes are reviewed. At a conceptual level, these descriptions are helpful, but in the functional arena where one makes decisions and implements actions, they offer ambiguous answers.

To Finish Up

In this chapter, we have explored another aspect of teaching that changes when instruction is learner-centered: the role of the teacher. Current instructional practice often finds us in the spotlight, at the center of the action, but our persistent position there compromises the learning potential of students. We need to move to a no less important but much more facilitative role. Metaphors and functional descriptions help us understand the role conceptually. The challenge comes at the point of implementation. Here much more is involved than two or three good techniques. We need an approach—one I have chosen to operationalize and illustrate with seven principles, but one with details still to iron out if we are to realize the full potential of these much more facilitative instructional roles.

Chapter Five

The Responsibility for Learning

In the preceding three chapters, the focus has been on what teachers need to change (the balance of power, the function of content, and their role in the classroom) in order to make instruction learner-centered. All of these actions involve and have many implications for students, but at their heart, these are faculty changes. With this chapter, the locus of the change shifts to action required of students. They must accept the responsibility for learning. This involves developing the intellectual maturity, learning skills, and awareness necessary to function as independent, autonomous learners. The faculty contribution to this process is creating and maintaining conditions that promote student growth and movement toward autonomy. To date, faculty have not accomplished these goals with much success.

To understand what makes our current approaches less effective than we might hope, we need to review the characteristics of today's college students. Students now arrive at college less well prepared than they once did. They often lack solid basic skills and now work many hours to pay for college and sometimes a car. Today's students are career oriented. They equate getting a good job with having high grades. Learning is often left out of the equation. Many students lack confidence in themselves as learners and do not make responsible learning decisions. Older students return to school when their lives are already filled with jobs and families. Having little self-confidence and busy lives motivates many students to look for easy educational options, not ones that push them hard. Significant percentages of today's college students have serious personal issues and experience emotional distress, characteristics well substantiated in data (Astin, 1998; Upcraft, 1996). Obviously, these descriptions are not characteristic of all students, but most faculty quickly agree that teaching college students today is far more challenging than it once was.

In response to college students who present these characteristics, we have taken action. For most of us, it has been a gradual, almost imperceptible realignment of instructional policies and practices. We deal with increasingly less mature and more dependent learners in two different ways. First, we respond by making clearer and more explicit the terms and conditions for learning. Our classrooms are now rule-bound economies that set the parameters and conditions for virtually everything that happens there.

We have institutional and individual policies that require attendance because students will not come to class without them. We assume that attendance in class positively affects learning and motivation. But we ought to keep better track of what the research says; its conclusions are mixed and decidedly more tentative than those of most faculty on this issue (St. Clair, 1999). We have strict policies on makeup tests and missed due dates. We have assignments submitted in installments because without those intermediate deadlines, students procrastinate and attempt to complete term-long projects in one night. We require participation. We have policies about coming to class late, leaving early, not talking, and not eating, drinking, or chewing gum. We stipulate page length and margin size for written work. We specify the number of references needed on a research paper and formats required for lab reports. These rules, regulations, and stipulations aim to bring student behavior in line with our assumptions as to what positively affects learning. In order to learn effectively, most faculty believe that students must be in class, meet deadlines, participate in class, follow the rules, and work according to prescribed formats.

And that is not all. We respond further to our poorly prepared, not very motivated, and almost always passive students with something else besides rules. We rely (now almost exclusively) on extrinsic motivators to move them to action. We use regular quizzes to keep them up with the reading, extra credit points for looking up a reference, bonus points if all the homework problems are correct, and a check plus for every contribution in class. Our classrooms are now token economies where nobody does anything if there are not some points proffered. We have created elaborate grading systems that specify point values for virtually everything a student does. Go into class, say you have a five-point extra credit project, and ask who might be interested in completing it. Be prepared for a sea of hands. The next day, make the same offer, but now the assignment is worth two points; there are still more volunteers than you need. I follow this routine with my students, and about the time I get down to .5 of a point, some of them begin to realize that I'm trying to make a point about what students will do for points and will not do without them.

Rule-based approaches and those that rely on extrinsic motivators do work. Lots of faculty who use reading quizzes report that they do keep students doing the reading regularly. And in surveys, students acknowledge this effectiveness; they understand their value and want them. But with requirements and extrinsic motivators, it is almost always about short-term gains and long-term liabilities. Do reading quizzes contribute to student appreciation of reading in the field? Is your textbook the one they do not sell back to the bookstore at the semester's end because through pop quizzes, they have come to appreciate the value of reading? Unfortunately, even after four years of college, most students harbor the same disdain for reading they had when they arrived. They do technical, challenging, informational reading only when required and only if awarded points for doing it.

The issue is larger than the effect of quizzes on attitudes toward reading. Despite our extensive reliance on rules, requirements, and extrinsic motivators, we almost never ask whether these rule-oriented and require-that-you-do-it approaches are having an overall desired effect. We know they seem to work in the short term, but are they creating intellectually mature, responsible, motivated learners—ones who when they receive an assignment can analyze it, break it into a set of separate tasks, move to complete those steps in a timely manner, and deliver a quality product? Are they effectively piquing student curiosity—the kind of interest that drives students ever deeper into content and issues? Is that what we see as we face seniors in seminars and capstone courses?

Most of us would say no. In fact, there is some support for a much more disturbing trend among students. The past decade has seen increasing concern about and research (Boice, 1996) that documents a rise in student incivility. Students show teachers and fellow students less respect than in the past. They quickly blame others, mostly the teacher, for their poor performance. They disrupt the classroom with behavior that compromises the learning efforts of others.

Often the eroding quality of life in college classrooms is attributed to a larger set of societal ills. That may be a contributory factor, but I wonder if the approaches we are taking with students might not also be part of the problem. The have us locked in a vicious cycle. The more structured we make the environment, the more structure students need. The more we decide for students, the more they expect us to decide. The more motivation we provide, the less they find within themselves. The more responsibility for learning we try to assume, the less they accept on their own. The more control we exert, the more restive their response.

We end up with students who have little commitment to and almost no respect for learning and who cannot function without structure and imposed control. To abandon all rules and motivational prods would be to put students in circumstances that doom them to failure. Early on in the transformation of my entry-level class, I created a wonderfully open-ended, exploratory log assignment where I envisioned students reacting to whatever caught their interest: content, an activity, something in the textbook, insights that came as they completed assignments, reactions to other students. It gave students the opportunity to take the course content to places where they were. It totally bombed. Students thought I was being deliberately vague (I was), but rather than being empowered and motivated by the opportunity, they could not figure out what to write, or they never got past the point of worrying about whether what they had written was "right." The current log assignment in Appendix A shows how far I had to retreat.

Nevertheless, these heavy-handed approaches do produce results. Students end up learning in our rule-oriented environments and as a result of the motivational sticks we apply. At issue is whether these are the only or best conditions for learning and whether their short-term gains are offset by long-term liabilities. I

think most of us would already agree that they do not foste.
growth and development of intellectually mature, responsible
learners. And I also think that most of us would agree that having to
be all over students about every detail of their learning experiences
does not make for particularly satisfying teaching experiences.

However, the proposal here and elsewhere in the book is not
about abandoning structure, rules, or extrinsic motivation. It is
about understanding the liabilities these approaches involve and
using them more judiciously. And it is about identifying other
approaches where faculty take leadership for creating climates and
conditions conducive to learning. With these approaches, they
work to build spaces in which students can begin to move, grow,
mature, and act responsibly about their own learning and toward
the learning of others.

Getting Students to Accept the Responsibility for Learning

When teaching is learner-centered, the classroom climate changes
in ways that accomplish two objectives. First, faculty aim to create
a climate conducive to learning, meaning that they work to establish an environment that positively affects how much and how well
students learn. Second, faculty aim to create environments where
without (or with fewer) rules and requirements, students do what
they need to learn effectively, develop themselves further as learners, and act in ways that support the learning efforts of others.
After examining research that has addressed climates that are conducive to learning, I propose a set of principles that more effectively motivate students to accept responsibility for learning.

Classroom Climates Conducive to Learning

In the physical world, the atmosphere, environment, and climate
exert powerful influences on our behavior. Classroom environments affect behavior, including the motivation to learn and the
willingness to accept responsibility for learning, in the same pervasive and significant ways. We sometimes teach unaware of these
forces or we take them for granted, but if the "weather" ever turns
nasty in a class, we quickly learn how powerfully classroom climate
can influence attitudes and actions.

Classroom environments have been studied empirically, first at the primary and secondary levels. Fraser (1986, 1989) moved forward the work on classroom climates generally and made specific applications to the higher education context. Classroom environment has more than metaphorical meaning.

Fraser's work rests on the premise that classroom climate results from a series of complex psychosocial relationships that exist between the faculty member and the students collectively and individually, as well as the relationships between and among students. Drawing heavily on work related to a larger concept of human environment, Fraser, Treagust, and Dennis (1986) developed and tested the College and University Classroom Environment Inventory (CUEI), which is designed to measure and compare preferred and actual classroom environments. This forty-nine-item instrument consists of seven subscales that can be thought of as the concrete components of classroom climate: (1) personalization (opportunities for interaction between professor and students and the amount of instructor concern for students), (2) involvement (the extent to which students actively participate in all classroom activities), (3) student cohesiveness (how well students know and are friendly to each other), (4) satisfaction (how much students enjoy the class), (5) task orientation (how clear and well organized class activities are), (6) innovation (the extent to which the instructor plans new and unusual class activities and uses new teaching techniques and assignments), and (7) individualization (to what degree students are allowed to make decisions and are treated differentially based on their individual learning needs).

Winston and others (1994) developed a similar instrument. They used six subscales, including two more "climate conditions" not on the Fraser instrument: inimical ambiance (for classroom environments characterized as hostile, highly, competitive, and rigidly structured) and academic rigor (for environments of intellectual challenge and individual responsibility).

The findings of Fraser and the Winston group strongly support the impact of psychosocial relationships on learning outcomes. Fraser (1986, p. 45) writes, "Use of student perceptions of actual classroom environment . . . has established consistent relationships between the nature of the classroom environment and various student cognitive and affective outcomes." When students are in a classroom environment that they prefer, they achieve more. Both instruments give a clear indication of those preferences by having students rate ideal classrooms and then comparing those with assessments of real classrooms. Students do not rate as ideal the common rule-oriented, requirement-driven, and teacher-controlled classroom.

Fraser has also used the instrument to measure faculty perceptions of their classroom and then compared those with student perceptions. The results (Fraser, Treagust, and Dennis, 1986, p. 45) are a bit troubling: "Teachers tended to perceive the classroom environment more positively than did their students in the same classroom." Fraser, collaborating with Giddings and McRobbie (1993), has developed a similar inventory for use in laboratory settings. Both instruments are included in the research articles and are valuable diagnostic tools that individual faculty can use to measure the success of efforts to create more learner-centered classrooms.

It is important to understand that these findings do not establish that a particular kind of classroom causes learning. It is not the case, for example, that if we frequently converse with students, they learn; rather, an environment where there is opportunity for instructor-student interaction creates a condition that is conducive to learning. It makes learning more likely to result. Much like being in the cold "motivates" us to bundle up, so the presence of certain conditions can move students to learning—indeed, so move them that learning becomes all but inevitable.

Another important lesson to be learned from this work is that climates conducive to learning are created by action, not by announcement. If you want this kind of climate in your classroom, you do not get it by including two lines in the syllabus saying that your class will have it. It results from actions (and sometimes inaction). You take action to create it and, once created, actions necessary to sustain it. And as we have learned about our own fragile physical world, the responsibility to preserve the classroom climate belongs to everyone within it. Early in my career, I heard a wise teacher once say to a class, "This is not *my* class; it is not *your* class; this is *our* class, and together we are responsible for what does and doesn't happen here."

Climates That Build Student Autonomy and Responsibility

In addition to creating climates that have a positive impact on student learning, we need environments that encourage students to become responsible, autonomous learners. Here, the work of those who study self-directed learners is helpful. Autonomous, self-regulated learners go by many different names, but a description by Zimmerman (1990, p. 4) introduces the attributes of these learners: "They approach educational tasks with confidence, diligence, and resourcefulness. . . . Self-regulated learners are aware when they know a fact or possess a skill and when they do not. . . . Self-regulated students proactively seek out information when needed and take steps to master it. When they encounter obstacles such as poor study conditions, confusing teachers, or abstruse text books, they find a way to succeed" (p. 4). I continue to be impressed by how little these descriptions fit my students.

And so the question is, How do we begin to move students toward becoming this kind of learner? I believe the place to start is with a set of principles that set the stage for student development. They create conditions that motivate students to begin accepting responsibility for the various aspects of their learning that we now impose as requirements. They also make it possible for us to create more positive climates for learning and teaching.

Principle 1: It's About Who Is Responsible for What in the Teaching-Learning Process

The approaches taken to deal with student immaturity and irresponsibility convey contradictory messages about who is responsible for what. Our actions, which set all the parameters and conditions for learning, create the impression that we are the ones ultimately responsible for student learning. We are not and never can be. The decision to learn is exclusively a student decision—one that we can and should influence, but never one that we can control. Clearer thinking about who is responsible for what in the teaching-learning process would benefit faculty and students.

I have a colleague who could metaphorically differentiate the lines of student and faculty responsibility quite clearly. He taught agronomy and used the familiar "you can lead a horse to water, but you can't make it drink" adage as the basis for his delineation. You can lead students to learning, he would say, but you cannot make them learn. His insight came in the way he characterized what faculty contribute. He said that it was the teacher's job to put salt in the oats so that once the horse got to water, it was damn thirsty. This dandy metaphor makes the principle conceptually clear: it is our responsibility to take explicit actions that will motivate student learning. The horse who has had salt put in his oats does not have to be forced to drink. He is thirsty, knows he is thirsty, and is looking for water.

In general, our instructional policies and practices do not make students thirsty. Rather, we tell students that they are thirsty—that they should be drinking. They remain unconvinced and so (mostly out of concern for them), we force the issue. We use rules, requirements, and sticks to try to hold their heads in the watering trough. Most do end up drinking, but a lot of them never figure out why water is so important. A few drown in the process.

Most of us would say that what compels us to take this very heavy-handed approach is the students themselves. Because they are unprepared and passive, make poor decisions about learning, and otherwise act irresponsibly, we feel compelled to act. We must do more, we believe, because they need more. And certainly we have professional responsibilities in this area. But what we have not sorted out or through is where the teacher's responsibility ends and the student's responsibility starts. When have we done enough? How do we know when a teacher's obligation to a student has been fulfilled? If a student refuses to accept responsibility for learning, that is his choice, and at some point, his decision is not our fault. But when has that point been reached?

Perhaps we could begin to clarify our thinking by specifying more precisely the domain of faculty responsibility. For example, we do have an obligation to show (not tell) students the value and necessity of learning. We have an obligation to make our content relevant, demonstrate its power to answer questions, and otherwise show its inherent intrigue. Once student interest is piqued, we have the responsibility to lead them to all the learning resources they need. As the student learns, we have the responsibility to monitor the process and offer constructive feedback and assessment.

And we might further clarify our thinking by explicitly describing the domain of student responsibility. Fundamentally, the responsibility to learn is theirs and theirs alone. We can try to force them into accepting that responsibility along with the obligation to grow and develop as learners, but we do them a much greater service if we create conditions and develop policies and practices that enable them to understand their responsibility and that empower them to accept it.

Principle 2: It Is About Logical Consequences, Not Discipline

We need to dispense with some rules and let students start experiencing the consequences of the decisions they make. There are any number of relevant issues and caveats, but before considering them, we must start with the most fundamental issue of all. The principle works only if there are consequences—if a student decision and the actions (inaction) that follow net some results or consequences.

I once had a class where a significant number of students arrived late. I had never had this problem before and was at a loss as to how to fix it. The problem persisted even after a positive request from me that I then followed with a firmly worded announcement. I adjusted by starting class more slowly. Why delve into the really important material when I would end up having to repeat it later?

When I complained to a colleague about this class, she caught me off-guard with a simple question: "Maryellen, are you ever consistently late for something?" I was: an administrative staff meeting where the person in charge always started with a litany of announcements mostly not relevant to me and easily summed up on a handout or now electronically. I could hear how I cajoled myself as I hoofed it across campus: "Oh, take it easy. You're not missing anything important." Was anything important happening during those first five minutes of my class? No. In fact, I had compensated by making sure that it did not. In contrast, I thought of a math class I once observed. I arrived five minutes before the class started, and most of the students were already there. The instructor was also there and on the overhead was the homework assignment (including some word problems not in the book). He left it up until about two minutes after class had started, then took it down and never put it back up. Any student who arrived late to that class missed the assignment and was then responsible for getting it from somebody else or seeing him after class.

The need for consequences is so obvious, and yet we have lost sight of it in instructional practice. Do students come to class not having done the reading? No doubt they have been told that they will understand more if they come to class prepared, and yet they still come unprepared. Why? In all too many classes, there are absolutely no consequences that students experience when they come to class not having done the reading. I observed in a class where the instructor began, "Has anybody done the reading?" When heads shook negatively, he continued, "Well, let me give you a quick review of the key ideas that relate to our topic today." In that class, the "punishment" for not doing the reading was actually a "reward": the instructor distilled thirty pages of reading in three minutes.

With consequences in place, we need next to consider how to deliver them. Our styles will vary. I am not comfortable with any response that might be interpreted as public humiliation. My goals for students are not accomplished when they drop the class out of fear or frustration. But in my class, there are consequences when students come unprepared. I bring my book to class and try to use it in ways that demonstrate and underscore what it contributes to our efforts to learn course content. I ask questions with the book open in front of me and encourage students to have their books out and open. If I ask a question on the reading and there is no response, I persist and am not reluctant to make the more mature and intellectually able students uncomfortable about their silence. I write the question on the board and recommend that students copy it in their notes. I ask them why it might be an important question—what the answer might enable them to do. These are not rhetorical questions; I wait for answers. If it is Friday and they are really not paying attention, I hint around about how it would make a mighty fine test question. If there is still no answer, I let the question stand unanswered, but with the promise that we will return, and when we do, I will be expecting more and better of them. I aim in these exchanges to be positive and patient but absolutely relentless.

To sum this principle, students will start assuming more responsibility for their learning once we start making them accountable for their actions. Obviously, there are complex issues involved when it comes to matching the number and severity of the consequence to a student's level of intellectual maturity. We tackle these developmental issues in Chapter Nine, but the place to start is by making sure that student decisions and actions have logical consequences that students experience. Note that *experience* is a deliberate word choice. This is not us yet again telling students about the consequences. And we make matters worse if we say certain consequences will occur and then they do not. For example, if you say, "Nobody gets better than a C on my exams if they study only the night before the exam," you had better have the evidence to prove it. This principle is about connecting students' decisions to and with results. Our role is to help them see those connections so that they can learn from them.

Principle 3: It Is About Consistency in Word and Deed

The essence of this principle is simple and straightforward and can be summed up in a well-known adage: actions speak louder than words. That adage has been confirmed and amplified in communication research (Knapp and Hall, 1992). When the sender contradicts a verbal message with a nonverbal one, the receiver believes the nonverbal message. You can write in the syllabus and say in class, "No late homework accepted," but if a student approaches with a litany of excuses as to why it is late and you acquiesce, your behavior says loudly and irrevocably that you accept homework late. No matter how clearly you have described the consequences for not getting work done on time, you have rendered all those messages mute by this single action.

The principle applies in many contexts. If we say we want student participation, that we can be interrupted with questions but then proceed at race horse pace to cover the content ground, commenting regularly about how much of the race remains ahead of us and finally pausing, breathless, for questions in the last three minutes, that behavior communicates more eloquently and persuasively than anything we could ever say that in this class, student questions are unwelcome interruptions.

Expectations for more responsible student behavior are conveyed not by what we say but by what we do. And we compromise what we say when what we do contradicts it. Two implications of this are that expectations for students need to be thought of in terms of actions that convey them, and we stop the cycle of dependency and irresponsibility with predictable logical consequences *and* with consistent coherence between faculty words and deeds. Faculty behavior models the kind of accountability expected from students.

Taken together, these three principles set the stage for the development of students into mature, responsible learners. They create an environment that clearly and consistently puts the responsibility for learning in student hands. Faculty offer a variety of supports. They create structured environments that do not give students more responsibility than they can handle. But the fundamental premise that the responsibility for learning rests in student hands remains an immutable reality in learner-centered classrooms.

In the Trenches: Policies and Practices That Create Climates for Learning

The goal with policies and practices is to create conditions within the classroom environment that positively affect student behavior on two fronts. First, we need policies and practices that create climates known to have a positive impact on learning outcomes, and, second, we need policies and practices that encourage students to take those actions necessary if they are to learn well and develop as learners. As in previous chapters, the examples that follow start the process. They are designed for students just beginning the journey to autonomy and self-regulation. Other kinds of policies and practices should be used with more mature learners. We begin with some ideas on creating and maintaining classroom climates conducive to learning and follow with ways that address student development and willingness to act responsibly within learning environments.

Creating and Maintaining Climates Conducive to Learning

There are many intriguing ways to create and maintain classroom climates conducive to learning. In the examples that follow, most seek to cultivate student support. Buy-in is important. Some examples include the kind of feedback that allows faculty to check perceptions and make adjustments. Still others aim to prevent problems more easily fixed before they emerge. All of these examples move the responsibility for learning back toward students at the same time that they clarify student and teacher responsibilities.

Involving Students in the Process

Consider devoting time on the first day of class to a discussion of classroom climate. Students might start by thinking about a class where they learned a lot and one where they did not learn much. How would they characterize the conditions for learning in each? Have them do some freewriting before beginning a discussion. Summarize the discussion by working with them to create the set of conditions for learning that they and you aspire to create in this class. Put the principles on paper, maybe post them in the classroom, incorporate them in the syllabus or on the course Web site, and occasionally have them on screen as students arrive or distribute them to students.

Goza (1993) proposes an interesting technique that could be used to launch this first-day discussion. She calls it a "Graffiti Needs Assessment." She writes ten sentence beginnings on the top of newsprint (one sentence per newsprint page) and posts them around the room. During the first fifteen minutes of class, students wander around the room meeting each other and writing sentence endings on the newsprint. She uses the exercise to generate information about student goals, ascertain levels of background knowledge, and begin to cultivate interest in course content. The exercise is equally effective at generating discussion about climate and conditions for learning. You could use sentence stems like:

"In the best class I ever had, students . . ."

"In the best class I ever had, the teacher . . ."

"I learn best when . . ."

"I feel most confident as a learner when . . ."

"Classmates compromise my attempts to learn when they . . ."

Equally important as efforts to create a climate are those needed to maintain it. The class should regularly revisit any principles they have agreed to. They can be transformed into a formative evaluation tool administered several weeks into the course. Let students offer feedback as to the presence, absence, and quality of the various conditions. Leave open the possibility of revising the principles, ratcheting them up if the class can be encouraged to assume even more responsibility for making the classroom a place where motivated and prepared people come to learn from and with each other.

If you have never explored these topics with students, those of us who have would assure you that students do not identify unusual or inappropriate climate characteristics, working conditions, and interpersonal relationships. The value of these activities lays not in the new insights students generate about conditions for learning but accrues from the process itself. These discussions develop student awareness at the same time they create a class history of addressing classroom environment issues. At some level, this is about an ounce of prevention being worth a pound of cure.

Any conversation or activity about conditions for learning needs to underscore the contribution of the class in making and maintaining constructive classroom climates. This is a whole class endeavor to which every individual is expected to contribute. If you open a new class by having students describe the characteristics of teachers who help them learn, respond with a discussion of the characteristics of students whom you have observed successfully acquire this particular kind of content. Do note that the conversation is not about the characteristics of teachers that students "like." Always keep the focus on learning. And do not be reluctant to mix the perspectives: you talk about characteristics of teachers that you think expedite learning, drawing from your own experience as a student, and students can discuss best and worst students they know and have observed.

Getting Feedback on the Climate

The CUEI instrument (Fraser, Treagust, and Dennis, 1986) is another tool useful in stimulating student thinking about classroom climates and learning, as well as to acquire feedback on the climate on your classroom. Early in the course, you could have students complete the instrument indicating their preferred classroom climate. Later in the course, have them complete the instrument again, this time assessing the climate as they perceive it in the class. Both evaluative events provide natural opportunities to raise and discuss classroom environment issues, especially if you let students or a subgroup of them compile and report on the results. Instruments completed from both perspectives provide a rich feedback source for faculty.

I have collected feedback on classroom climate using an adapted version of an assessment technique proposed by Garner and Emery (1994). They have students take a sheet of paper eight and a half by eleven inches and divide it into three columns, labeled "Start," "Stop" and "Continue." Under "Start," I have students list things not present in the classroom environment that if present would enhance their learning. Under "Stop," they list aspects of our classroom climate that are detracting from their learning experiences. And under "Continue," they list things we are doing that contribute positively and should be retained.

Tackling Troubling Behaviors Constructively

Rather than the standard syllabus admonitions against behaviors that erode climates for learning, consider using the work of Appleby (1990), who asked 43 faculty and 214 students, "What three behaviors of your students/teachers most irritate you?" Faculty identified thirty behaviors, but the following nine accounted for 77 percent of the responses: talking during lectures; sleeping during class; chewing gum, eating, or drinking noisily; being late; cutting class; acting bored or apathetic; not paying attention; being unprepared; and creating disturbances. The thirty-five faculty behaviors most often identified by students fell into several categories: communication problems, like monotone lecture delivery and too many seemingly unrelated digressions; not responding to students' needs, like keeping the class late or arriving to class late; and having a condescending attitude most often exemplified by treating students like children (shadows of our admonitions to avoid always telling students), but also exemplified by always presenting the faculty point of view as the best or correct one.

You could ask students the what-most-irritates-you question and tally and report the results at the same time you report your answer to the question. The Appleby work provides a useful comparative benchmark as you press the class to make a commitment: "In the interest of creating a more positive and constructive classroom, could we agree not to irritate each other in these ways?" One final interesting sidelight of this work is that Appleby found a number of parallel behaviors where reciprocal actions will solve the problems. Both students and teachers are irritated when the other arrives late to class. Teachers are irritated when students skip class, and students are annoyed by faculty who cancel or do not show up to class.

For one final concrete answer to the question of what to do (and not do) when you want to create and maintain climates conducive to learning, see Hilsen (2002), who has developed a handout that clearly and specifically identifies relevant faculty behaviors.

Policies and Practices That Develop Maturity and Responsibility

We need policies and practices that encourage students to encounter themselves as learners, motivate them to become more than what they are, and provide the resources, experiences, and skills they need if they are to move forward in their development. The examples that follow do that. Note how each applies the principles proposed. I encourage you to adapt and alter them to fit your own instructional situation.

Facing Poor Exam Performance

The first exam is over, and you have a number of students who have done poorly. If class size permits, see what you can do to get them to come for an individual meeting during office hours. You might invite the student with a personal note on the exam or withhold the grade until the student meets to discuss it with you. There is a need for salt-in-the-oats thinking here: What will bring the student to you? The coming is a necessary first step in the process of assuming responsibility for exam performance. However, do not set unrealistic expectations. Not all students will come, and part of the clear thinking about who is responsible for what involves your understanding that you cannot help students who do not want help.

When a student does come, the conversation you do *not* want to have is one where you tell the student what she needs to do. In your part of the conversation, raise the relevant questions: How did you study? How much did you study? What did you study? Why do you think your approaches didn't work? Was there anything that did work? And it is a conversation that focuses on the future: "So, what do you think you need to do now to prepare you better for the next exam?" Encourage the student to develop a game plan and put it on paper. Offer feedback on the plan and encourage the student to get feedback from professionals in the learning center. Provide options, but let the student make the decisions about what she will do. Express confidence in the student's ability to do what needs to be done. Ask for progress reports. If the student's class attendance improves, participation in class increases, more notes are taken in class, and more homework problems are submitted, note the progress, and reinforce it with positive feedback.

Over an eight-year period, McBrayer (2001) conducted 547 conferences like these with students and reports that on average, their next exam score in his introductory psychology course increased by ten points. Students who needed to schedule such a conference but did not showed no consistent signs of improvement on the next or subsequent exams. Tell students about studies like these, and let the facts motivate student participation in the process.

Accepting Responsibility for Assignment Details

The interest here is to get students to understand and accept assignments, especially those that they find challenging or that involve new and unfamiliar learning experiences. (Issues of resistance are addressed in detail in Chapter Seven, and those discussions are relevant here too.) Writing about assignments that promote critical thinking, Keeley, Shemberg, Cowell, and Zinnbauer (1995) offer a useful set of suggestions based on psychotherapy literature. They recommend presenting the rationale behind the assignment and the benefits that will accrue from completing it. They advise that instructions be clear and that students be asked to paraphrase their understanding of what the assignment requires. Let dialogue about the assignment be continuing and ongoing. Help students understand that problems are a natural part of doing something difficult or new. And when the assignment is completed, let students debrief the experience.

Taking quite a different tack, Sessoms (2001) reports positively on her experiences of letting students set due dates for papers. She gives them the first couple of weeks of the course before they submit their due dates. They may not have more than one per month. Papers may be due on any weekday, even days when class does not meet. And students may request an extension for one paper, provided they make that request a week before the paper is due. Like the business faculty member reported on earlier, she likes the system because it effectively distributes her grading work across the course.

Clarifying Student Responsibilities

The most effective way to make these responsibilities clear is to involve students in the process of establishing them. Introduce a group project by having students discuss how they would like the group to function. Ask for this description in the form of a memo from the group to you, signed off by all participants.

Longman (1992) has developed a "Bill of Rights" for study groups that she shares with groups as they begin their work together (it is provided in Appendix B). It addresses both what individuals must contribute to the group and what the group owes its members. This particular "Bill of Rights" could be distributed as a working document, with the challenge to groups being to revise and adjust it to meet their goals and objectives. Or ask groups to develop their own description of group and member responsibilities, using this one as a model.

The benefit is the same one accrued when the class has explicit discussions of conditions conducive for learning. If a student study group has identified the annoyance and frustration felt in groups when the social interaction overtakes the task agenda, that might be enough to prevent the group from getting socially sidetracked, or it might be what it takes to empower one group member to point out when that is happening to the group.

Making Logical Consequences Real and Compelling

Siegel (1993) reports on a compelling encounter with consequences that occurred in her business course. She had assigned a paper on theories of quality control in production and operations management. Students handled the content fairly well, but their papers were replete with the usual spelling and grammatical errors. Siegel decided to turn that problem into a quality control case without divulging to the class who was involved. She asked the class to discuss a small manufacturer who had twenty-two workers, each producing one batch of product per day, with each batch consisting of an average of seven units. A quality control consultant documented that there were approximately 1.44 defects per unit, 9.73 per batch. "Students were adamant in their insistence on quality standards as crucial to competitiveness" (p. 5). They went so far as to suggest that workers with the most defects should be fired. Finally Siegel revealed to students that they were the "case" being discussed: "A pin drop would have echoed loudly in that classroom! Nothing I could ever say about the importance of good writing—the quality of the presentation of their work, regardless of subject matter—could have had greater effect" (p. 5).

Empowering Students to Fix Problems

Nowhere else is the inability and outright reluctance of students to accept responsibility clearer than in groups when problems emerge. Despite the sizable pressure that groups can exert on individuals, it is as if everyone in the group rolls over and has their productivity compromised by dysfunctional individual behaviors. Teachers often find themselves intervening, fixing serious problems that could have been prevented if group members had acted responsibly earlier in the process.

There is a simple principle I go over and over again when my students are working in groups: no group member does any behavior in a group unless the group allows it. No person performs a silent and noncontributory role unless the group lets him or her. The problem of individuals' not contributing, not showing up on time, and not doing their work is equally an individual *and* group problem. Groups can exert lots of pressure on individuals. It is tough to remain a silent member if fellow group members regularly ask for opinions and insights. Groups have the responsibility to try to deal with individual members whose behaviors have a negative impact on group functioning.

I once worked with a faculty member who used a semester-long group project about the design and delivery of a health promotions campaign. It was a difficult and complicated project used in an upper-division majors course. Her solution to group process issues was to have each group appoint a group process liaison. The liaisons from each individual group met with her every two weeks to discuss group process issues. I observed in one of those sessions. She used simple scenarios (like a group that is falling behind its set of deadlines) to prime the discussion pump. How could a group address this problem? How could they deal with individual members who missed deadlines? The discussion started out on hypothetical issues, but very soon, liaisons were talking about what was happening in their own groups. She kept the focus on concrete solutions. After each meeting, group liaisons returned to their groups, reported on the discussion, and raised issues they felt relevant to their groups.

To build climates conducive to learning, we need policies and practices that involve students in the process of creating and maintaining them. We must aspire to relationships with students and classes that are constructive—encounters that build students' self-confidence and move them to places where they learn more, accomplish that learning more efficiently, and do so by setting their own rules and conditions. The policies and practices highlighted here can be used to start that process.

Questions That Emerge When Students Are Encouraged to Accept Responsibility for Learning

Questions emerge when we move to make students responsible, and like the questions at the end of previous chapters, these are numerous and difficult. I will consider three that raise important philosophical and practical issues. I believe the success of learner-centered approaches is related to our ability to answer questions like these wisely and well.

The approaches I have used to encourage students to accept more responsibility raised questions about the whole process of weaning both them and me from the strong reliance on the rules, structure, and extrinsic motivators that have so long been a part of our instructional practice and educational system. You cannot move a baby from milk to solid food overnight. So what are the instructional equivalents of "soft" foods—those that allow the immature student to grow and in the process prepare him for solid food? Is it a matter of doing away with some rules and retaining others but ending up with less overall? How do you determine which rules stay and which ones go? Is it a matter of revising rules in ways that make them less stringent and restrictive? Or is it some combination of deleting, retaining, and revising?

We have done little research work or wisdom-of-practice scholarship that address these questions. In the context of individual practice, you can by trial and error derive some answers that work for your students in the content area you teach, but collectively we need a more complete understanding of the process involved in successfully moving away from rules and extrinsic motivators.

A second and related set of questions involves the logical consequences principle. Begin with the question of how many: How many consequences should students (especially beginning students) be allowed to experience? If you know from classroom research evidence that attendance strongly affects performance in your class, is letting students make the decision about whether to be in class an ethically responsible one, especially if they erroneously decide that attendance does not matter? Should we let students get in trouble their first year in college because that is the time they need to learn who is responsible for what even if that means they end up having to spend a fifth year at college or drop out?

In addition to knowing how many consequences it takes to get the message across, there is a second question that involves the relation among three variables: the nature of the offense (what the student did wrong), the consequence (what happens to the student), and the student's level of maturity (meaning what the student can handle without getting seriously hurt). Does a student who comes to class not having done the reading and not able to answer a question about it deserve a public rebuke? Should the student who arrives late and disrupts the class (not all classroom configurations make late arrivals disruptive) be criticized in front of the entire class? Should a beginning student with inaccurate expectations of what it takes to succeed in college and this course receive evaluative feedback only at midterm and on the final?

The caveat that needs to guide our punishment-fits-the-crime thinking is the effect of the consequence on subsequent motivation and personal development, and there is much relevant research on this topic. Covington (1997 for a summary of his work) has devoted his career to studying motivation, especially as it is influenced by failure experiences. He summarizes how students deal with failure by identifying four different categories of students. First, there are the failure-avoiding students. These students harbor serious doubts about their abilities and therefore work hard to avoid personal blame for failure. "I wouldn't be doing so poorly in this course if I had a decent teacher," they might say, or, "This is a required course, not in my major; I don't care how well I'm doing." Overstriving students may in fact have plenty of ability, but they are plagued by self-doubt that seriously compromises their ability to study and perform. Even when these students succeed, they attribute their A's to luck. They study hard but are so tense that they freeze during exams; their minds go blank, and they forget what they knew very well before the exam. Failure-accepting students have given up. The more failure they experience, the more convinced they become that there is no hope; nothing they can do will make a difference. Success-oriented students learn from their mistakes. They believe in themselves and are comparatively less anxious about performance events. Covington points out that students often move between and among these categories.

Research like this can help faculty avoid damaging students and help in efforts to repair them. Students must understand that their actions produce results and that different actions are likely to produce much more desirable results. It is about destiny being in their hands—not about a faculty member's undermining their intellectual and personal worth.

And finally, there is a kind of existential question with practical ramifications. Is there any legitimate place for teacher-imposed structure or sanctions when the environment is truly learner-centered? Is the ultimate goal for every student to structure and regulate tasks in ways that work for them? How does assembling them together in an organizational structure like a class limit, transcend, or otherwise affect the learning proclivities of individual students? If one student works well against a set of deadlines (even though they might be self-imposed) and another functions best without the pressure imposed by deadlines, does the teacher allow deadlines for some and not for others? What of notions of fair and equitable treatment for all students? The question is philosophical at the level we seek to position individual rights within a collective context and pragmatic at the level where we must decide if we can or should have different rules for students enrolled in the same class.

To Finish Up

This chapter rests on the premise that students must take responsibility for learning. Functionally, that means they need to assume a role in creating and maintaining the kind of classroom climates conducive to their own and fellow students' learning. If immature, disruptive behavior occurs, it should not be in response to teacher-imposed restrictions but should be viewed as the action of an individual against the entire class. Students come to understand that a causal relationship exists between actions they take and the learning that results. And students start wanting to develop their skills as learners and ultimately come to resist when prevented from making decisions that legitimately belong to them.

Most college students today are the antithesis of autonomous, independent, self-regulating learners, and I believe that faculty have had a hand in making them so. But we are equally able to take actions that set in motion a different set of learning parameters. With students, we can create classroom climates more conducive to learning and to their development as learners. In learner-center teaching, this is our responsibility.

A long journey lies ahead, but once we get students headed in the right direction, at some point they start traveling with us, and then another powerful cycle comes into play. The more independence and autonomy we give, the more they take, and the more they handle responsibly, the more we can give. We start at the top of the hill by forming a small snowball. We push it around until it is a reasonable size. Then we move it to the edge and shove it down the slope. It starts off slowly but then gathers speed, and all of a sudden it rolls forward with more momentum than we can stop. Compare that with our current efforts at the bottom of the hill where we are trying to form dry snow into a ball and push it up hill. We may make it happen (most of us are very determined), but that ball will never go anywhere on its own.

Chapter Six

The Purpose and Processes of Evaluation

Rounding out the changes necessary to make teaching learner-centered are those that relate to evaluation. Currently, when faculty consider evaluation, what typically comes to mind first are grades. In fact, students, parents, society, and faculty regularly focus on grades more than learning. The learning is assumed; it occurs automatically, an all but inevitable outcome of the evaluation process. Learner-centered teaching abandons tacit assumptions about automatic learning. Evaluation is used to generate grades *and* to promote learning. The new purpose is larger and better balanced.

Along with this revised purpose, evaluation processes change as well. Today, faculty, almost entirely and exclusively, evaluate student work. In learner-centered teaching, faculty still evaluate and grade student work, but evaluation activities that involve students are included in the process. Students learn how to assess their own work and participate in the evaluation of work done by their peers. These self- and peer assessment activities develop skills that independent, self-regulating learners need. Current educational practice does little to develop these skills and lots to feed the focus on grades.

Learner-centered teaching does not deny the importance ascribed to grades. They function as gatekeepers in, through, and out of our postsecondary institutions. The more selective the college or university is, the higher the entrance grade point average (GPA) required. An increasing number of institutions control enrollment in majors. Getting accepted in the major depends in large part on GPA. At the other end, GPA stands at still more entrances: to virtually all postsecondary educational opportunities, including graduate school and professional education, like medicine and law. Many employers use it to decide who does and does not get a job interview. Grades matter very much in the short term, and only naive faculty make proclamations to the contrary. But learning still matters more, especially in the long run. How long has it been since you have been asked to report your college GPA?

Some of the short-term importance ascribed to grades rests on what should be solid assumptions. Grades purport to measure learning, and that inseparably links the two. But assumptions made about the nature of that relationship get us into trouble. Consider three such beliefs that make the links between grades and learning more than what they are.

First, some people assume that grades measure learning precisely. However, measuring learning turns out to be a complicated process. Some kinds of learning, like memorization of facts and the rote recall of details, grades can measure well. But higher-order thinking skills, the ones we most want to develop, like the ability to analyze, synthesize, and judge, and even other ways of knowing, are much more difficult to assess. A classic article, "Angels on a Pin" (Calandra, 1968), tells the story of a physics student arguing for more exam credit, but it is actually a damning critique of how our evaluation methods fail to measure some important kinds of learning.

The precision of grades is further compromised by the fact that not all of us use the same grading standards. Few of us have the nerve never to give A's (or give them only once every twenty years, as a professor I had did). More of us give many A's, but let us not step into the murky waters of grade inflation at this juncture. The point is simply that the different standards faculty use to determine grades make them imprecise measures of learning.

Second assumption: Grades are objective measures of learning. That is not true. Students play games to get them. No one makes that point quite as eloquently as Pollio and Humphreys (1988, p. 85): "Grading outstrips both intercollegiate athletics and intramural sports as the most frequently played game on the college campus. It takes place in all seasons and everyone gets to play one position or another." Sometimes students win at the grading game: they get the grade by unduly influencing their all-too-human evaluators.

The third assumption is that grades and evaluated assignments promote learning. Both successfully promote encounters with content, but whether those encounters produce high-quality learning experiences is quite another question. Because grades are so important, students are highly motivated to figure out how to get them and end up "learning" what they need to get the grade. They will memorize details, learn certain problem solutions, repeat key terms, regurgitate professor opinions, or figure out the multiple-choice format if that is what it takes. Recent research (Church, Elliot, and Gable, 2001) confirms that students are more likely to adopt performance goals as opposed to mastery goals (those likely to be associated with deep learning) when the professor emphasizes the importance of grades and performance and when the grading structure is perceived to be excessively difficult. In those kinds of environments, students may get "good" grades, but they leave the experience with little else. Content remains where they encountered it: in the course.

With these more tentative links between grades and learning, it would make sense to view grades with healthy skepticism, but that is not how most people, in and out of academe, see them. Because grades open doors to so many future opportunities, they powerfully motivate and influence student behavior and do so in some counterproductive ways. Consider three examples: cheating, beliefs about ability, and grade grubbing.

Pressure for grades results in cheating. Documentation that supports the steadily increasing pervasiveness of cheating can be found in many sources and contexts. McCabe and Trevino (1996), for example, replicated key questions from a 1963 survey of five thousand students at ninety-nine campuses in a 1993 survey of six thousand students at thirty-one campuses. In the original study, 63 percent of the students admitted to cheating behaviors; 70 percent in the recent study did so. In 1963, 26 percent reported they copied from another student's exam; 52 percent in the recent study did so. Less impressive were increases from 49 to 54 percent who reported that they copied material without footnoting and from 16 to 27 percent who said they used crib notes. (The 1996 reference is to a succinct, nontechnical summary of this large survey. It contains references to the original 1963 and 1993 research studies.)

Genereux and McLeod (1995) studied the circumstances most influential in spontaneous and planned decisions to cheat. Depending on grades for financial aid and the impact of course grade on long-term goals were in the top five for both decisions. A recent study of business students (Allen, Fuller, and Luckett, 1998) using an interesting mechanism involving simulated behaviors suggests that self-reports of cheating tend to underestimate the actual number and percentage of students who cheat. Certainly not all cheating results from the pressure to get grades, but a sizable amount does, and this much cheating raises questions about the integrity of the whole academic endeavor.

On quite a different front, grades strongly influence students' beliefs about themselves. They equate grades with ability and come to believe that the grades they receive are not influenced by the efforts they expend to learn the material. Consider here the work of Perry (1997), who has studied perceived personal control. This psychological construct involves the extent to which individuals believe they can or cannot influence or control events. It has been studied in a variety of contexts and situations, such as overcrowding, marital relations, health, aging, stress, and depression. Perry studied how it influenced academic achievement. Working with a number of colleagues, he has documented that if students perceive a loss of control, that orientation strongly affects their academic performance. In one study (Perry and Magnusson, 1987), it even superseded the influence of effective instructors. In other words, even the presence of an outstanding teacher could not dislodge the powerful effects that result when students believe academic outcomes are predetermined by factors external to them, such as the abilities they were born with.

The Perry and Magnusson findings corroborated earlier work by Covington and Omelich (1984), who asked students to rate their ability to deal with content in a course taken the previous semester, estimate how hard they had worked, and report the grade received. Estimates of ability accounted for 50 percent of the variance, with course grade and amount of effort expended a distant second and third. If you have not gotten very good grades in math and have come to the conclusion that you cannot do it, you should not bother trying to learn because those efforts will not make a difference. The importance placed on grades is causing students to come to the wrong conclusions about what they mean.

And finally, as much as faculty decry excessive grade orientation, they actually contribute to the grade grubbing mentality now seen in so many of students. I believe we do that with elaborate and detailed grading systems that put a point value on absolutely everything that students do. We have designed these systems as a means of clarifying expectations, which they do, but not without creating something a bit monstrous in the process. A student who rarely contributes in class comes to the office to discuss certain items on the test. He throws out ideas, arguments, and insights that demonstrate more command of the content than expected. We warm to the intellectual exchange and counter with other evidence and different arguments. The volley continues, and we relish all it might signify. But as the conversation ebbs, the student bluntly returns us to reality: "Well, do I get two more points, or don't I?" This dialogue was not motivated by a developing affinity for intriguing content.

Our point systems (and I use one) convey a powerful message: the only learning worth doing is learning that you get points for doing. What of that intensely satisfying pleasure derived from and through the sheer joy of learning? Will students ever fall in love with learning if they do it only for points? I often tell my students I will know that I have died and gone to instructional heaven when I pass back an exam and rather than hearing everyone buzz, "What'd ja get?" students ask each other, "What'd ja learn?" They laugh.

Recent research documents that faculty think students are excessively grade oriented, and this study found a more surprising result: most students think that they and faculty are too grade oriented. Of that finding, the researchers (Pollio and Beck, 2000, p. 98) write, "Basically, the present situation seems to be that both students and professors want the same changes—stronger emphasis on learning, weaker emphasis on grades—and both seem to hold the other responsible for the present, less than ideal situation."

Extensive cheating, wrong conclusions about ability, and this grade-grubbing mentality attest to the negative impact of an overemphasis on grades. The purpose for which we evaluate must be realigned so that we better use assessment to promote learning. Evaluation processes also need to change if teaching is to become learner-centered. Faculty should not be the only ones doing assessment work. It is yet another way we make students dependent learners. When students hand in a paper, ask them if it is a good paper and see what they say. Mine are confused when I ask the question and counter with these typical responses: "Why are you asking me?" "How would I know?" "You're the one who'll decide that." Or they think I have given them a public relations opportunity: "Oh, it's definitely an A paper. You remember that when you grade it."

The ability to evaluate one's own work accurately and constructively does not develop automatically. The more intellectually immature students are, the greater the chance is that their personal investment will bias what they see when they look at their own work. Without self-evaluation experience, the less likely students are to use appropriate comparative criteria. And they struggle with external feedback. Do they solicit it? From whom? Only the safe sources? Recently, I had my business students complete a leadership evaluation. They were to ask two others for feedback on their leadership skills so that they could compare their self-assessment with feedback from others. I was amazed how many chose to solicit input not from persons who saw them in leadership roles but from their parents. And having received feedback, learners must learn to interpret its conclusions accurately and constructively deal with what needs to be changed.

Students are not born knowing how to assess the work of others or how to deliver assessments that improve the work and skills of others. How many of us have had job experiences with a boss who could not accurately assess performance or deliver the necessary feedback constructively. Some of us have academic leaders who lack these skills.

Being without good self- and peer assessment skills is a professional liability. Most of us have known colleagues without the skills and have seen firsthand the consequences of not being able to render judgments. From the colleague who cannot let go of professional papers in a timely manner, to the article reviewer who delivers only brutal critique, knowing how to make accurate self- and peer assessments makes for a more successful and much less stressful professional and personal life. Current educational practice offers students few opportunities to develop skills in these areas.

In sum, there are two problems with the way evaluation is used in higher education. First, our policies and practices, coupled with a larger societal interest, place a disproportionate emphasis on evaluation for the purpose of grading. That emphasis has serious consequences that compromise learning outcomes. Second, our policies and practices exclude students from evaluation processes. They deny students opportunities to learn important self- and peer assessment strategies. When teaching becomes learning centered, it makes changes in both areas.

How the Purpose and Processes of Evaluation Change

Change in the evaluation arena occurs on two fronts. First, evaluation activities are used in ways that enhance their already inherent potential to promote learning. Second, evaluation processes are opened to students in ways that give them opportunities to develop self- and peer assessment skills.

Elements of Evaluation Experiences That Promote Learning

We can build on the power of grades to motivate students and connect these summative assessments to content in two productive ways. First, we use the motivation that drives students to get grades. We ride along with it and in the process attempt to redirect it—to harness it to more productive outcomes. Student understanding of grades needs to be broadened and put into a larger context. They need to see that encounters with content are worth more than points. They can and should take from exams, assignments, and ultimately the course itself something more enduring than the grade. What faculty must do with the student motivation to get grades is to bring a liberating message: learning matters more than grades, especially across the span of life.

Second, we work to maximize the encounters with content that occur as a consequence of evaluation activities and strive to shape those experiences so that they result in rich, transformative learning experiences that change not just what students know but how they know it. Both goals can be accomplished in a variety of ways, but consider four potentially productive areas, illustrated with a variety of examples.

Focus on Learning Processes

Add elements to evaluative experiences that make students aware of the learning processes involved. Consider structures that make students mindful of what they are doing, question why they are doing it, and expose them to alternatives (potentially more effective approaches). Much as I proposed using content to develop learning skills, now we want to use evaluative experiences to accomplish the same end.

The subtle but significant difference already pointed out is relevant again. This is not about telling students how to study but about challenging them to explore their approaches and presenting alternatives at times when you have their attention. Initially, students will try study alternatives if they think those approaches might result in more points. Ride along with that motivation, but try to help them see alternatives as part of developing their prowess as learners.

Reduce the Stress and Anxiety of Evaluation Experiences

Students find evaluation the most stressful aspect of college life. One study (Sarros and Densten, 1989) asked students to rate thirty-four potential stressors. Nine of the top ten related to evaluation activities, including the number of assignments, taking exams, and receiving low grades on them. Afraid, anxious, and stressed students do not easily focus on learning objectives. We need to reduce the stress, not eliminate it. A certain level piques performance, but most students would perform better and learn more if they constructively coped with stress.

Experiences that prepare students for what is to come help them manage stress. With exam reviews, this means using authentic, bona-fide test questions, not ones that would never appear on an exam. With papers, it means access to samples that illustrate appropriate topics and levels of treatment. Some faculty are reluctant to provide samples because students work so hard to copy the models. If the models are good, that might not be such an undesirable outcome. And sample topics can be removed from the list of acceptable ones.

Anxiety falls when the stakes are lower—when there are more than just two tests or one paper in a term or opportunities to redo or do more. Arguments for and against extra credit have been around for a long time. (Student experiences and attitudes are explored in Norcross, Horrocks, and Stevenson, 1989; faculty opinions in Norcross, Dooley, and Stevenson, 1993; and more opinions and a variety of extra credit options in Weimer, 1990.) Many faculty object to giving extra credit because if students are doing extra credit, then they are not spending time on the regular course assignments. However, if the extra credit offers more opportunities to interact with the same content, seeks to develop the same learning skills, and is at the same level of difficulty, why should this venue for connecting with content be prohibited? Remember that in a learning environment, the top priority is learning. I have one colleague who lets students redo papers forever, even after the class is over, as long as each time they redo, the paper improves and the grade is higher.

Some faculty have a problem with letting students have more than the one try it takes accomplished learners to get it. Slow learners are not as capable, and we apparently have some need to verify that during the educational process. Does it matter how long or how many tries it takes if students ultimately learn the content? Sometimes, perhaps, it does, but not always. It took me "forever" (my husband's judgment) to learn how to build a fire, but now I can get one going when it is windy, dark, and wet, and I have yet to have anybody ask how long it took me to learn. On darker days, I think our reluctance to let students keep trying smells more like intellectual elitism than a commitment to standards.

Remember that the goal is to reduce and better manage the kind of stress that inhibits and prevents learning. Opportunities to redo or try again are effective tools in the pedagogical repertoire of the learner-centered teacher.

Do Not Use Evaluation to Accomplish Hidden Agendas

Some of these agendas are hardly offenses; others raise serious ethical issues. I once observed in a class where the faculty member was querying students about content from an earlier part of the course. "Remember when we talked about X?" Students were slow remembering. Their lack of response prompted this comment: "We covered it just before the first exam." Memories were not triggered by positioning content in relation to course concepts or other material but as that content existed in relation to an evaluation experience. The hidden agenda here involves organizing content around exam events. Though a minor offense, it illustrates how the importance of evaluation events permeates our thinking.

Much more serious is the occasional faculty member who uses evaluation to show the class how much she knows or how inherently difficult the content is. Faculty members have no business using courses or exams to weed out students who by some set of subjective standards "cannot do" physics, engineering, math, or any other discipline. Students may learn through courses and exams that their interests and talents lie elsewhere, but courses and exams should never be designed to accomplish this end.

Moreover, we do not establish the reputation for rigor or enhance the credibility of a course by making exams excessively difficult. Only two conclusions can be drawn in classes where the faculty member has made a good-faith effort to explicate the material and students have made a good-faith effort to learn it but 75 percent of the class has still failed the exam: the faculty member cannot prepare good tests or cannot explicate the material. Maybe all the students cannot study, but I am more inclined to see this as a faculty problem.

Using evaluation to demonstrate the rigor and complexity of the content demotivates students and encourages them to see success in terms of ability, not effort. I believe that few faculty use evaluation in this way, but perceived problems with grade inflation reopen this inappropriate solution. Rigor and standards belong in courses. They challenge students and result in more learning, but there is a point of diminishing returns.

A bit less egregious ethically but still questionable as an agenda are faculty who use evaluation experiences to test how far students can take content. They include questions or problems totally unlike anything students have seen or solved before. The solution is not the opposite extreme—including only problems done in class or assigned as homework—but some place in the middle. Evaluation events can be used to measure application and critical thinking skills, but they promote these skills more effectively if students have the opportunity to work on them in class or on homework first. During this formative period, faculty can guide the process, illustrating how it is done, and the students are more likely to learn problem-solving processes and critical thinking methods as they develop application skills.

Designing exams that promote quality learning outcomes requires skill and experience. It also helps if faculty understand some basic exam construction principles. Those are ably presented in a first-rate book by Jacobs and Chase (1992) on developing and using tests effectively.

Incorporate More Formative Feedback Mechanisms

Finally, we can improve the learning potential of evaluative experiences if in addition to the grade, we include feedback that aims to improve the next performance. Grades are summative feedback, highly judgmental, and comprehensive in their conclusions. And they often get in the way of learning. Return a set of papers with careful and complete comments throughout and a grade at the end, and watch the students. They quickly flip to the grade, only glancing briefly or not at all at those comments. You see papers stuffed in cluttered book bags, dropped off in the trash on the way out of class, or never retrieved from the stack outside the office door, and you begin to understand how much the summative context compromises the learning potential of the formative feedback.

It is usually best to separate the two as you would if you return the papers with the comments and then require a written response to those comments before giving the grade. Hogan (1994) reports on a method like this that he devised for returning papers. He requires students to read his feedback and begin to see the basis for his evaluation of the paper before they find out the grade. Or try putting the feedback in a different format. Finkel (2000) writes persuasively of his experience delivering feedback in individual letters he wrote to students.

On occasion, entirely separate the feedback from the summative evaluation. In our busy lives and classes with too many students, we often do not have time for one-on-one feedback, but we ought not to underestimate the power of a comment to have a significant impact on a student. I am a college professor today because my favorite professor said to me one day, off the cuff and in passing, "Have you ever thought about teaching college?" At that point in my life, the thought had never crossed my mind. I do not know if it ever would have.

Also important in the formative feedback arena are the well-established principles of constructive feedback. Feedback should be directed toward the performance and not the person, should use language that describes more than it evaluates, and should not overload the receiver. Its effectiveness is enhanced if it is immediate and well timed.

Each of the four areas considered has the potential to change the kind and quality of learning that results from evaluation events and experiences: (1) calling attention to the learning processes associated with evaluation experiences, (2) reducing the anxiety experienced as a consequence of them, (3) not using evaluation to accomplish hidden agendas, and (4) providing formative feedback through structures and formats that separate it from the summative context. If these are incorporated in evaluation activities, we will be well on our way to reclaiming the ultimately more important purpose for which we evaluate students: to promote learning.

The Case for and Goals of Self-Assessment

Given the fact that faculty evaluate student work so entirely, the idea that students should be involved in the process strikes many faculty as a radical alternative. Quite expectedly and justifiably, they question its feasibility and legitimacy. Can students responsibly self-assess? Doesn't the "need" for grades totally compromise students' abilities to be objective? Can they be involved in self-assessment activities without compromising faculty responsibility to certify what they know and can do at the course's conclusion?

Learner-centered teaching is not about faculty's abdicating legitimate grading responsibilities. Rather, it is about students' developing skills that enable them to self-assess their work accurately. However, there is no question that student involvement in self-assessment activities will be more intense and rigorous if these activities "count." But can we responsibly make changes in a domain where faculty have such serious responsibilities?

Student self-assessment has been studied empirically and to a greater degree than most faculty would expect. The most definitive work in the area has been done by Falchikov and Boud (1989), whose meta-analysis of forty-eight studies draws together much of what is known about student self-assessment. Some of the results are what we expect. For an entry-level required course, the correlation between student-assigned grades and teacher grades is low and does not justify having students grade their work. In an upper-division course for majors, if the grading is done against specified criteria and students have a chance to compare their assessment with that of their teachers, the correlations are much more promising.

Work done since this meta-analysis continues to confirm the ability of students to self-assess accurately under certain conditions. For example, Kardash (2000) looked at fourteen research skills purportedly developed by undergraduate research experiences in science. Students rated themselves on these skills before and after an undergraduate research experience. Their faculty mentors also rated them on the same set of skills. Kardash reports striking similarities between the ratings, with both faculty and students giving highest ratings to the same five skills.

Because the notion of student self-assessment seems so on the edge, work in this area has always been low profile, but the idea is not new. MacGregor (1993, p. 1) explains that student self-evaluation "has a long history in alternative colleges. Faculty members there have always wanted to evaluate their students more extensively and qualitatively than they could by assigning grades, and at the same time they have wanted—and expected—students to claim the value and meaning of their learning in their own words. At more traditional institutions as well, some faculty have engaged their students in self-evaluation and have encouraged the active participation of their students in the process." (For an excellent compilation of ideas on student narratives that evaluate learning and reports of some programs that use the approach, see MacGregor, 1993.)

Given the empirical justification and successful experience, what goals can self-assessment activities be used to accomplish? Ultimately, students should be able to do an accurate self-assessment to identify relative strengths and weaknesses, determine what next needs to be improved, develop an improvement plan, implement it, and finally use an assessment of its effectiveness to position themselves for the next round of improvement.

Accurate self-assessment is contingent on the ability to deal with external feedback. Through evaluation experiences, students need to learn when their lack of objectivity mandates that they include outside feedback. They should have a repertoire of mechanisms they can use to solicit that feedback. They also need to be able to interpret and evaluate the feedback from others accurately so that it does not harm inappropriately and so that poor-quality conclusions can be rejected. Finally, they need to be able to incorporate the conclusions of viable feedback into their overall self-perceptions and plans for improvement. In learner-centered environments, students are taught skills that accomplish these goals.

The Case for and Goals of Peer Assessment

Like self-assessment, the case for peer assessment rests on the importance of these skills in professional contexts. That importance is clearly seen in the goals that peer assessment activities ought to accomplish. When students do peer assessment, they learn how to use (and ultimately generate) criteria to gauge their reaction to the work or performance of others. They learn how to identify and otherwise point to aspects of the work or performance that support or illustrate the larger conclusions drawn. And they learn how to deliver evaluative messages using the principles of constructive feedback.

What makes peer assessment difficult for students relates directly to self-assessment issues. Students question their qualifications: "I'm just another student. What can I say about somebody else's writing?" They question their self-assessment opinions compared to the experience and expertise of a faculty evaluator. And with peers, there is the struggle involved in delivering the feedback, especially anything negative. "What if the peer recipient doesn't like me any more?" they worry.

Because self- and peer assessment issues are so tightly linked, experiences in one area contribute to the development of skills in the other area. Getting students involved in reacting to each other's work synergistically develops their ability to self-assess. It teaches them how to make judgments and helps them to gain confidence in their opinions, especially if they can document those conclusions with evidence. Their ability to give criticism helps them learn how to take it. They see the value of an outside perspective. They learn what kind of feedback most helps as they see others try to grapple with what they deliver and try to make sense of what they receive.

Evaluation changes when teaching is learner-centered. I have proposed a move away from using evaluation events only to generate grades and a view of them as some of the course's most potent learning opportunities. In a learner-centered environment, evaluation occurs for the purpose of grading *and* learning. I have further proposed a move away from thinking that views evaluation exclusively as a teacher activity. Evaluative events can and should be used to develop student self- and peer assessment abilities, yet another part of their development as learners.

In the Trenches: The Policies and Practices of Assessment and Learning

This collection of policies and practices is structured a bit differently from some of these sections in previous chapters. I felt it might be more useful to explore a smaller number of options and cover them more fully. Successful implementation of these changes in evaluation purpose and processes can be accomplished by redesigning, refocusing, and better connecting a series of instructional activities and assignments—all parts of a single evaluation event. I have chosen three common instructional activities and describe how evaluation in each can be restructured to accomplish the changes being proposed. I identify a variety of ways that exams and the events associated with them can be reconfigured so that they more effectively promote learning, describe how the evaluation of participation can be designed to include a variety of self-assessment activities, and discuss group work and the role that peer assessment can play in the evaluation of it.

Using an Exam to Promote Learning

A series of activities that enhance the learning potential of exams can be incorporated into this common evaluation event. Consider them in more or less chronological order beginning with the need for regular ongoing review. Students should be encouraged to review, not told to do so by the teacher, with short activities that help them revisit content regularly. You could start with activities described in Chapter Three on the function of content. Use the last five minutes in class to have students work on summarizing the content, figuring out what is most important and what is mostly likely to appear on an exam.

Green (1997) builds this into something more elaborate, thoughtful, and detailed. She has each individual student, for credit, generate one test question (short answer or multiple choice) for each content module. Once the module material has been presented and questions on it submitted, Green enters all the questions in a database, prints the questions, and puts them, without answers, on reserve in the library. She uses these student questions for about 75 percent of the exam and identifies the question's author on the exam.

The Review Period

Some faculty do not believe that they should devote a class session to review; that leaves less time for covering the content, and they see reviewing as basically a student responsibility. I might be able to accept the student responsibility part of the argument if my students knew how to review, but many of them do not. In addition, integrating, summarizing, synthesizing, and otherwise pulling together disparate pieces of information are sophisticated learning skills that merit attention and development. Sahadeo and Davis (1988) propose thinking of the review session's purpose as one of content integration, with the focus being on organizational patterns, structures, and relationships that exist between content segments, so in a sense it is new material. If that assuages your conscience, so use the review session. If you continue to be concerned about content coverage, it may be time to revisit Chapter Three on the function of content when teaching is learner-centered.

In my entry-level class, I use the review session to try to teach students how to make accurate decisions about what content will be on the exam. We focus on the reading, since they almost always indicate they are least confident about material that we have not "gone over" in class. I put them in groups and assign each group a section of the reading. Each group has a transparency and a marker, and their task is to write three multiple-choice test questions from that section of reading. Beautifully formed questions do not emerge out of this activity. That is not actually the goal, although I think there is great virtue in getting the students to think about questions and not just focus on answers. My students memorize all sorts of answers, giving little thought to what questions they answer.

I put each group's transparency on the overhead. Students answer the questions individually, and then we vote on the answers as a class. I vote right along with the students. Some of the questions are confusing and difficult to interpret, but we work through the semantic clutter to make the question and options clearer. I tell my students that a good test question is like a clean window: it does not get in the way of seeing what the student does and does not know. Then we do what I consider the most important activity: we rate, on a scale of one to seven, how likely we think we are to see a question like this on the exam. After the students have rated the question, I rate it. This activity generates good discussion about the kinds of questions and level of knowledge students need for the exam. I remind students of this exchange when we debrief the exam.

Using the Exam Itself Better

Here the goal is to enhance the learning potential of the exam itself. You can use the group exam experiences or some variation of them described in Chapter Four on the role of the teacher, or consider some simple changes that make for more and better learning mainly by alleviating anxiety and building confidence.

When I started teaching and lacked confidence, I worried endlessly that students were not taking my class, and thus its exams, seriously. To make the point, I put a very difficult question first. To help my highly anxious, not very confident students, I now do the exact opposite.

Any number of faculty have experimented with letting students prepare and use a crib sheet or card during the exam (for an example, see Janick, 1990). Students may include on the card any information, facts, or formulas that they think they might need to answer exam questions. The preparation of the card itself has significant learning potential. Janick (1990, p. 2) observes, "The development of a good crib sheet resembles its antithesis: studying." When Cassini (1994) has students respond to an essay question in class, he distributes the question and then lets students collaborate for twenty minutes. They may review their notes and discuss the question with other students in class. Any notes or outlines prepared during this interval may be used during the next ninety minutes when students write the essay. The rationale behind both of these approaches (and that of take-home exams) rests on the fact that access to information is seldom denied in professional contexts. The ability to find and quickly organize information matters more than whether you can carry it in your head.

Extra credit questions or redo mechanisms are another way to relieve anxiety and promote learning. If you do not want students working on the extra credit questions when they should be working on the main questions, put the extra credit questions on a separate sheet and give them out only after students have turned in the test. Rusth (1996) reports on a two-try testing scheme he devised. Students in his advanced financial accounting course first do the exam problems individually in class. The exams are designed so that the average student scores about 50 percent. For the second attempt, groups of students work as a team on the same exam for a week outside class. Typically, the teams score 100 percent. Rusth averages the two tries. He includes data documenting that this approach improves individual performance on the standardized final used at the end of the course.

There are many other options. I have a colleague who leaves one question blank and lets students write that question. They are instructed to write a question they expected to see on the exam but is not there and one that they are prepared to answer. Approaches like this, as well as essay tests where students have a choice of questions, do raise reliability issues. Because you cannot guarantee that all questions are equally difficult, you are essentially evaluating learning with a number of different tests and so should not compare student performance as a curve grading scheme would.

Some faculty are creative when it comes to mechanisms that let students experience at least some success with what they know. Instructor Lance Gordon described to me (Weimer, 1988a) a cost-benefit approach used in a math class (it probably would work best with problem-solving exams). A student who got stuck on a particular problem at an interval during the test could "buy" information (a hint, a clue, or maybe a full or partial formula) from the instructor. The "cost" was taken out of the test question's worth. So a ten-point question might be reduced to seven points for a student who needed to buy a particular part of a formula.

To take the creation of test questions to an extreme place, probably justified only after giving students extensive experience writing questions, consider two other options. Barton (1994) has students individually or in groups submit test questions and problems. He constructs the exam so that 80 to 90 percent of the content consists of student-generated items. His list of ten advantages accrued by the approach makes it worth considering. Instructor Viji Sundar outlined for me (Weimer, 1989) an end-of-course option where students develop a final exam. She did this in a math course, but it would work well with different kinds of content. She graded on things like the problems developed (in terms of their propriety given the objectives of the course), the solutions, and the point value assigned the problem (given its relative importance in course content). Interestingly, a number of students reported that they spent more time making the final than they would have studying for it.

In sum, the exam itself will promote better learning if there is less anxiety associated with it. (For additional background on the negative effects of test anxiety and still more ideas on ways to help students constructively cope with it, see Mealey and Host, 1992.)

Debriefing the Exam

Finally, consider how exam results should be reviewed. Most important of all, consider having a debriefing session and making it longer than the last five minutes of class. Also move away from simply "going over" the exam. Consider some of the options proposed in Chapter Five on the responsibility for learning as vehicles to develop student awareness of logical consequences of their study decisions. And welcome discussion that challenges what you have designated as the right answer, provided these conversations occur within certain parameters. If students see that persistent and passionate protests can be used to gain more points, you reinforce grade-grubbing behavior and can sacrifice the exam's integrity.

If students think that option B is correct, I make them work hard to prove that: "Show me something in the book that justifies that answer" or "Read me something that you have in your notes that led you to believe B was correct." And when they present an argument for B, I argue back and push them to respond: "How would you answer the point I made about x?" And I work everybody who wants credit for B. "How many of the rest of you had B? I need to hear from some of you. Explain your thought processes. What evidence would you offer?" And I work those who have selected the answer I have given credit for. "Let's say both B and D are technically correct. Which one is the better answer? Why?"

Faculty should work diligently not to respond defensively when students challenge test questions. Protect yourself in three ways. First, recognize that you will on occasion write a bad question. If more than half the class has missed the question and it is answered wrong on more than half of the top ten scores, eliminate it. Second, ask students to observe the golden rule of feedback: give unto the teacher feedback in the form you would like to receive it. And to ensure that my thinking is clear, I always defer the decision. I do not make it right there in class but in the quiet of my office. After I have had a chance to think about what they have said and review my notes and the book, I decide if I am accepting a different answer. I announce my decision in the next class and do not discuss it further in class. Of course, any student may see me during office hours to talk more about it. If you do not want to have this discussion in class and give the extra points to everyone—even those who made lucky guesses—consider a mechanism whereby students can justify alternative choices in writing, including persuasive arguments documented with evidence.

Participation and Self-Assessment

All sorts of course assignments and activities can be used to develop self-assessment skills. In this section, we will consider one in detail: participation. I chose this particular learning activity for several reasons. Evaluation of participation is common, although most faculty do not use objective or carefully thought-out systems. More germane here, I can use this example to illustrate the level of attention to design details necessary when you begin developing student self-assessment skills. Finally, this example, even though it is primarily a self-assessment activity, illustrates how peer components can be incorporated into most self-assessment activities, with the effect of benefiting skill development in both areas.

In Chapter Two on involving students in course- and learning-related decisions, I described how my public speaking class establishes the participation policy. Once that is in place, I have students set concrete (that is, measurable and observable) participation goals for themselves. They select these goals based on an analysis of how they currently participate and what participation skills they next need to develop. They propose goals that are consistent with and advance the class-generated policy.

The peer contribution to this self-assessment activity happens early in the course. Shortly after having developed their goals, I assign everyone doing this option a participation partner. The partners exchange their individual participation goals in writing. Over the next several weeks, the partners observe each other, looking for participation behaviors specified by the goals. What happens during these weeks is extraordinary. I have more participation and student involvement than at any other time in the course, with students doing things they have never done before. I am regularly amazed at how effectively peers motivate behavior change.

At the end of the two-week period, the partners write each other a letter giving feedback—not generalized, evaluative conclusions but descriptive details—on what they have observed. The letters are uniformly positive and constructive, often including encouragement if behaviors in support of the goal have not been observed. Students then use this peer feedback and their self-assessment as the basis of a memo to me in which they evaluate their progress toward the goals and assign themselves the number of points they think they have earned at this midpoint of the course. I assign the points (formatively only; I do not record them) that I think they have earned before they submit their memos. On their memos, I indicate my point total, making extensive comments when there is a significant disagreement in our totals. If students are well on their way to accomplishing their goals, I try to encourage them to revise their goals for the rest of the semester by making them more challenging. I do not offer more points if they do in a small effort aimed at making them see the value of doing things that benefit their development as learners. They will be using these participation skills for years to come, I point out.

At the end of the course, students do a final self-assessment memo. I expect their conclusions to be documented with evidence— very concrete references that identify the dates of their contributions and summaries of their substance. I keep track of their class contributions in a log that I write in for five to ten minutes every day after class. I quickly enter in my computer everything that I can remember that students did. If anybody does anything unusual, I almost always note that.

Their final memo ends with students saying how many of the fifty points they believe they have earned. Once again, I assign their points before I read their memos. If their self-assessment and my assessment are within three points of each other, I record the higher score. If we are not within three points, the student and I have a discussion, and one or both of us revise our totals. To my amazement, in about 85 percent of the cases, we are within three points of each other. And when we are not, the most frequent problem is an underevaluation, more often than not by female students.

I believe this system works well because it uses the conditions Falchikov and Boud (1989) identified as those most conducive to accurate self-assessment. I know the system makes students much more aware of their contributions in class. I also know that it has significantly improved the caliber of the exchanges I now have with students in class. As with all other instructional strategies, I am hardly the first or only faculty member to have searched for better ways to promote learning though and about participation. Lyons (1989) and Woods (1996) offer two other examples. Woods's example is especially intriguing because he has students develop the criteria that will be used to assess their participation. He conducts the assessment, but getting students involved in generating the criteria is another effective way to change their perceptions of evaluation purpose and processes.

Many other activities can be used to develop student self-assessment skills. One of the oldest and most effective involves the construction of a portfolio or collection of work selected and organized by the student. To have to assemble your five best drawings, ten strongest paragraphs, or six most persuasive contributions to an electronic discussion forces students to differentiate among their work samples using a quality criteria. And if the portfolio assignment includes a written justification for the work selected, self-assessment skills develop even more.

Group Work and Peer Assessment

With peer assessment, as with self-assessment, there are many venues in which peer involvement can occur. Best documented and most extensively described in the literature is work within English composition, much of it written as part of the Writing Across the Curriculum movement, on the role of peers in the critique and evaluation of writing. The rationale, justification, and a myriad of examples exist. I am partial to the collection presented by Bean (1996).

Much less work has been done on the role of peer assessment in groups, despite the contribution it can make, especially to one of the most serious objections that both students and faculty raise about course-related group work: one or two members end up doing all or a disproportionate share of the work for the group.

Advocates of cooperative learning believe strongly that any group work needs to retain individual accountability. In other words, grades are measures of individual mastery and should never be assigned to a whole group. There is nothing on a transcript indicating that a B course grade resulted from participation in a group that bombed. (For a succinct and well-reasoned summary of this position, see Kagan, 1995.) Some faculty divide group grades into parts: a designated percentage awarded for the group's product (everybody in the group gets this grade) and another designated percentage for what the individual contributed. In the second case, that grade might be based on work the individual completed, provided individual tasks have been clearly partitioned, or, germane to our discussion here, it might be based on what the individual contributed to the group as assessed by other group members. The more deliberate this process is, the more likely that it develops students' peer assessment skills and improves the functioning of the group.

When first assigned to assess peers, students typically respond by claiming that everyone in the group performed equally—this despite extensive research documenting that in almost every group, people contribute differentially. One way around this conundrum is to have group members rank and rate the contributions of others against a specified set of criteria. I tell my students that if they all contributed equally, the numbers will show that. They in fact rarely do.

Contributions in a group need to be measured against a set of criteria. If students are new to this process, you might to want to start by providing the criteria, derived from general information about effective group members, the discussion individual groups may have had about how they hope to work together, or based on the specific contributions necessary to complete this group project. As students become more experienced and comfortable with the process, let the groups identify their own criteria. They need to do this at the start so that the criteria clarify expectations before the group starts working together.

Also consider including a formative component to the process, especially for group projects that extend over the entire course. I recommend having the students use the same criteria they will use at the end of their work. Have them evaluate and submit all assessments for all group members, including themselves. Then return to each individual a summary of other members' assessments, looking for those individuals whose self- and group assessments widely differ. In those cases, it might be well to meet individually with the student to discuss the differing perceptions.

You can enhance peer assessment within groups by involving groups in assessment tasks related to the work of other groups. Start simply by giving all groups the same problem and then having them compare and contrast their solution with those of other groups. Or you can have groups directly critique the work of another group; they can raise questions about it or apply some set of evaluative criteria to it. Let groups then revise based on the feedback provided by other groups as a last step before formal submission.

For groups comfortable with group work and peer assessment, there are some intriguing possibilities. I have a colleague who takes the group exam strategy to a next level. He has groups prepare the third of four unit exams in his course. He provides the format: twenty multiple-choice questions, ten short answer, and three essay questions. Experience with the first two exams in the course gives students some standard to work against. He also provides resources on test construction and item preparation. The groups then prepare the test and provide him an answer key and outlines of essay responses meeting the requirements for an A. All individuals in one group take an exam that has been constructed by another group. He grades the individual exams. The peer assessment activity involves groups' "grading" the exam they have taken, after it has been graded and returned to them. They evaluate things like the clarity, propriety, and worth of the questions. He also "grades" the exams and uses a combination of his and the group's assessment to derive a final grade for the exam. It becomes a group grade, recorded in addition to the individual exam score.

How does he keep students from conspiring to write simple exams? He tells me it has never been a problem. He reserves the right to intervene and take action if groups do not complete the assignment thoroughly. On the whole, he rates the student exams as tougher than his, but the range of scores is consistent with his exams. He thinks students do better because writing an exam is such good preparation for taking one. Student feedback confirms this conclusion.

We have explored ways of emphasizing the learning potential of exam experiences and options with participation and group work that develop self- and peer assessment skills. All three examples illustrate what happens when the purpose and processes of evaluation change. In addition, the examples illustrate the even greater benefits that accrue when self- and peer assessment activities are combined.

Questions That Arise When the Purpose and Processes of Evaluation Change

The most important question that arises out of the changes proposed in the purpose and processes for evaluation is the ethical one: Should students have any involvement in the actual grading process? Evidence included in the chapter documents what most of us already know: the pressure for grades makes it impossible for students in entry-level courses to grade their own work reliably. But the same empirical work opens the door for student self-assessment in upper-division courses. However, neither that work nor anything else I could find in the literature addresses the ethical issue: Is it academically responsible to let students make these judgments? Some faculty do and report surprising results. Clark (1994) describes his experience with more than 350 students. He offers feedback and assessments along the way, but students determine their grades. To track how the system works, he also assigns the student a grade: "Nearly 50% of the grades have matched exactly. Some 30% have assessed themselves a half grade higher, and 2% a full grade higher than I have. Another 2% have awarded themselves a full grade lower" (p. 2). He estimates that roughly 5 percent take complete advantage of the system but notes, "This percentage is not appreciably higher than in a traditional system—and I judge the trade-offs to be easily worth the risk" (p. 2).

I have described and proposed strategies that give students a piece of the grading action—a partial but less than full stake in determining their course grade. But the ethics question remains relevant because these approaches still give students a legitimate piece of the action. Is it ethical to give them even this small part?

The reason for bona-fide student involvement in the grading process hearkens back to the benefits accrued when we ride along with their motivation to get grades. They take self- and peer assessment activities seriously if they "count." The intensity of their involvement makes the self-and peer assessment skills easier to develop. If you divest students of any involvement with assessment that counts, it is correspondingly more difficult to get them involved and to achieve much in the way of skill development. So there is motivation to work within the course's grading structures. Do those reasons offer enough justification? What we need to know is how closely we can walk to the edge without falling into practices that are ethically compromised.

If we are responsible, self-regulating practitioners, we can answer these questions for ourselves and probably be safe, although we are not likely to answer the same way. But we are not all equally reflective and scrupulous. Moreover, we have some collective professional responsibility to set standards and offer guidelines against which individual practice can be benchmarked. Here again, if the practice of learner-centered teaching is to move forward and gain credibility and more widespread use, then we need more and clearer thinking about an appropriate relationship between teacher and student assessments.

To Finish Up

Consider what about evaluation needs to change if teaching is to be learner-centered. The purpose for which we evaluate must become enlarged and better balanced so that evaluation activities are used not just to generate grades but to promote learning as well. The processes of evaluation must also become enlarged so that evaluation events can be used to develop the self- and peer assessment skills of students. Now consider what does not change, even in learner-centered teaching environments. Grades are still used, and the important gatekeeping roles they play are upheld by continuing commitments to fair, equitable, and rigorous standards. Also remaining is the faculty responsibility as the ultimate summative assessor. The changes proffered here will strike many faculty as dramatic, but what stays the same should provide enough comfort and security to motivate exploration of the changes.

Part Two

Implementing the Learner-Centered Approach

Chapter Seven

Responding to Resistance

This chapter and the next two are about making the approach laid out in Part One happen. They deal with the nuts and bolts of implementation, that is, doing learner-centered teaching in your class, with your content, and for your students. They are the chapters I wish I had been able to read before I started making learner-centered changes in my teaching.

Once convinced, many faculty respond to learner-centered approaches enthusiastically. They begin to create new assignments, develop classroom activities, and realign course policies, and as the work progresses, their commitment to the new approach deepens. They excitedly launch a new course, new activity, or new assignment—only to discover that students do not respond to the changes with corresponding enthusiasm. In fact, they resist either passively or openly, making their preference known for the way things used to be.

The student response is disheartening and feels like a personal affront. Perhaps the new approaches should be reviewed with a colleague. The reaction there may be equally negative. The colleague questions what is being done and bluntly points out that it would never work with his students. And so now the faculty member faces a real quandary. What seemed so right, so good, and so exciting now seems less so. Does it even make sense to proceed with changes this unpopular?

Consider this chapter forewarning: student and faculty resistance is all but a guaranteed response to learner-centered teaching. It is a common, typical response, not some dreadful anomaly expressed exclusively by your students and your colleagues and resulting from your instructional inadequacy. This chapter aims to help you deal with resistance from students and colleagues. We consider student and faculty resistance separately, but being prepared and able to handle the resistance of both is related to the same three areas. First, it helps to understand why students and colleagues resist. What is the source of their resistance? What fuels and feeds it? Second, how does the resistance manifest itself? What will students do and say that indicates they are resisting? How will faculty object? Finally, and most important, the chapter proposes some strategies for dealing with resistance. With students, there is good news. Their usually negative initial responses can be answered. Their hostility diminishes, and ultimately most students come to endorse learner-centered approaches. With colleagues, the results are more mixed. In both cases, it helps to expect the resistance and to have considered some ways of responding.

Why Students Resist

Student resistance has been studied by researchers and written about by faculty who have experienced it. I strongly recommend a fine article by Felder and Brent (1996) aptly titled, "Navigating the Bumpy Road to Student-Centered Instruction." (My copy is dog-eared and almost completely underlined. I keep it with my course materials and have a note in my first-day folder to read it before proceeding to class.) Felder and Brent make the fundamental point about student resistance very clearly: "It's not that student-centered instruction doesn't work when done correctly—it does, as both the literature and our personal experience . . . richly attest. The problem is that although the promised benefits are real, they are neither immediate nor automatic. The students, whose teachers have been telling them everything they needed to know from the first grade on, don't necessarily appreciate having this support suddenly withdrawn" (p. 43).

Students resist learner-centered approaches for a variety of reasons that can be listed and discussed separately even though they are related and cumulative in effect. If faculty understand the sources of resistance, their knowledge can be used to enlighten students who may not fully understand their own reaction. Consider four of the most common reasons students resist learner-centered approaches. Although resistance for these reasons applies directly to learner-centered approaches, students have and do resist other aspects of instruction—sometimes for the same reasons.

Learner-Centered Approaches Are More Work

These approaches are more work for faculty, who now face complex instructional design issues, but the students resist because they quickly realize that this means much more work for them as well. If students need five examples to illustrate a concept, the easiest and most efficient way to acquire them is to have the teacher list them on the board or in a handout. It is much more difficult and much less efficient to sit around with a group of peers and generate the needed five examples. It is probably as simple as the old pleasure-pain principle. The resistance is an objection to the pain associated with the hard work of learning.

Resistance that is based on the increased amount of work is resistance for the right reason from the teacher's perspective (and someday perhaps from the student's as well). It ends up being proof that these approaches effectively engage students with content. Consider resistance based on this reason as a sign that the approaches have been successfully designed and are accomplishing their desired objective. They are engaging students with content and developing their prowess as learners.

Learner-Centered Approaches Are More Threatening

Students also resist these approaches because they are afraid. The old familiar scenario, played out across years of educational experience, with its predictable roles and expected student and faculty behaviors, no longer applies, or applies less, or applies differently, so what are students supposed to do? How are they supposed to behave? Who is responsible for what now? The teacher has opened Pandora's box and let out all sorts of unknown and unfamiliar policies, practices, assignments, and expectations not regularly encountered in other classes.

The fear becomes a major anxiety for students who face learning tasks without confidence in themselves as learners. Keeley, Shemberg, Cowell, and Zinnbauer (1995, p. 141), who write about student resistance to being taught critical thinking skills but note that similar resistance is likely engendered by other learner-centered approaches, draw from psychotherapy literature to explain: "Teachers of critical thinking and psychotherapists both *require* individual responsibility and self-direction from their students/clients, who often lack self-confidence. So students/clients must try things they are not yet good at. Relying on oneself rather than the expert is frightening. Becoming a successful critical thinker or client means taking risks and fighting fears of failure and of the unknown." Candy (1991, p. 382) believes the threat is related to not being able to figure out what the teacher "really wants" in an environment where so many of the learning parameters have been changed. In sum, some student resistance says more about self-perceptions than it does about the approaches.

Learner-Centered Approaches Involve Losses

Kloss (1994, p. 155), who charts students' resistance to intellectual development (and as we will discuss in Chapter Eight, these approaches really jump-start intellectual development), points out that whenever you move from one level of understanding to another, something is lost: "We as teachers need to remember that growth creates a sense of loss in students, the loss of certainty that has sustained them and been a refuge in an increasingly complex and confusing world."

Most of us can recall those moments on the road to maturity when we finally realized we had to make the decisions for ourselves. I remember speaking with my father about what seemed an especially important and unclear decision. He said he would offer advice and give me his opinion, but I would have to make the choice. I remember weeping when I hung up the telephone. I liked it so much better when Dad just told me what to do.

These approaches take our students to new places where the responsibility and the ownership for what does and does not happen is much more obviously theirs. One of my students wrote in his journal, "In this class your destiny is very much in your own hands. I keep thinking that I should like that, but I don't. I miss having things decided for me." Some student resistance is about loss and longing for the simpler way things used to be. They may understand intellectually that the new approaches are good for them and foster their personal development. But the feeling of loss is an emotional one that sometimes manifests itself as resistance.

Learner-Centered Approaches May Be Beyond Students

I had never considered the possibility of constructive resistance until I discovered the work of Kearney and Plax (1992), who have studied student resistance to a variety of instructional actions and approaches. Their point is that if teachers are unfair to students and unethical or ask students to engage in ethically compromised behavior, then we should hope that students would resist, despite the fact that they may do so at some personal risk. Most faculty are not unethical or unfair with students, but the learner-centered techniques selected may ask students to take approaches, complete work employing methods, or use particular structures that are beyond students' abilities to handle. Chapter Eight considers the complex issues of development, how we prepare students for and then push them toward levels of increased responsibility and autonomy, but in most cases we are starting close to ground zero. Our students are passive, disconnected, not always responsible, dependent, and not very confident learners. Some of the strategies, assignments, and policies described in this book require a level of intellectual maturity that they may not possess in the beginning. Part of their resistance may be in response to that, and so we need to listen closely in order to ascertain if the resistance is against more work, based on fear, or about loss or a legitimate objection to something the student is not yet prepared to handle.

Knowing Resistance When You See It

Kearney and Plax (1992) document that student resistance is widespread. The resistance they describe and that has been confirmed in the experiences of many of us is to instructional specifics. My students do not object to the approach. They are not against learner-centered philosophies. They respond to the details—the policies, practices, assignments, and activities that I use to implement the approach. It seems to me a case of my students not seeing the forest because they have a problem with what looks like a tall tree directly in their path.

The work by Kearney and Plax is especially valuable because from their data, they have created a nineteen-category typology of student resistance techniques. They have identified exactly what students do when they resist. They did not study resistance only in the learner-centered context, but some of their categories are especially likely to be associated with learner-centered approaches. Consider three of these.

Passive, Nonverbal Resistance

This frequently appears as an overwhelming lack of enthusiasm for what you have proposed. For example, I describe to my class a group activity that I use early in the course, and once I explain the task and procedures, I say to students, "Join with three or four people sitting near you, and form a group." I have done this in classes where there has been absolutely no visible response to that request. The students just sit there, looking at me, looking around, looking at the clock, gazing out the window. I persist: "I need you to get into groups. Please circle up your chairs, and start introducing yourselves to each other." This request might be met with what I would characterize as a minimalist response: some students start looking at each other. They do not speak but make tentative nonverbal queries, for example, looking inquiringly at others. Still nobody moves any furniture. I now venture out into the class, smiling cheerfully, seemingly unaware, and certainly undaunted by this less than enthusiastic compliance. "Bunch," I say. "Bunch. You folks a group? Well, get your chairs together. Want me to arrange some for you over here?"

Their message is perfectly clear: "We don't want to get into groups." But no one has spoken this resistance. There is less risk involved when the message is communicated nonverbally. If the teacher directly asks you, "What's the problem, Fred?" you can make a verbal denial: "No, problem. I'm going with these guys." Passive resistance is a way to object without having to own the responsibility of doing so. It presents the teacher with special challenges because students can maintain that it is not happening.

Passive resistance may take other forms too. Students may not do assignments because they object to what they are being asked to do, but when confronted, they offer other excuses—for example, "I had to work overtime" or "I had two tests to study for." They may resist by faking attention, appearing to take notes while actually working on material from another class. They may passively resist by refusing to participate. They may be fully prepared but not ask or answer questions. Sometimes they refuse to look at the teacher or do so with a face just shy of comatose. With passive resistance, the objections are made behaviorally as opposed to verbally—the kind of actions that can be denied or explained alternatively if directly questioned about them.

Partial Compliance

This resistance is often what students do if the teacher ignores their passive resistance and keeps after them until they comply. Now they resist by the way they complete the task. They do it poorly, or half-heartedly, or very, very quickly, especially if they might get out of class early. The thinking (or maybe it is not thoughtful but more a subconscious response) goes something like this: *If we do a really crummy job with this, just barely, barely do what she wants, maybe, just maybe, she will figure out that this isn't working and won't try it again.* Student response is never simple to figure out, so the possibility that students do not have much experience working in groups, do not have very good group skills, and therefore do not perform a group task well should not be ruled out.

Partial compliance as a resistance technique also takes many forms. Maybe the student does come to class prepared, but any divulging of that preparation is done with total and absolute lack of enthusiasm—perhaps a mumbled three-word answer to a marvelously open question. Maybe the student does some of the homework but not all of it. Maybe the student is very bright but puts forward only minimal effort.

Partial compliance may also be indicated by a preoccupation with procedural details—endless questions about what "you want us to do," discussion of alternative approaches, or questions of interpretation. The students comply by focusing on the task; they resist by discussing it to death. Once again, there is a question to ask: Is this endless discussion a form of resistance, or is there something unclear and confusing about the task?

Open Resistance

These are the students who openly object to the approach or the policies, practices, and assignments associated with it. In the best-case scenario, the disgruntled student comes to your office and lays out his objections. Most do not deliver the feedback that constructively, however. They pop off with some kind of remark in class: "No other teachers expect us to work like this" or the comment I got three weeks into this semester, "What's with this class? I don't get it."

Some of the objections to learner-centered approaches are difficult to answer on the spot. For example, adult students frequently resist when asked to work in groups with eighteen- to twenty-two-year-old undergraduates. They want to be in a group with other adults, and their objections are full of insinuations: "I don't know a lot about this, but I don't have time to sit around with a bunch of kids who know less about it than I do," or, "I'm paying tuition to be taught by an expert. You're the one who should be answering these questions." The message is, "You're not doing your job. You're supposed to teach us. What are you getting paid for when we sit around in groups trying to figure something out that you could just tell us?"

When they openly resist, students frequently rally the support of others in the class: "Nobody in the class wants to do this" or "Everybody thought the exam was unfair and tricky." They may complain to other students, other faculty, or the department chair. They may challenge the teacher's authority. They may argue, "I know how I learn best, and I learn best when the teacher lectures" or "I need the teacher to go over the material in the text." There are good answers to all these objections, but they do not always come to mind the moment after an irate and especially eloquent student has articulated them. It helps to think through responses beforehand.

Also distressing to many faculty is the fact that the students who offer these objections are frequently the brightest ones. Often the concern behind the resistance is the grade. When you consider, according to a recent survey by Gaultney and Cann (2001), that 64 percent of students preferred fun and interesting academic tasks on which they can get a good grade as opposed to 15 percent who preferred academic tasks that let them learn something new, that 53 percent preferred multiple-choice tests over 10 percent for essay tests, and that 83 percent want their grade determined by a curve or modified curve system, it is not surprising that grade-oriented students have some concerns about learner-centered evaluation processes and procedures. Most have developed a formula for success, and if it does not appear that the formula can be used for this class, they panic and protest.

When behaviors like these occur and messages like these are heard, chances are good that it is resistance. It is not a response to be taken personally. Although students may object to something you did or did not do, fundamentally, that is not what this is about, and it is most certainly not something to which you should respond defensively or emotionally. You need to put the fire out, not fuel it. Understanding both the sources and manifestations of resistance, we are ready to consider responses that help students accept and overcome their feelings of resistance.

Overcoming the Resistance

Overcoming the resistance is not something the teacher does for the students; it is something the teacher works to help students accomplish for themselves. The best solutions involve communication—a free exchange between and among everybody involved. Consider four characteristics of this communication.

The Communication Is Frequent and Explicit

The rationale behind learner-centered approaches to teaching needs to be discussed openly and regularly. Nothing should be kept secret, and nothing about the approach should be assumed to be obvious. Students' emotional involvement and anxiety may prevent them from seeing things that are perfectly clear and obvious to the instructor. This is not a population that has spent a lot of time thinking about learning processes.

Be prepared in the beginning to spend some time selling students on the approach, activity, or assignment. This is more than explaining how something works. It is an open, forthright attempt to persuade them on the basis of merits that may not be obvious. There is no need for endless hype, but students do need to hear about the good and compelling reasons that justify this approach— what you think a particular assignment will accomplish and why.

Shortly after, I find myself justifying the approach: "We both want the same thing: a course that is worth the money you have paid for it. My goal is to design a course that promotes learning— a lot of learning, deep, enduring learning, and learning about the learning process. I understand that this is more work for students. I could tell you all the answers, but how does that prepare you for the future when you will be expected to figure things out on your own?"

Overlapping and not entirely separate, I also hear myself defending the approach, not defensively but constructively: "I don't care if you like this course or this activity. As far as I'm concerned, that's not a relevant criterion. I care about how this activity is strengthening your learning. Talk to me about how much and how well you learned from this activity." "No, you cannot form your own groups. In most professional contexts, we don't get to pick the people we work with. We are assigned to teams, groups, and committees and expected to be able to work productively with fellow professionals." So whether persuading, justifying, or defending, I am communicating in ways that explain more about the reasons and rationale behind the approach.

The Communication Encourages and Positively Reinforces

In my experience, resistance because of more work dissipates first. Students can see the logic behind being able to figure out what is important in the reading, what is likely to be on the test, what examples illustrate the concept, and what key points summarize the chapter. They become convinced quite quickly once they discover that repeated complaints do not prompt me to tell them what they need to know. The more enduring resistance springs from the anxiety, the fear of not knowing how or if they can do it.

Encouragement from the teacher helps individual students and the class as a whole cope with their anxious feelings: "I know that this is pushing you, but I wouldn't be asking if I didn't think you could step up to the plate and do what needs to be done. Frustration and mistakes are positive parts of the learning process. See what you can learn from them."

And right along with the encouragement, there needs to be positive feedback when it is deserved. It is not deserved when it dishonestly praises behaviors, actions, or contributions that do not merit acclamation. It is deserved even when what worked, went right, or meets high standards is a small part of the total project. In fact, it is more needed when much of the feedback has to be negative.

To be authentic, teacher encouragement needs to rest on a firm and absolute belief in students' abilities to learn, figure things out, and develop into mature, autonomous learners. True, not all students can or do. Sometimes they fail and let us down. But that should not shake our faith in the ability of most students to learn well by and through these approaches. It is much easier to offer the kind of encouragement they need when you believe in them.

The Communication Solicits Feedback from Students

This communication characteristic relates to content in Chapter Five, where I propose that we jointly work with students to create the kind of classroom environment that promotes learning, and Chapter Six, where I recommend we actively involve students in assessment activities. It is about providing opportunities for them to talk about their experiences as they are having them. For longer projects, schedule a time for discussion during which students describe (descriptions are more helpful than judgments at this point) how things are going, what they are doing, and how these experiences are affecting their learning. If they need to, let them vent. After that, the discussion is about options that might help with the frustrations, solutions, or changes that might rectify and make the rest of the project a more profitable learning experience.

Students also need to debrief at the end of an experience. What happened? What worked well? What needs to be improved? If we want it to work better next time we do it, what should we change? This debriefing might be an in-class discussion, it might occur on-line, it might be written, it might be that some group of students is assigned evaluation of the project as part of their task, or any combination and rotation of these methods so long as students are regularly describing their experiences with the learning processes and structures of the class. If they make good suggestions, implement what they suggest and then get more feedback on these revised structures.

It helps to think of all the activities, assignments, and events of the course as work in progress, expecting that they will evolve and change in response to student feedback. This keeps the instructional designer from responding defensively, from being hurt and feeling incompetent when something does not work. For students, the process of providing feedback and offering input builds assessment skills and gives them a sense of ownership. It also begins to prepare them for the time when they will design their own learning experiences.

The Communication Resists Their Resistance

Unhappy, whining, complaining students get on the nerves of most faculty. If it continues, it tends to wear us down, which is exactly the response students want, especially at the beginning of this endeavor. However, some faculty reactions can intensify student resistance. Kearney and Plax (1992) found that if faculty display cold, uncaring attitudes and lack of enthusiasm, students resist more—so don't become part of the problem.

The solution to student resistance, in this case their complaints, rests on the commitment we make to the changes. You cannot try learner-centered approaches half-heartedly. If you are not totally committed to their execution, the first time you waver, student resistance will grow. You may feel like retreating to a safer place, but when you are before the students, pursue learner-centered goals with relentless determination.

This is not to say that student resistance should be ignored in the hope that it will fade away. It will vanish much more quickly if you point it out, encourage students to discuss it, and suggest remedies. Do bear in mind that this total and absolute confidence in the approach does not assume that everything you try with students will work right and well. The confidence is in the theory and research on which the approach rests and your ability to (with students' help, of course) make better whatever did not work well.

In the beginning, faculty new to these approaches may not feel as confident as they need to appear, but Keeley, Shemberg, Cowell, and Zinnbauer (1995) point out that resistance does fade when students perceive that the teacher knows what she or he is doing and why. They make an important distinction: behaving like an expert is not necessarily the same as feeling like one. They describe the behaviors: "The expert teacher seems interested and relaxed; talks at the students' level and is not arrogant or defensive; carefully listens to students, has an inflective and lively voice and changes facial expressions, speaks fluently, is well-prepared, asks direct and/or thought-provoking questions, points out contradictions in reasoning, restates the student's comments, and communicates security by a willingness to admit fallibility" (p. 141).

You have the testimony of many of us who have implemented these approaches. The resistance fades and then goes away as student confidence grows and successful experiences accumulate. And you will be pleased by what replaces it. Just as those of us who have adopted these approaches find that we cannot return to the way we taught before, students find they do not want to return either. They chafe in classes where there are no choices, no focus on learning, no responsibility or autonomy. I still give ten-minute lectures in my course, but as the semester progresses, students object and politely point out that they have their work to do and this content is covered in the reading. The first time that happened I was offended and then thrilled.

Faculty Resistance

Students are not be the only ones who resist these approaches. Some colleagues and administrators will object as well. Their resistance will be just as disheartening; it might be professionally threatening too. As with students, it is important to analyze the basis of their resistance. On what grounds do they object? Then consider how a faculty member committed to learner-centered approaches and anxious to implement them can deal with resistance at this level.

Sources of Faculty Resistance

The objections that colleagues raise come primarily from two sources. They object (as some students do) because they find the approaches enormously threatening. Of course, almost no self-respecting academic would admit to such an emotional, potentially irrational reason. You will have to figure out if this is what the resistance is really about. But do not underestimate the strong emotional reaction of some faculty to these ways of teaching. Learner-centered approaches test a teacher's level of self-confidence. They deal with issues of power and authority. They take us away from an exclusive reliance on content expertise and move us into the new and unfamiliar domain of learning skills. They raise questions about common instructional practices. As we will discuss in the next chapter, just as with students, there are development issues for faculty. The position taken there is that you have to be at a certain point in your pedagogical development before you can even consider approaches like these. So for colleagues who object, ask yourself whether this is about learner-centered approaches or about where this particular colleague is in terms of his or her development. Most of us can name at least one or two (some of us more) colleagues who will never be able to do what is being proposed in this book.

Some colleagues resist for much more objective reasons. They are concerned about what these approaches do: diminish the amount of content in courses, let students set course policies, devote class time to developing learner skills and awareness, employ fewer rules and requirements, and involve students in assessment activities. For many faculty, these are radical ideas, and they raise quite legitimate questions about them. This is why it is important for those of us using these approaches to understand something of the empirical, theoretical, and experiential bases on which they rest.

And as with some kinds of student resistance, these are objections for the right reasons. These are questions we can answer, and they provide us opportunities to inform, educate, and move more faculty forward in their thinking about learning and the kind of teaching that promotes it.

Dealing with Faculty Resistance

Like student resistance, that of faculty is not quickly dissipated with easy answers. It is likely to persist, and that makes it important for the learner-centered teacher to have some strategies for dealing with it. Consider five such strategies.

Be Mindful of the Politics

Faculty can be idealistic. Once they are convinced they are right, they sally forth with all the commitment of a crusader. If you are old, tenured, and without much to lose, go forth and win the resistance war for the rest of us. But if you are not, do not ignore the political realities of your situation. If you do not get tenure, you will not be around at your institution to practice these fine approaches. If you end up on the outs with your department chairperson, you might find your merit raise disappointing. Academic freedom is a wonderful thing, but we still live, work, and must survive in very political organizations.

Use the Autonomy of Your Classroom

We are simultaneously blessed with and cursed by the privacy of our classrooms. In this context, classroom autonomy is a blessing. What you do in your classroom is pretty much your own business, so even if the climate at your institution is not pro-learner-centered teaching, no one is likely to stop you from trying some of the policies and practices outlined in this book. You do not need to post a sign on your classroom door that announces what you are doing. Just do it. I am not proposing that you be dishonest. There is no reason to lie about these approaches. But you can also be a learner-centered teacher without announcing to the world that you are making significant changes in some aspects of your instruction.

Do Not Seek to Convert the Masses

The motivation to do missionary work on behalf of learner-centered teaching derives from two sources. First, when most of us started using these approaches, we were unsure of ourselves and the outcomes. It is nice to have company on trips to unknown destinations, so there is a tendency to want to get others to come along with us. That is fine if you have some like-minded colleagues; see if they would like to join you. But do not let your commitment to the approach be dependent on getting the whole department on board. If there was no resistance before, you will create it by proposing that all sections of the entry-level course involve students in assessment activities.

The second reason derives from success. Faculty become enthusiastic about the approaches and start sharing their excitement with others. Sharing the excitement is fine, but it is an easy transition from "this works" to "you ought to try this." The need to have others doing as we do may derive from lingering questions and self-doubt. Something always feels better if everybody is doing it. Be wise here. Learner-centered approaches are not made right because others do them. They are right because they are grounded on empirical, theoretical, and experiential evidence. Let those facts do the persuading. Proselytizing is not an effective way to deal with resistance.

If faculty find themselves dealing with colleagues and administrators who strongly object to these approaches, then trying to convert them is not a productive way of dealing with that resistance. Remember the basic principle of learning: you cannot learn anything for students. The same principle applies to instructional change: you cannot improve anybody else's teaching for them. And trying when they are not ready spells trouble.

Document the Impact of Your Approaches

Colleagues and administrators are persuaded by evidence. Rather than tell them about what these approaches are accomplishing, collect evidence that demonstrates it. In Chapter Nine, we discuss a variety of assessment strategies teachers can use to obtain feedback as to the impact of these approaches. Use them. Then when someone challenges that students are learning less, answer with something more than your opinion. This is especially relevant in the case of institutions that use student rating forms that solicit feedback to traditional instructional methods. Faculty using learner-centered approaches will find that many of the items do not apply or assume instructional goals they no longer support. Alternative forms and approaches should be used. If they cannot be substituted for the regularly used form, data should still be collected so that the information can become part of the documentation assembled to support the outcomes of learner-centered approaches.

A concrete example illustrates an alternative approach. VanderStoep, Fagerlin, and Feenstra (2000, p. 89) report some interesting research results acquired when they used an open-ended query at the end of a number of courses: "As part of my research on college students' memory for course concepts, and also as a way to improve my teaching of Introductory Psychology, I am interested in what students remember from this course. Let your mind wander freely as you do this assignment. Think back on the semester as a whole and report to me the first 10 things that come to your mind as you answer the question: *What do you remember from this course?*" Use this prompt, and see what your students list. If colleagues who teach the same course (or even ones in the same discipline) challenge that your approaches diminish the quality of learning, challenge them to use the prompt, and then compare what their students list with what your students list. Now we are not exchanging assertions with colleagues but looking at a concrete set of learning outcomes. What do you suspect these researchers found that students remembered? In a majority of cases, they listed course content that had been presented through some activity.

The point here is that resistance diminishes in the face of evidence. You need feedback to accomplish your objectives. It helps you and students improve so that next time, it promotes even more learning. You also need it to document the legitimacy of this approach and persuade other colleagues to consider it.

Find Like-Minded Colleagues

You may be the only person in your department exploring these approaches, but you are not alone at your institution or anywhere else in higher education. Many faculty are experimenting with the instructional strategies described here. They may not have assembled them together in an approach called learner-centered teaching, but they are open to discussing, using, and learning about policies and practices that have an impact on learning. Find those colleagues.

Most of us are not in the instructional closet. We are out, perhaps not going head to head with senior colleagues in the department or our division heads, but other faculty know that we are exploring approaches like these. So ask around, and seek us out. And do not be put off just because we do not teach the same content as you do. As with any other instructional strategy, there are unique content issues, but there are also generic issues, resistance being a good example. Colleagues from other departments may be able to help with political issues, and they can certainly provide the encouragement and support you need to deal with faculty and student resistance more effectively.

To Finish Up

Student and faculty resistance will keep us honest about what we are doing and why. It helps to see it positively—the rub that reminds us to continue exploring the theory and research, as well as the experience of colleagues. Many of us will tell you that student resistance fades and is then gone well before that of colleagues. Lots could be said of that, but the net effect is that once students are on board, there really is no turning back. They will move you forward, despite the objections and resistance of some colleagues.

Chapter Eight

Taking a Developmental Approach

Developmental issues are not front and center in faculty thinking about students, learning, or instruction. We know that students mature, and most develop intellectually in college, but how that occurs, what processes are involved, and how we might constructively intervene in the process all remain pretty much unknown. As a consequence, most faculty use basically the same approaches, assignments, and activities with all students, from those in their first year to seniors. They might work seniors harder, but not much differently from the others. (In the early 1990s, Stommer and Erickson [1991] authored an excellent book titled, *Teaching College Freshmen*. I advocated for a series of sequels on teaching sophomores, then juniors, and finally seniors in the interest of making faculty aware of developmental issues and their impact at various points during the college years.)

Against this backdrop of little faculty awareness of developmental issues generally, we must consider the issues uniquely associated with the progression from dependent, passive, often not confident student to autonomous, motivated, responsible, and empowered learner. Although something is known theoretically, empirically, and practically about how students develop as learners, the impact of particular instructional approaches on that development has not been studied extensively.

However, we should start with what is known, and that includes some important fundamentals. For example, this transformation from dependent to independent learner is gradual; it does not happen all at once as a consequence of a few learner-centered assignments or courses. It is a sequential process and mirrors other kinds of growth. There are moments of insight, growth spurts, and times when no changes are apparent.

We also know that the transformation of students into autonomous, self-directed learners is not the inevitable outcome of educational experiences, even learner-centered ones. Some other kinds of growth and maturation do happen automatically or without much in the way of planned intervention. In the case of development as learners, Candy (1991) points out that giving students the opportunity to become independent is a necessity, but it is not a sufficient condition for the development of autonomy and self-direction in learning.

Because learner-centered approaches are not prevalent in the curricular experiences of students, it is especially important that faculty who use these approaches do so in ways that are effective for students' growth and development as learners. To develop that effectiveness, I will consider developmental issues in three contexts. First, we examine the levels or stages of growth associated with development as learners. Then we can explore how instruction can be tailored to promote that growth. Second, development as a learner happens in the context of other kinds of growth and maturation. We need to see it as related to and dependent on other changes that occur both within and outside the learner. Finally, developmental growth issues present faculty with a number of instructional challenges. I identify those and explore some ways they might be addressed.

Understanding the Developmental Process

Not much literature addresses the actual process of becoming an independent, self-directed learner. The presence, relevance, and importance of developmental issues are uniformly recognized, but the sequence of the developmental process, its speed, how it interacts and might be dependent on other maturation processes, how instruction prepares and moves students to different levels, and how instructors match instruction to developmental levels are addressed only sporadically and tangentially. I share what I have discovered and then use a couple of models to illustrate how assignment sequences might encourage the growth and development of learning skills and learners.

How the Developmental Process Works

Grow (1991) proposes a set of stages from dependence to self-direction. His continuum of growth borrows key concepts from situational leadership models. He offers his characterization "not as a definitive thing, but as another statement in the ongoing conversation of those who encourage self-directed, lifelong learning" (p. 147). His model is the only detailed description of how learners develop that I have run across. That may explain why it is so widely referenced, but I take the referencing as indicative that these ideas strike many people as a sensible description of the progression.

Grow (1991) sees students' abilities to handle learner-centered teaching at four different stages. In the first stage, students are dependent, not self-directed. He writes that they "need an authority-figure to give them explicit directions on what to do, how to do it, and when" (p. 129). He suggests that these students respond well to teachers who coach them. For these students, he recommends keeping them "busy learning specific, identifiable skills. Set standards beyond what students think they can do, then do whatever is necessary to get them to succeed" (p. 130).

At the next level, he describes students as being interested; they are moderately self-directed. To move through and beyond this stage, they need teachers who bring "enthusiasm and motivation to the class, sweeping learners along with the excitement of learning" (Grow, 1991, p. 131). At this level, students are ready to begin goal setting for themselves. Both their confidence and learning skills can be built at this level. They appear to internalize the teacher's enthusiasm and confidence and thereby find their own motivation by the end of this stage.

In the third stage, students are involved and at intermediate levels of self-direction. They begin to see themselves as participants in their own education. At this level, they are especially amenable to learning how they learn, applying and adapting generic learning strategies to their own efforts to learn and finding out what works for them. They are also more open to learning from and with others. They develop further at this level if their teachers function as facilitators or co- or joint participants in the decision-making process as it pertains to their learning. Students might make interim reports, with the teacher giving them more and more latitude as they make good decisions and appropriate progress on the learning task.

Finally, students reach a level where they can be identified as self-directed, setting their own goals and standards. Grow (1991, pp. 134, 135) says that they "thrive in an atmosphere of autonomy." At this level, teachers do "not teach subject matter but . . . cultivate the student's ability to learn." The teacher acts as a consultant, reviewing criteria students have developed, time lines, lists of potential resources, and possible productive collaborations, for example. Grow writes, "A Stage 4 teacher might set a challenge, then leave the learner largely alone to carry it out, intervening only when asked to help—and then not help meet the challenge, but instead empower the learner to meet the challenge" (p. 136).

Grow (1991, p. 127) makes an interesting observation at the beginning of his article: "A theory doesn't have to be right to be useful. Nearly every action we take results from a workable convergence of misconceptions." He may be right about the stages he has laid out, but they do provide a good introduction to developmental ideas. We can use them as a benchmark in observations of our own students. Most important, the model makes clear that the role we take with students, the kind of interactions we have with them, and the nature of the learning tasks we ask them to complete can positively or negatively influence their development as learners.

With any model that positions people at different levels or stages, there is a tendency to get trapped in a kind of linear thinking about the development that is occurring. If our instruction is successful, there will be a general forward progression, but it will not necessarily be in a straight line with stages entered and exited at regular and predictable times. The lines between stages are blurred, if they exist at all, with students moving forward and back and being at different levels depending on the issue.

I try to expedite movement to a new level by making or using an assignment or activity that pushes students to a place of discomfort and anxiety, has them function there for a while, and then lets them return to a place of greater security and confidence. I also try to encourage movement to new levels with a collection of assignments that offer a range of familiar and novel learning experiences. Because students select assignments in my course, they decide how much innovation they can handle. For students at Grow's first level, there are traditional assignments like multiple-choice tests, but not so many that they can be the entire learning diet in the course.

Sometimes the growth is in spurts, with a series of insights or understandings that quickly move a student to new confidence and competence. We understand the phenomenon more metaphorically than actually. We describe seeing students "when the light goes on," when that look of understanding finally floods their faces. Usually, we think about this in relation to content acquisition, but it also happens as students first struggle with learner-centered approaches and then finally see how and why they work. Some research documents the existence of these moments of insight and learning when all at once a variety of things make sense and come together for a student. O'Neill and Todd-Mancillas (1992) have studied turning points, or pivotal moments, in the development of a student-faculty relationship and found that often a single event will crystallize or come to characterize the nature of that relationship.

Grow's stages provide a useful conceptual framework on which to hang a general understanding of how students mature as learners. But it is a framework and to my knowledge has not been empirically verified. That makes it especially challenging to design instruction with "guaranteed" impacts, but based on certain assumptions, there are some sequences that stand a good chance of moving students forward in the development of skills and as more mature learners.

Assignment Sequences That Develop Independent Learners

If students develop as learners incrementally, then the assumption is that assignments, activities, events, indeed, courses can be sequenced so that the order in which they are experienced expedites growth. Not a lot of research can be summoned to support the assumption, but several examples can be offered as potential models of how it might work. They illustrate how assignments can build on each other, leading to more complex levels of learning.

Consider a couple of strategies that help students learn how to organize content and see relationships between parts of it: matrices and concept maps. Matrices work especially well in disciplines like biology where content is categorized and characterized. Concept maps work well in fields where content is less tightly configured, like literature and philosophy, although both strategies have broad applications.

Matrices involve a grid with defining characteristics across one axis and categories on the other. Specific examples fit in the cells where the characteristics and categories intersect. The goal is for students to see the value of this device for organizing content and to learn how to construct matrices on their own. Consider how a sequence of experiences might accomplish those goals. Begin by giving students a matrix with categories and characteristics specified but the cells empty. Use it as a vehicle for summarizing content at the end of the period, working with students to complete it. The next time, give students another matrix with empty cells, only this time let them complete it on their own. Have several students share their matrices and with the class construct one with the cells filled in correctly. Next, give half the class a matrix with categories but no characteristics and the other half one with characteristics but no categories. Have students in pairs work to complete the matrix, and then let the two sides exchange and compare their products.

At some point here, you may want to have students work to complete matrices using text material instead of content presented in class. At this level, you could also give students a matrix with the cells filled in and make their task identification of the categories and characteristics. Then you might have students in groups create matrices for other groups to complete, encouraging them to discuss and assess the matrices created by other groups. From the group context, move back to the individual, assigning creation of a matrix on text material as a homework assignment or using a partially complete matrix on a quiz and end with matrix creation or completion test questions. The value of any learning strategy is potently reinforced when it becomes incorporated into the assessment mechanisms of the course, as we learned in Chapter One.

Concept maps (sometimes called mind maps or knowledge maps) allow students to create organizational structures that make content meaningful to them, which means there is much more room for variation with this strategy. (Dansereau and Newbern, 1997, review research on the effectiveness of the strategy, explain how knowledge maps are constructed, and offer a variety of ideas for using them in class.) Begin with an example: present material in class, and then end by distributing a concept map that visually illustrates relationships among concepts. Some propose a structured way of creating concept maps with rules about connecting lines, circles, boxes, and language. If you opt for this approach, share those rules with students. Next, give students the opportunity to create a concept map, and share various examples with the class.

With concept maps, learners develop structures that portray relationships; some concept maps explore and explain relationships better than others. The goal is to teach students to make maps with the most explanatory power. Once students are comfortable with creating concept maps, have them take their individual maps into a group setting and challenge the group to integrate the maps or select the one most meaningful to the group, and then explain their rationale. Also in the group context and using text material, have the group create a concept map (to expedite the process, give them sheets of newsprint and sticky notes so that they can easily position and reposition concepts). Have them share the completed concept map with another group and ask that group to critique it. Initially, provide or develop with students a set of criteria that can be used to guide the critique. With take-home exams, students can be given reading material and asked to create a concept map that illustrates relationships within the text. They might, in addition, be asked to explain or justify the structure they have developed.

With an individual learning strategy like matrices or concept maps, it is fairly easy to see how and why a sequence of experiences develops student confidence, skill, and commitment to the strategy. The ultimate goal is to have students reach a point where, when confronted with text material they need to understand structurally and relationally, they automatically think of these organizing devices (or whatever other learning strategy you are emphasizing). The strategy becomes part of the repertoire of approaches they use to complete learning tasks.

This model using matrices and concept maps illustrates a comparatively simple developmental sequence. When the goal is acquisition of more sophisticated skills, the order of and interaction among a set of learning experiences is much more complicated and dynamic. Perhaps the goal is for students to learn how to organize a complex task—say, a semester-long group project. Here the progression should not be thought of as exclusively linear, with assignments designed so that they overlap and build on each other. One assignment may be designed so that it helps accomplish several different goals. With more complex learning goals, it is the cumulative impact of the learning experiences, not just the order, that is important.

Begin the planning process for an integrated sequence of learning events with the learning objective: What should students know and be able to do? If the goal is for students to learn how to organize a complex learning task, for example, they should be able to partition it into a sequence of steps, judge the time and person-power involved in those steps, identify and evaluate the resources needed to complete the task, and assess when and how well the task has been completed. What kinds of assignments and activities in what order might be used to develop those skills?

You might start with a group project that can be completed in three one-hour meetings. As a first task, have students prepare a memo to you that outlines the steps they plan to take to complete the task. Provide feedback on their memo. If you have a paper assignment in the course, introduce it with a class discussion where students brainstorm and then prioritize the resources necessary to complete the paper. Encourage individual students to use this discussion to guide their decision making about resources. Then use another group project, this one more complex than the previous one. Again have students begin by identifying and ordering the steps necessary to complete the task. This time, have them assign those tasks to individuals, working to identify specifically what each individual is required to submit. You might challenge them to justify why they have assigned certain tasks to certain individuals (making them aware that different group members have different experiences and skills that make them better qualified to complete some tasks and not others). Move back to the individual paper assignment, and have students write a description and critique of the process they used to complete their paper. In the light of your feedback and their experiences, how would they revise and refine their process? Assign the next paper, and let part of the grade be the process students identify and follow in preparation of that paper. Note in this sequence that not all of these activities and assignments are devoted exclusively to developing skills related to partitioning complex tasks. Rather, this objective is incorporated into assignments that are being used to expedite content acquisition and the development of other learning skills.

With complex learning goals that transcend individual assignments, the movement to ever more responsibility needs to be in an overall direction, but it need not be a rigidly fixed sequence, and various course activities and assignments may contribute a little or a lot to the goal's accomplishment. Do not interpret this to mean that your usual collection of assignments in some undifferentiated way will accomplish these developmental goals. Learner-centered teachers are careful and deliberate instructional designers, able to identify specifically what each activity, assignment, and course event contributes individually and what the group accomplishes collectively.

We know that there is a developmental progression that learners move through on their way from dependence to autonomy. Grow (1991) identifies some possible stages or places along that continuum. But we need to understand that as with any other human growth, development is not linear, predictable, and exclusively forward. Nevertheless, even given that fact, instruction can still be designed so that it has an impact on student development. Certain kinds of assignments, in sequence and cumulatively, can be powerful developmental tools. They prepare students so that movement to the next stage or level becomes all but inevitable.

Development of Learners in Context

It would be nice if the only concern for teachers was the development of students as learners. But life (including life in the classroom) is never simple, and the development of students as learners is only one maturation process of several that occur during the college years. We next consider two maturation processes relevant to students and then one that involves faculty in the interest of putting development as a learner in the more complicated and dynamic milieu in which it occurs.

Related Student Growth

Two major areas of student growth pertain directly to instruction and classroom experiences: intellectual development and interpersonal maturation. They will serve to illustrate that growth as a learner happens in the context of other kinds of growth and growth in all areas overlaps, interrelates, and reciprocally influences.

Begin with the kind of intellectual development students experience in college. Here, models describe the growth. Best known is the work of Perry (1968, 1999), who, based on a large and in-depth study of Harvard College males, concluded that most students go through four phases, each depicting how the student understands knowledge and knowing: dualism (it's either right or wrong), multiplicity (everybody has a right to their own opinion), relativism (what's right depends on the situation), and commitment in relativism (it does depend, but some answers are better than others). The work of feminists in the 1980s and later added some gender balance to Perry's work (for examples, see Belenky, Clinchy, Goldberger, and Tarule, 1986, and Baxter Magolda, 1992).

Kloss (1994) proposes how an instructor consciously and deliberately tries to design assignments and experiences that move learners forward in their intellectual development. He writes in that context, but his description of the teacher's task is relevant when the goal is development of students as learners: "My goal is to create environments and tasks that invite right/wrong thinkers [the dualists] to change for themselves" (p. 153). The development of students as learners also needs to be thought of and approached in this way. Dualists believe there is a right and a wrong answer to everything; there is no middle ground, and there are no gray areas. To dislodge this kind of polarized thinking, Kloss has students analyze readings that present two or three conflicting, mutually exclusive points of view. For their assignment, they explain in detail the reasons that they reject a particular point of view. His commitment is to creating an environment and designing tasks through which students change on their own, coming first to see and then to accept multiple perspectives.

At the same time as exposure to content can facilitate intellectual growth, students undergo a variety of psychosocial changes, some related to identity and self-esteem development and others to interpersonal relations, personal adjustment, and maturation. Pascarella and Terenzini summarize and evaluate the research documenting psychosocial changes in their definitive *How College Affects Students* (1991). The research is scattered across many fields and not integrated with a coherent model or schemata that identifies distinct stages, but changes occur nonetheless, especially in the area of external relationships. Most of us can attest experientially to the powerful influence that peers play in almost any classroom dynamic.

But my point is not to delineate development in these other arenas, only to make teachers aware that what we propose to expedite in terms of developing students as learners cannot be dealt with as an isolated phenomenon. How the various developmental processes interact has not been explained, and what precisely and specifically a teacher should do about development on multiple fronts is not clear, but if teachers ignore its occurrence, their analysis of student reactions may be wrong; at the least, they will be incomplete. Teachers will make better decisions if they take into account all that is happening to and with students developmentally.

Related Faculty Growth

As complicated, interconnected, and dependent as these various kinds of student growth are, the classroom locks learners and teachers into a relationship where what is happening to one party influences what is happening to the other. So faculty are affected by student growth (their resistance, frustration, anxiety, and lack of progress on the negative side), but students are also affected by growth and development that may be occurring within faculty members. Given where most of us begin, how the cultures of our disciplines and institutions orient us to teaching, there is no question that for most faculty, learner-centered teaching requires change that is not at all unlike what students may be experiencing.

There is a general sense in the literature that as teachers mature, they move from an almost exclusive content orientation to a more student-centered approach. The sense is that this move is gradual but widespread across teachers, although we all have colleagues for whom no instructional world beyond content exists. Some work describes our growth in ways especially relevant in the learning context. Biggs (1999a, 1999b), for example, identifies three stages of teacher growth, and Hebert and Loy (2002) present a related typology.

At the first level in Biggs's typology, the focus is on student differences. New teachers quickly discover that some students are intellectually gifted and some are not. At this stage, teachers conclude that those levels of ability have nothing to do with them or the way they present content. If students do not learn, it is their fault—the likely result of inability, poor attitude, absent study skills, or no motivation. At this level when learning does not occur, teachers blame the students, never thinking that the teaching might have some impact on what students are or are not learning.

From here, teachers progress to a second level, where the focus is on what the teacher does. The attempt now is to have a positive impact on student learning with a repertoire of instructional strategies, techniques, gimmicks, and approaches. The emphasis is on the "how to" of teaching. Biggs (1999b) notes that the how-to advice is useful but is "concerned with *management,* not facilitating learning. Good management is important for setting the stage for good learning to take place—not as an end in itself" (p. 62). And when students still do not learn, the tendency at this level (popular with many administrators) is to blame the teacher. If faculty just knew how to teach, goes this thinking, students would learn.

At the third level, according to Biggs (1999b), the focus is on the student: "It's not what *teachers* do, it's what *students* do that is the important thing" (p. 63). This puts the teacher's emphasis on what it means to understand concepts and principles within the discipline and what kind of teaching-learning activities enable students to reach those levels of content understanding. Biggs says that this makes education about "*conceptual change,* not just the acquisition of information" (p. 60).

Biggs believes that development along this continuum is facilitated by constructivist theories of learning that encourage individual reflection and analysis (much like that described in Brook-field, 1995). But our interest is how faculty growth and development affect what is happening with students. Grow (1991), who would put teachers on the same developmental continuum he proposes for learners, makes the most straightforward application. Tension, trouble, and considerable frustration will occur if a mismatch exists between the level of teaching and the level of student development. This means that although as a teacher you may be self-directed in your own learning and have similar expectations for students, you may need to modify those expectations in terms of where those students are in their development as learners. Learners can and should be pushed, but only to the extent they can handle constructively.

The interaction between teacher and student development may make some mismatch unavoidable. Kloss (1994, p. 158) explains: "No redwood resists becoming gigantic. But we have all repeatedly witnessed students resist learning, refusing . . . to grow. The biological metaphor applied to education cannot adequately account for the complexity of our species." You may design a learner-centered class that is appropriate to the developmental level of most students and still have in that class some students who refuse to move forward. Recognizing that faculty growth occurs along a continuum can be equally important in understanding why some colleagues may so vigorously resist these approaches. They may not be pedagogically mature enough to handle them. Some of our failure with students and colleagues may be attributable to developmental mismatches.

The interaction between the various developmental vectors that converge in the classroom over learning experiences has yet to be explicated and the practical implications explored. We are on our own here but need to proceed by understanding that the developmental issues affecting students as learners occur in the context of a lot of other developmental happenings.

Responding to the Challenges

Based largely on my own experience, I believe that one of the most challenging aspects of learner-centered teaching involves knowing how to respond to the developmental issues described in this chapter. It is not difficult to see that they are important and should be addressed. But how can that be done, especially given the paucity of theoretical, empirical, and experiential work? Very little has been written proposing how to plan and implement instruction based on what is known about development. About the best we can do here is identify a specific set of challenges that need to be considered in any plan to implement learner-centered teaching.

Challenge 1: Understanding the Development Process in Context

We begin with where we have been. What needs to happen to learners as they progress through a set of learning experiences designed to cultivate their confidence and competence will happen in the context of other kinds of development. That development occurs within each student, among peers, and within the teacher.

The old adage that knowledge is the best defense is about all we can do for advice on responding to this challenge. Faculty need to understand that student response—resistance, an unexpected growth spurt, or something else—may not entirely be the result of attempts to promote their growth as learners. Other factors may well be influencing what we see. All faculty should be encouraged to posit some theories of their own as to how development as a learner might be influenced by these other forces and then observe and test those theories.

Challenge 2: Responding to Students at Different Levels

So far, our focus has been on the development of an individual student and how that is likely influenced by a confluence of forces. But the challenge is quite different when a teacher is faced with a class of students who are not at the same level of development: some ready to set goals and make many more decisions; others resistant, anxious, and basically unwilling to decide anything. How does a teacher respond to very different learning needs within the same class?

Here some relevant resources do exist. Instruments that measure the extent to which students are independent and self-directed have been developed (see Oddi, 1986, for example). One of those could be used diagnostically to provide students and the teacher with baseline data as to the various levels at which students might be located. In my experience, individuals at different levels have been less a problem early in the course. My entry-level beginning students all start at about the same place; they are passive, unmotivated, dependent learners who think I am not doing my job if I ask them to make any decisions. As they gain exposure to learner-centered approaches, they develop abilities to handle those approaches at different rates, so there is more diversity in individual levels by the end of the course than at the beginning.

As the course progresses, I try to apply the same principle some wise person gave me about pace. We make a mistake when we think about the pace of instruction as a single "speed"—a kind of average rate that allows most students to keep up—albeit always too fast for some and too slow for others. Alternatively, based on where students are and the importance of the content (or, in this case, learning skill), present the most important content or skill so that as many students as possible have a chance to learn it. But with less central, perhaps more sophisticated content, then quicken the pace even if it may leave some behind. In other words, routinely change the pace at which content and skills are delivered. And if in a learner-centered environment, students are making decisions for themselves, is there any reason why some cannot be making more sophisticated learning decisions than others?

Challenge 3: Designing a Sequence of Learning Experiences

The general principles of design apply. The challenge is at the level of individual instructor application. It involves being able to answer questions like these: How many of a particular kind of assignment or learning activity do you give students before you can reasonably expect that most of them will be ready to move on? What assignments and learning activities work particularly well at what level of development? And are there particular combinations of assignments and learning activities that more effectively promote learning development than other combinations? Can relationships between two assignments that work well be extrapolated and applied to other assignments?

We might also consider questions that relate to how far and how fast we should push students. Sometimes I have students do work that is out of their comfort zone, sometimes even beyond their abilities as learners. When I do that, I always wonder how long I should let them be there. How much frustration and anxiety are motivational, and when do they become debilitating and destructive?

Ongoing diagnostic assessment helps to answer these questions. I like to think of it as keeping my finger on the pulse of the class—talking with students frequently about how the content, activities, and assignments are affecting them and having them think and write reflectively about their feelings and insights regularly throughout the course. Their feedback provides answers for that class and those students. I have not found that the answers always generalize to other classes, nor do I believe that their feedback answers the questions for others.

Challenge 4: Designing a Learning-Centered Curriculum

We have not been here. The book is written for the individual faculty member who aspires to offer learner-centered instruction, but clearly one or two learner-centered courses are not going to promote the level of development that would be reached by a whole curriculum. (For a not totally unrelated and fascinating example of curriculum work focused on a value-oriented set of learning outcomes, see Mentkowski and others, 2000, a powerful and thoroughly documented example of what a learning-focused curriculum can accomplish.) The curriculum challenge is really twofold. First, how do we get colleagues and administrators on board and supportive of this way of teaching and learning? It will be easier if the focus in higher education stays on learning and if we accumulate lots of successful individual experiences using the approaches.

The second challenge involves how to design an entire curriculum that seeks through a sequence and progression of courses to move students to a place of independence and maturity as learners. What role would content play across that sequence? What kind of assignments would be used in the beginning as compared with the end? In terms of courses themselves, what would the first year of that curriculum look like? How would it differ from the final year? Could this kind of curriculum be more individualized and less organized around time-dependent course structures? What kind of faculty member would most effectively teach the first year and the last year? Would the role of the teacher change across the curriculum? Would the role of the student change? How, when, and in what ways?

No doubt there are many questions that would need to be answered on the way to designing learner-centered curricula, but what an enjoyable and rewarding task to tackle. Perhaps as more individual faculty begin teaching this way, their collective influence on curricular development will grow. In the meantime, this area presents individual faculty members with a challenge. What if the instructor's course is the only truly learner-centered experience in a curriculum? How can the instructor maximize that experience for students?

To Finish Up

The conclusions of this chapter are not like those offered at the end of other chapters, where I have described learner-centered teaching in ways that require faculty to explore and use "new" instructional strategies. But although some of those strategies are new, most are familiar to faculty, and none is difficult to implement successfully. In those chapters, I have proposed a different conceptual orientation to instructional tasks, and faculty do need time to consider and question the new conceptual framework, but faculty are good at conceptual thinking. They can make the adjustments a new one requires.

By contrast, in this chapter, successful response to developmental issues requires a level of knowledge that does not yet exist conceptually or pragmatically. What is known does establish the importance of developmental issues and offers a place to start. We know that development as learners is not automatic, although some does occur without much intervention. However, there is the tantalizing possibility that much more is likely if that development happens in the context of carefully planned, sequenced, and interconnected learning experiences. Even more may occur if it builds off related developmental processes. But how it all fits together at this point remains a mystery, a case to be solved through our collective efforts and experiences.

Chapter Nine

Making Learner-Centered Teaching Work

Two concerns motivate the inclusion of this chapter. First, instructional improvement is frequently a solitary endeavor that occurs in climates not always conducive to exploration, innovation, or other forms of instructional risk taking. There may be colleagues with traditional orientations to teaching who resist those who change in the directions proposed; pressure to publish may be competing for the time and attention good teaching demands; or the administrative climate may be focused on evaluation, productivity, and economic bottom lines. These factors, singly or in combination, may persuade faculty to tackle instructional projects alone, unaided, and in private. If a book is a teacher's main companion on the road to change, it needs to offer help not only as the approach is contemplated, but at that even more important point when the faculty member starts making changes.

Second, and not totally unrelated to the first concern, I aspire to write a book that makes a difference. Too many books occupy space on bookshelves; they may be read a bit or leafed through on occasion, but basically they live on the shelf. I want a more active life for this book. Books that make a difference change what faculty do with students in and out of the classroom. Part of supporting that change includes offering advice on how what is being proposed will work when *you* do it with your students, your content, in your classroom, and at your institution.

This chapter assumes that you are ready to start using more learner-centered approaches and offers advice in two areas. First, I propose some guiding principles. Consider them operating premises that need to orient the whole process of making instructional changes, whether you are making the changes proposed in this book or some other set. Some of the principles are supported empirically. Others are grounded in the wisdom of practice—what those of us who have worked with faculty on improvement agendas have learned about the instructional change process.

Then I propose a learner-centered approach to implementing the material in Chapters Two through Six. In what I hope will be an interesting and useful twist of perspective, I will assume that an independent, self-directed learner needs to learn how to teach using more learner-centered approaches. What would that learner do? How would he or she approach the task? And how does that approach differ from the ones faculty typically take?

Principles of Successful Instructional Improvement

Once faculty decide to make instructional changes, generally they just do it—a laudable approach that does not always achieve the desired results. In my first book on faculty development (Weimer, 1990), I used a metaphor to characterize the approach: faculty do instructional improvement a bit like children play Pin the Tail on the Donkey. They get a new idea and become convinced that it is worth trying right away. They take this instructional tail and blindly attach it to whatever is happening in class tomorrow. Although the results may not be quite a humorous as the game, the chances of getting the new instructional tail positioned where it fits and functions effectively are not very good. Consider the following guidelines as principles on which a more productive process might rest.

Get Beyond Techniques: Think Approach

The impact of this book will be diminished if faculty respond to it only as a collection of techniques and not as a new way of thinking about teaching and learning. The book is filled with ideas, but if faculty do only one or two of them, the overall impact on students and learning will be small. The piecemeal addition of new techniques does not transform teaching.

Techniques seem to me the blessing and curse of the instructional improvement process. Faculty like them, probably because most of us started our careers without enough of them, and so we gravitate toward practical content offered in books, newsletters, and workshops. New things to do rejuvenate teachers and sometimes students. Effective techniques are the nuts and bolts of successful teaching. There is nothing wrong with them.

But the problems emerge when the quest for better teaching involves nothing more than the pursuit of new techniques. Inherent in every technique are assumptions about teachers, students, and learning and the role of each in the instructional process. When the criteria for selecting a technique are "neat idea," "I like it," and "this would work," then instructional practice evolves into a hodgepodge of isolated, unrelated techniques. Individually, they are all good ideas, but taken together, they do not reflect a set of internally consistent assumptions, nor are they a collection that advances an overall approach to teaching or one that exemplifies a certain philosophy of education.

The straightforward solutions proffered by techniques add to their appeal. Their simple answers come to reflect the not very intellectually robust ways we think about teaching. They move us further in the direction of details. And so rather than a profitable exchange about where learning takes place and what role (or right) faculty have to "require" learning in certain locations, we discuss attendance policies and whether they should allow for two or three excused absences per semester. No right answer exists to that question, and no single technique (or even a couple of them) constructively solves attendance problems. The problems and issues are much more complex than the questions that techniques lead us to ask.

We need something in addition to techniques. We need an approach that comes to reflect an integrated, coherent philosophy of education and one with enough intellectual muscle to work on the problems we face. This book offers that kind of approach. But what it proposes has got to be implemented as an integrated and coherent plan, not a few new techniques blindly pinned on here and there.

Approach Change Systematically

Systematic change means change that is planned, prepared, and then implemented according to some process. There is room for individual variation and adaptation. What I will highlight here are plans and implementation processes known to work well. They should be molded to fit how you plan and prepare. The principle that applies uniformly is the need to be systematic no matter how you execute the details.

With learner-centered teaching, systematic change ought to begin with, or at some place include, a complete instructional assessment, that is, a major analysis of how you teach. It makes no sense to implement a set of changes unless you understand clearly what they are taking you from. The second section of this chapter offers suggestions on developing that level of pedagogical insight. This complete instructional assessment should be the basis on which an overall plan for change is developed. Perhaps it helps to think of starting with a complete description of where you are, following that with an equally complete analysis of where you want to be, and finishing up by developing a plan for how you will get from here to there.

As for the implementation process itself, there is no one right, best, or most effective method so long as you implement it according to some plan that moves you through the process in an orderly way. Steps in the process of implementing instructional change have been laid out, useful for consulting if you have never used them or would like to compare what you do with what has been proposed. I am partial to one I developed (Weimer, 1990) but also recommend the set of steps Menges (1994) proposed. With planning, preparation, and implementation, advice can be simply summed: do all three systematically, and adapt processes so that they work well for you.

Approach Change Incrementally

When educators get persuaded about a particular approach, it is hard to keep them from having a kind of instructional conversion experience. One faculty retreat participant told me that our time together had been transformative, a watershed in her teaching experience: "I made a list last night. I'm going to do fifty-eight things different in my classes this fall." That amount of behavior change is very difficult to sustain, especially as enthusiasm fades and energy wanes. Soon only twenty-four of the "new" things are happening, and a feeling of failure dampens efforts to continue. By the end of the semester, instruction is about back to the way things used to be. After one or two failed "conversions," most faculty end up cynical about instruction born anew.

How much you should change and how fast depends on you and your ability to deal with instructional change. How much do you have time for? How much can you execute with poise and confidence? It should also be affected by the climate for change at your institution. What happens to innovators? Are they encouraged or ostracized? I recommend that you start with what feels right and fits with where you are in your thinking about this approach. Changes implemented with commitment stand a much better chance of succeeding.

At the same time, I strongly encourage making some changes (probably only a few, though) that take you to the edge. What is gained by instructional risk taking? For starters, the nature of the teaching task—same content; same courses; same students, administrators, and colleagues—makes it all too easy to get into instructional ruts. Then change that is just about like what we already do does not bump us out of the ruts and onto a different piece of the road. When we opt for change that is not comfortable and is entirely out of the ordinary for us, we open ourselves to teaching as a learning experience, a point of personal development. In this case, wander back through this book, and look for ideas that struck you as really intriguing and not at all like what you currently do. Give them a second look.

Opt for planned, incremental change. Make changes in one course, not all of them. Make changes in two assignments, not all six of them. Change assignments but keep the text and basic course outline. Change what happens for two weeks, not all twelve. This may seem to be advocating incorporating a few isolated techniques, and I have objected to that. I believe that what I am proposing here is different because it starts with an overall plan, the agenda is large and transformative, and it is implemented systematically and incrementally so that the teacher and students have the opportunity to grow into it.

Plan to Tinker

Tinkering with teaching is another favorite metaphor of mine. Start out assuming that you will have to tinker before and during the process of implementation; then view it as those who tinker do: an activity of intrigue, challenge, frustration, and satisfaction. A tinker enjoys the process of analyzing what happened, speculating on problems, hypothesizing about what needs to be changed, making changes, and then seeing what kind of results they bring. A good part of the past three days, my husband has fussed around with an old motorcycle he bought for $150. He has had it apart five or six times now—cleaning, repairing, timing, adjusting, and otherwise figuring out how it should run. This morning, it sounds like a totally different bike. Most instructional strategies come to us equally used, adjusted by and for somebody else, not new or running smoothly. To have to adjust techniques before and as we use them is not a sign of incompetence. To figure out what is wrong and fix it so that it runs well for you and your students is a sign of pedagogical prowess.

All the farmers in the valley where I live tinker endlessly with their old equipment, mostly out of economic necessity. They cannot afford machinery that runs well. And so they are always checking, listening, and observing, ever alert to subtle changes that may indicate problems. None of them is smug about finally having gotten an old tractor to run. Their job is to keep it running. That means regular maintenance checks, replacing old parts with newer ones before they break down; it is a never-ending job, and not one for the complacent. How like the work required to keep instructional strategies always effective, always facilitating as much learning as possible.

Those who tinker work tirelessly when something can be repaired, but they also know when to give up. In our very disposable society, we trash things quickly, including instructional techniques. Generally, we do not work on them enough, compared to the tinker who does not trash anything before a considerable expenditure of energy. However, there are strategies that even after endless tinkering still do not work, and they need to be discarded. Whether you are finally getting a technique to work well or finally figuring out that a particular approach will not, you need to celebrate or despair briefly and then move on.

Tinkering involves taking a generic strategy or one that somebody else has used with different content in another context and making it your own. It involves adjusting the strategy so that it fits your instructional proclivities, your content and context, and your students. Mostly we do this by an intuitive sense of what will work. I wish we were more reflective and explicit in our understanding of this adjustment process. It is a complicated one, and most of us cannot explain how we do it.

Nevertheless, we recognize the elements involved. We know that the way content is organized has pedagogical implications. Faculty who teach the periodic table do not discuss it the same way faculty who teach literature discuss themes in a novel. But the questioning techniques employed to ascertain whether students understand quadratic equations are not just for use in a math class. Those of us who regularly observe instruction hear the history professor using the same techniques. The tinkering metaphor implies an orientation of adaptation and adjustment, of making techniques work in the unique and dynamic milieu that is your conceptual and actual instructional home.

Set Realistic Expectations for Success

We do not always set realistic expectations. A participant in one of my workshops announced, "Group work doesn't work." The exchange continued on something like this: "How do you know?" "I tried it once, and it didn't work." "What did you do?" "I put students in groups, gave them problems to solve, and the smart kids did all the work." I could make many points about his comments, but one germane here is the idea (I am tempted to call this a preposterous idea) that you could try a pedagogical strategy as complicated as group work once and decide on the basis of that single experience that a whole method does not work when there is solid and extensive empirical evidence as to its effectiveness supported by the classroom experience of many faculty who regularly and successfully employ it.

That is an example of how we set unrealistic expectations for the success of new techniques. Why do we do this? Perhaps because the old ways of teaching are safe and comfortable. We do not want to change unless we have to. And if the alternatives are not as effective as what we currently do, we can certainly be excused from doing things differently. Perhaps it goes back to our quest for techniques and the assumption that a "good" one totally solves an instructional problem. Or maybe it is that we are such high achievers that we cannot deal with anything less than success.

Some of these explanations illustrate how we not only set unreasonably high standards for the techniques, we set them for ourselves. A national study (Gmelch, 1993) involving twelve hundred faculty from across disciplines identified the top ten causes of faculty stress. The top one is imposing excessively high self-expectations. We own successful implementation entirely and place blame for less-than-perfect execution squarely on our own shoulders. Part of the blame belongs there if we did not plan and prepare carefully, but virtually all the techniques being advocated in this book involve students. Students thus become part of the success or failure equation, and the role they do or do not play is often beyond our control. We do need to be hard on ourselves, but we also need to be realistic about any instructional approach. Some are better than others, but none is perfect. No technique will ever work equally well for all students, for all classes, and on all days, regardless of how brilliantly it is executed. Perfection is an elusive ideal, and the pursuit of it will cause us to reject many potentially effective techniques and ultimately diminish our commitment to improvement agendas.

I have proposed five principles that if used to guide improvement efforts will help to ensure the successful implementation of a new approach to teaching. The principles collectively will have an even greater impact if the whole improvement effort is approached positively and constructively, and the focus on more and better learning provides that perspective. Do not base efforts to change teaching on premises of remediation and deficiency. I have said so many times to the various faculty I have worked with that all teachers can improve, and most should.

Taking a Learner-Centered Approach

One way to implement instructional change is to use the learner-centered approaches espoused in this book. This approach differs from the way faculty normally go about incorporating change. I will characterize the learner-centered approach to developing learner-centered teaching in three ways, highlighting how each differs from current instructional practice.

Study the New Approach

Even faculty who care about teaching pay a dismaying lack of scholarly, intellectual attention to it. We devalue teaching practice by failing to do the kind of homework needed to make us informed practitioners. Our knowledge base rests almost exclusively on our individual experience and the equally uninformed reflections of colleagues. This is not to discredit the wisdom of practice or the insights of colleagues but to say that the knowledge base for learning is much broader than this, and we miss much when we teach oblivious to it.

There are many reasons that we remain so uninformed. Our conditioning begins early. I once heard a graduate student confess amazement at having discovered that an entire book had been written on teaching. He could understand some articles, but a whole book? And it continues with no or few expectations that faculty will keep up with pedagogical developments as they are expected to stay abreast of advances in their disciplines. There are equally few or no rewards for pedagogical scholarship and many assumptions about its inferiority. I wrote this book during a six-month leave and hoped to have most of the first draft finished by the time the leave ended. When I shared this with a colleague, he observed that no book of intellectual merit in a discipline could be written in six months but that he thought that might be enough time for a book on teaching.

You are reading this book, but how often do you find time to read? Do you read intellectually challenging material, or is it mostly more on how-to approaches? How well would you do on an exam covering the latest educational research findings? The kind of learners this approach seeks to develop know how to study and find the motivation to do so when faced with a learning task. I do not think we lack the study skills, but we struggle with the motivation.

If you are about to implement more learner-centered approaches to teaching, this should not be the only book you read. Many excellent references appear throughout the book, and organized and annotated reading lists are provided in Appendix C. This material illustrates the kind of knowledge base that supports learner-centered teaching. I hope it motivates further study of an intellectually rich and fascinating area. In sum, then, a skillful learner would not go about implementing an approach that requires as much change as this one without learning a great deal about it. And that learning would continue as changes are made.

Develop Deeper and More Accurate Self-Knowledge

Skillful learners are adept at self-assessment. They are able to analyze and reflect in ways that result in detailed and accurate self-knowledge. And effective efforts to improve instruction start with a complete and accurate understanding of the instructional self. How much do you know how you teach? Can you accurately and in detail describe what you do to promote learning? Can you explain the connections that exist between the proclivities of your style (what you believe you do well), the configurations of content in your discipline, and the learning needs of your students? Can you identify the assumptions inherent in the particular set of policies, practices, and behaviors you use in the classroom? Do you know what you believe about teachers, learners, content, and context and their respective roles, responsibilities, and contributions to the educational enterprise?

The level of self-knowledge necessary to answer those questions is not something most faculty possess. I believe three barriers stand between us and accurate self-knowledge. First, we do not study teaching and learning. As a result, we cannot benchmark our practice against any external standards. Second, as we will discover shortly, assessment is misused. It fails to give us the descriptive, diagnostic sense of detail on which accurate self-knowledge builds. Third, accurate instructional self-knowledge is precluded because we dismiss and otherwise ignore the emotional involvement that is inherently a part of teaching. Let us deal with that barrier now.

Teaching exposes much of who we are. We try to pretend that being professional protects us, but the fact of the matter is this: every professor is a person, and everything done in the classroom reveals something about that person. That level of vulnerability makes objectivity about how we teach difficult to achieve. Perhaps a metaphor will make the point more clearly. Take a flashlight into the woods at night, and shine it around. You may see animals, but they will not behave as they normally do, and precious little of the light ever shines on you. Unaware of the emotional baggage we carry, we often try to understand students, classes, and ourselves using this flashlight-in-the-night approach. The way we respond to what we "see" proves that our vision is impaired. Let me make the case with three examples.

Our first and almost automatic response to whatever we see in the classroom is judgmental. About activities we conclude, "It worked" or "It didn't work." About a day in class, "It was good" or "It was awful." About students, "They like me" or "They hate me." Some of these judgmental responses result from the evaluative environment in which many of us work, but it is more than that. Many of us find it is almost impossible to think about our teaching in anything but evaluative terms. If you do not think that is true, try completing this assignment I give my graduate students. Write a page-long description of how you teach, and use only language that is neutral and descriptive. In virtually every paper, I still find words and phrases that reveal the writer's evaluation of what is being described. Until we are able to separate what we do from an emotional assessment of it, we will have difficulty developing accurate self-knowledge.

For a second example of how emotional involvement impairs accurate self-knowledge, consider the frequency with which we respond defensively to feedback. How often do we respond to student rating results by criticizing the rating process? "If they used a decent instrument or if students took the process seriously . . .," we say. And how many real and perceived instructional failures do we lay on student doorsteps? "If they were smarter," "if they came to class," "if they prepared," "if they listened," "if they did what I told them." And finally how often do we use the "it's not my fault" explanation for instructional failures or difficulties? "If my classes weren't so large," "if I didn't have as many course preparations," "if my department head was supportive," "if my institution rewarded teaching," "if I didn't have to do so much research." Any or all of these may be legitimate reasons that explain a given performance, so they are not the problem. The problem is a level of emotional involvement that impairs our ability to separate reasons from excuses.

And finally, there is the consistent tendency we have to overreact to negative feedback. Which do you remember better: the two or three evaluations where students said you walked on water and gave you perfect scores or the two or three who criticized everything about the class? I worked with so many faculty I felt were overreacting to negative feedback that I wrote an article in the newsletter I edit about the problem. That same semester, I had the best graduate class I had ever taught. I could hardly wait to see the ratings. I knew they would be splendid, and any number of them were. But one student gave me the lowest possible score, on every single item. Devastated, I spent all evening trying to figure out who it was, complained about it at length to my husband, lay awake in bed thinking about what went wrong, and was still mulling it over in the morning before I remembered that I had just written a piece about how faculty overreact to negative feedback.

I am prepared to rest my case: we are emotionally involved with our instructional selves. Unless we get better at recognizing our vulnerability and find ways to compensate for it, our chances of building an accurate understanding of how we teach and might more effectively facilitate student learning will continue to be severely compromised. So how would a skillful learner develop the degree of objectivity necessary for deeper and more accurate self-knowledge?

The learner would begin where we have been by recognizing that emotional involvement stands in the way of that objective self-knowledge. The learner would make a concerted effort to cultivate more objectivity. He or she would work to think and speak more descriptively and less evaluatively about teaching and learning. The learner would be much more careful about conclusions drawn and generalizations made. A set of descriptive details may lead in the direction of a conclusion, but it is thought of and offered tentatively. And the generalizations are bounded by the set of circumstances to which they apply—for example, "The four group activities I tried in this course this semester did not produce the results I had hoped for." Generalizations and conclusions need to leave room for the almost always mixed results that instruction produces.

In addition, given the difficulty of attaining objectivity, sophisticated learners would look outside themselves for things that would prompt more and deeper insights. It might be a book or article. Some learners gain insight through inventories. Angelo and Cross's Teaching Goals Inventory (1993) is an outstanding tool to clarify instructional priorities. In the spirit of this book, if you have never taken a learning styles inventory, you should. A simple one (Fleming and Mills, 1992) can be found and scored on-line at www.active-learning-site.com/inventory1.html.

Developing complete and accurate self-knowledge begins with a recognition that we are emotionally involved with our teaching and that involvement clouds our objectivity in some unavoidable ways. You walk through that dark instructional woods alone. You hold the flashlight that lights your way. But even given that, we can cultivate more objectivity. We have explored ways of developing the levels of self-knowledge necessary to understand how we teach and how we might want to change. We continue with others.

Alter Attitudes Toward Assessment

Learners gain deeper self-knowledge when they use assessment constructively. Unfortunately, instructional evaluation more often than not compromises instructional improvement agendas. So many faculty have had so many dismal and frustrating experiences, ranging from data that are not meaningful to comments that are hurtful, that even when in charge of their own improvement efforts, many do not collect assessment data. How is it that instructional evaluation has so poisoned this very important feedback well? There are many reasons. Consider some of the major ones briefly.

End-of-course ratings and peer reviews are mostly summative evaluation activities. They offer overall, comprehensive judgments about instructional effectiveness. The items used are often highly inferential ("instructor's attitude toward teaching the course"), and although low scores may motivate improvement, the items themselves do not provide the diagnostic, descriptive details that help faculty make informed choices about what to change. A comparison of the evaluation item above with one that rates the extent to which the "instructor's presentations facilitate note taking" illustrates the difference. If you have never used a low-inference behavior-specific instrument, I recommend one developed by Murray (1983) because his research links the behaviors on the instrument to teaching effectiveness.

It is ironic that of all the instructional events and activities within the higher education domain, nothing has been studied more than the evaluation of instruction. (Any number of fine nontechnical summaries exist. For a recent example, see Hobson and Talbot, 2001.) But despite a wealth of research, practice lags far beyond. Rarely are policies and procedures employed that make the collection and dissemination of rating data useful for faculty. For example, summative and formative evaluation efforts should be separate. Ratings that generate the overall assessments are useful in promotion and tenure decisions. Ratings that provide diagnostic descriptive details are useful in improvement efforts. You cannot collect both kinds of data on the same instrument without compromising the potential of each to accomplish its designated purpose. Just as the grade-oriented environment compromises students' ability to deal with formative feedback, so the data collected for promotion and tenure or a merit raise create a context that compromises the value of improvement information.

We poison the well further by the way peers are used in the evaluation process. Violating norms of collegiality, they do "commando raid" observations: they drop into class, not knowing what happened yesterday or is planned for tomorrow, observe, having had no training and sometimes no experience, and then evaluate using their own idiosyncratic standards of instructional excellence. Research has consistently documented (Feldman, 1988; Marsh, 1984) that there are reliability issues when peers are used in this way. Researchers continue to raise questions about peer assessment and challenge those who make policy to let peers evaluate those aspects of instruction that students are not qualified to judge (for example, whether the textbook is appropriate given the goals and objective of the course). Otherwise, let them function as colleagues and work collaboratively on improvement efforts.

Faculty response to evaluation feedback might be characterized as a kind of stoic, macho toughness: "This is the way they give it to me—I can take it. If I'm hurt, I'll just suck it up." Faculty, especially those who are new, need counsel and advice when interpreting the results of their evaluation. They need options and alternatives when considering changes. Minus that and in a highly evaluative context, they draw their own and often erroneous conclusions. In sharp contrast, consider a critical reflective narrative offered by a young faculty member who describes his own experiences at coming to grips with student evaluation results (Gallagher, 2000).

As a consequence of our summative orientation to evaluation, our failure to deliver formative feedback in more constructive contexts, our misappropriation of peer contributions, and macho "nobody-will-know-it-hurt-me" attitudes, faculty have come to view evaluation as a foe, not a friend; an adversary, not an advocate. This must change if individual efforts to improve are to be at all successful.

Skillful learners rely on feedback mechanisms to understand accurately, in this case, the impact of instructional policies, practices, and behaviors. Its data provide the bits and pieces of information on which accurate self-knowledge and good choices about change build. How do we move faculty learners from the place where they fear and avoid feedback to a place where they take advantage of all that assessment can contribute to their efforts to make teaching more learner-centered? I have four suggestions derived from our knowledge of how mature learners handle assessment. I will apply each in the instructional context and discuss them in terms of faculty soliciting feedback from students.

Sophisticated Learners Want Specific, Focused Feedback

They let others worry about global assessment. In the instructional context, if you are trying something like a group exam or a student-generated participation policy, or you are involving groups in establishing assignment criteria, have students offer feedback on that activity and that activity alone. Any aspect of the course can profitably be the object of fixed and focused feedback: the reading material, the exams, the papers, the quality of the feedback you provide, the group work, the quizzes, the infusion of technology. This narrower frame prevents the kind of threatening global assessments (for example, "How does this instructor compare with all others at the institution?") that are so difficult to deal with. A focused assessment is narrow and specific.

Do not be afraid to devise your own feedback mechanisms. Part of the positive legacy of the classroom assessment movement is that it has persuaded faculty that they can write their own questions, use their own formats and scales, and analyze their own data. In a learner-centered environment, let this be a shared activity with students. How did this work, and how do "we" make it better? The evaluation is not always about what faculty need to do differently or change. It may very well identify targets of change that involve students' doing something differently as well.

Self-Regulating Learners Make Data-Based Assessment an Ongoing Activity

Do not wait until the end of the course to solicit the feedback. The quality will be better if you get student reactions when the experience is fresh in their minds. And after you have gotten some feedback and changes are indicated, discuss those with the class, implement them, give everybody a chance to experience them, and then solicit feedback again. Students take the feedback process much more seriously once it becomes clear that the information will lead to changes in this class, this semester.

Experienced Learners Ask the Right Questions

Do not ask students if they "liked" a particular activity. That is an irrelevant criterion, and their responses will cause you to revisit all that emotional baggage you want to put aside. The questions you need answered are these: "How did that activity [or event or policy] affect your learning?" "What about it needs to change so that if we do it again, you will learn more?" The right kinds of questions encourage responsible, mature student response, not potshots aimed at aspects of instruction over which you have no control. Let the golden rule apply as you and your students exchange feedback: give unto each other (students to faculty, students to students, faculty to students) the kind and quality of feedback you would like to receive.

Sophisticated Learners Make Selective Choices About Peer Involvement

Pick your instructional peer collaborators carefully. Let them be people with whom you can have open, honest dialogue, and let that dialogue be about substantive educational issues. Let them be informed about teaching and learning. Let them be fellow learners. Pick ones who will come to your class as a colleague and ones who will let you visit their class. Let them be ones with whom you can share and critique course materials. Let them be ones with whom you can discuss failures, quandaries, and difficult students.

Do not rule out colleagues outside your discipline. They bring fresh perspectives and are more likely to see your content as the students see it.

Some faculty are lucky enough to have a group of close colleagues with whom they discuss many things, including teaching and learning. Sometimes all that these groups need is an agenda—a specific framework for talking about teaching that can ratchet up the quality and impact of the exchange significantly. Beaty (1999, pp. 51, 52) proposes just such a mechanism. She calls it action learning and defines it this way: "Action learning is a continuous process of learning and reflection, supported by colleagues, with an intention of getting things done. Individuals work on real problems and learn from reflection on their practice over time." She justifies the approach with this observation: "In order to improve, a teacher needs to learn from experience over time. Experience does not of itself improve instruction. Rather, thoughtful and critical reflection on previous practice invokes the necessary learning and change."

Peers can contribute a great deal to individual efforts to improve. It is a tragedy that we have come to define their involvement so narrowly and inappropriately. A wonderful collection of resources and information (Chism, 1999) illustrates the positive and constructive ways that peers can come alongside individual efforts to understand and improve teaching and learning.

Independent, self-regulated learners would learn about and then implement a new instructional approach differently than most faculty currently approach instructional improvement. They would study the approach, cultivate the ability to see and understand accurately how they teach, and use assessment constructively throughout the implementation process.

To Finish Up

This chapter is a good one with which to end the book. I see it as the bridge from thought to action, from thinking about a way of teaching to starting to teach with learning the explicit outcome. My quest to become more learner-centered is now in its fifth year. Both my thinking and my practice are considerably different, more refined, and more effective (I certainly hope) than when I started. It has been the most remarkable journey of my pedagogical career. I used to think that someday I would finally be a learner-centered teacher. Flachmann (1994, p. 1) changed my mind about this and offers advice that fittingly summarizes this chapter, perhaps this whole book: "Good teaching is a *journey* rather than a *destination*. It's not like a subway stop where, once you are there, you can cease moving forward. . . . Inertia is an insidiously powerful negative force in teaching—the urge to keep doing things the way we've done them for years. It's a bit like belonging to the pedagogical equivalent of Alcoholics Anonymous: there's always a poor teacher in us waiting to emerge. We have to resist the temptation to stay as we are, to rest at the bus stop."

| Syllabus and Learning Log

Welcome to Speech Communications 100A, a course that aims to develop your communications skills. Because everyone communicates all the time, the content of this course is relevant to you today, as well as after you graduate. In this course you will become more aware of how you communicate and better able to communicate effectively. The course combines theory and practice, giving you the opportunity to apply what you have learned.

Text

The course text is *Communicate* by Rudolph F. Verderber. Reading assignments should be done before coming to class. Please bring your text with you to class, as regular discussions of text content will occur during class.

Course Assignments

In this course, assignments are handled differently: you select what work you complete, with one exception: all students must give an informative or persuasive speech. Review the following options bearing these rules in mind:

1. At least 50 percent of the total points possible for each individual assignment must be earned; otherwise, *no points* will be recorded for the assignment.
2. Once the due date for an assignment has passed, that assignment cannot be completed.

Exams

1. Test 1—A multiple-choice and essay exam including material from class and the text. (80 points possible)
2. Test 2—A multiple-choice exam including material from class and the text. (80 points possible)

Presentations

1. An informative or persuasive speech (5–7 minutes long) and a speech preparation sheet. THIS IS THE ONLY REQUIRED ASSIGNMENT IN THE COURSE. (speech, 50 points possible; prep sheet, 10 points possible)
2. Interviews (10–12 minutes long) conducted by classmates representing hypothetical corporations and organizations with open positions. You select the positions of interest and are interviewed by the group. See Small Group Experience 3 for more details on the groups. (two interviews, 15 points per interview, each summarized in a short paper, plus 5 bonus points if you get the job)

Small Group Experiences

1. Test 2 study group—be a member of a 5–7-person study group who will jointly prepare for Test 2. After taking the exam individually, the group will convene and complete a group exam. Group exam scoring options will be described on a handout. (? bonus points possible)
2. This assignment also includes a 3-page typed paper which analyzes what happened in the study group in terms of (1) what the group did/didn't do that contributed to its success or lack of it and (2) what the individual group members did that contributed to the group's success or lack of it. NOTE: THIS PAPER MUST BE COMPLETED IF EXAM BONUS POINTS ARE TO BE AWARDED. (30 points possible for the paper)
3. Interview group—with 5–7 other classmates be employees of a hypothetical corporation who will write a job description, prepare interview questions, and interview up to 8 candidates for the job. A group grade will be based on a final report, which

includes (1) the job description, (2) interview questions, (3) a summary of interviews conducted and justification for the person hired (30 points possible), and (4) an assessment of how well the group conducted the interview based on feedback from those interviewed (10 points possible). In addition, individual members' contributions to the group will be assessed by other members (20 points possible). (This makes the interviewing part of the assignment worth up to 60 points total.)

Learning Log

This assignment encourages students to explore how the course content relates to their individual communication skills. Each entry is written in response to a series of questions provided by the instructor. Entries may be handwritten or typed and should be about two pages long if handwritten, a double-spaced page if typed. Collections of entries are due on the dates specified in the course calendar. You may prepare all, one, or some of the entries. However, once a due date is past, those entries may not be submitted.

Entries are graded using the following criteria: (1) their completeness (meaning all the questions for a particular entry are addressed); (2) the level of insight and reflection (evidence of thoughtful responses); (3) the support provided for the observations and conclusions; and (4) the extent to which relevant course content (from class and the text) is integrated in the entries. (10 points possible per individual entry)

Speech Critiques

You will provide constructive feedback to eight classmates on their informative speeches. You will use a form provided by the instructor, and after your critiques have been graded, they will be given to the presenter. NOTE: YOU MUST DO ALL EIGHT CRITIQUES. (80 points possible)

Participation

Using the class-authored participation policy and a set of individually generated goals, your contributions to class will be assessed.

NOTE: PARTICIPATION CANNOT BE ADDED AS AN ASSIGN-MENT OPTION AFTER THE THIRD CLASS SESSION. (50 points possible)

This assignment also includes a 5-page typed participation analysis paper, submitted in installments, due dates indicated on the course calendar. *Installment 1:* one page, which reacts to and assesses the class-generated policy and in which you generate your participation goals for the course; *Installment 2:* three pages, one of which is a letter to your designated partner providing feedback on his or her participation as you have observed it and two pages consisting of a midcourse progress report; *Installment 3:* one page, which contains a final assessment of your participation in the course. A more detailed handout describing this assignment will be distributed subsequently. NOTE: THE PAPER MUST BE COM-PLETED IF POINTS FOR PARTICIPATION ARE TO BE EARNED. (50 points possible for the paper)

Bonus Points

1. On several unannounced days, attendance will be taken. Those present will receive 5 bonus points. (up to, but not necessarily 25 points)
2. There will be some additional bonus point options offered at the discretion of the instructor.

And Finally, About Developing a Game Plan for the Course

For the purposes of planning, circle the assignments you are con-sidering, and then total the points possible. Be realistic. It is highly unlikely that you will get all the points possible for the assignments. Check your total with point totals needed for each grade. Be sure that you're planning to do enough assignments to get the grade you desire in the course. Keep track of your points as the course progresses (a points grid sheet will be provided subsequently) so that you will know if you need to add more assignments.

Test 1	80 points
Test 2	80 points

Informative or persuasive speech and preparation sheet	60 points
Interviews	30 points
Study group test bonus	? points
Study group analysis paper	30 points
Interview group experience	60 points
Learning Log, 22 entries at 10 points per entry	220 points
Speech critiques	80 points
Participation	50 points
Participation analysis paper	50 points
Attendance bonus	25 points
	765 points TOTAL

Grades

Grades for this course are assigned according to the following scale:

525 and above	A	378–412	C
499–524	A-	343–377	C-
482–498	B+	309–342	D
465–481	B	292–308	D-
448–464	B-	291 and below	F
413–447	C+		

[A day-by-day calendar of all course meetings follows. It lists content topics, activities scheduled for the class session, reading assignment, and assignment due dates.]

Learning Log Entries

Entry 1

Develop a game plan for the course indicating which assignments you plan to complete. Why have you selected these options? What do you think your choices indicate about your learning preferences? Why do you think a teacher would give students a choice about assignments? How do you think this strategy will affect your performance in the class?

Entry 2

Why does the university require a course in speech communication? If this course wasn't required, would you take it? Why? Why
not? Overall, how would you assess your communication skills?
Reread pp. 22–23 in the text, and set at least one goal for yourself
in this class.

Entry 3

Write about your participation in college courses (or high school if
you have no or limited experience with college courses). How much
do you participate? Is that as much as you'd like to contribute? If
it's not as much, what keeps you from saying more in class? What
role should student participation play in the college classroom?

Entry 4

Think about your experiences working in groups. What made
those group experiences effective or ineffective? What responsibilities do individuals have when they participate in groups? Can
individual members do anything to encourage other members to
fulfill these responsibilities?

Entry 5

Take a look at the definition for leadership that appears in the
chapter in your textbook on leadership in groups (pp. 241–259).
Summarize the definition in your own words, and write about the
notion of leadership as exerting influence. Are you comfortable
with that? How is it different from telling people what to do? Content from the rest of the chapter should be used in addressing that
question. How would you characterize your potential as a leader?

Entry 6

In the light of the material we've discussed in class and that you've
read in the text (on roles and leadership, for example), analyze

your small group communication skills. What roles do you typically fill in groups? Are there any skills you'd like to develop further? How often and in what context do you think you will have to work in groups in your professional life?

Entry 7

React to our in-class discussion of sexist remarks and gendered references. Is this "much ado about nothing"? On what terms and in what ways do you think language influences the way you think and act? Provide some examples. So, if you marry, will you or your spouse change your last name?

Entry 8

Where are you in terms of choosing a topic for your informative speech? What sort of feedback did you get from classmates in the class activity Tuesday? Analyze the strengths and weaknesses of the topics you are considering in terms of your qualifications and interest in the topic, the relevance of the topic to the class, and the suitability of the topic given the occasion and setting. (Text material on pp. 265–285 should be used in this entry.)

Entry 9

Write me a letter that answers the questions and/or supplies the additional information requested in my letter to you about your first set of log entries.

Entry 10

You have been asked to address an audience of inner-city high school students on why they should attend college. What things about this audience would you like to know before you plan the content of your speech? What issues do you think might be important to raise? How likely is this audience to believe you speaking on this topic? Any things you might be able to do to enhance your credibility?

Entry 11

Take and score the communication apprehension quiz. How does this feedback compare with how you feel about doing the speech? What ideas in the text (pp. 373–379) might help you overcome the anxiety you associate with speaking?

Entry 12

Take stock of how you are doing in this class so far. How many points do you have now? Revisit your game plan described in Entry 1, and discuss any changes you plan to make. Is this course structure and grading system having any impact on your learning? Include some examples to illustrate the impact you have described.

Entry 13 (write the period after you do your speech)

So, how did it go? Using the critique form, assess your speech. Answer the questions at the bottom of the page. SUBMIT THE COMPLETED CRITIQUE FORM WITH THIS ENTRY.

Entry 14

Describe an experience you've had trying to persuade someone to change his or her mind about something. Were you successful? Analyze your success or failure in terms of the eight principles of persuasive speaking, text pp. 417–441.

Entry 15

Take and score the Uncritical Inference Test (I will distribute it in class). Report and comment on your score. What do you think an exercise like this is trying to teach you? Is this an important lesson? Why? Why not?

Entry 16

Compare and contrast your analysis of your speech with the feedback provided by your classmates and the teacher. Any noticeable differences? Any feedback from others that strikes you as particularly constructive?

Entry 17

Use the ad you brought to class, or pick another one and analyze it in terms of fallacies and propaganda. More important than correctly naming the fallacy or propaganda technique is being able to explain what is wrong with the argument being made. Also write about the ad in terms of the nonverbal messages it portrays. INCLUDE THE AD WITH THIS ENTRY.

Entry 18 (write this entry only if you plan to take Test 2)

Develop a study game plan for Test 2. If you took Test 1, think about what you learned from that experience. If you didn't, write about content you expect to see on the exam and how you'll go about preparing yourself. Include in the entry a time line identifying how much time you'll spend and what you'll do each day leading up to the exam.

Entry 19

Return to the text, pp. 327–351, the chapter on organizing speech material. Prepare a 2-page study guide that identifies material from the text that you believe will appear on the exam. Describe how you could or would use the study guide to learn this material.

Entry 20

You have your exam back. Did you do better or worse than you expected? If you developed a game plan, analyze how well it worked, including how closely you did or didn't follow it. If you were in a study group, explain how the group efforts dovetailed with your individual preparation. If you took the exam as an individual, were the group scores posted in class higher or lower than you expected? How do you account for this? Next semester, what one thing could you do that would most improve your performance on multiple-choice exams?

Entry 21 (to be completed only if you've written entry 2)

Return to the assessment of your communication skills offered in entry 2. How would you describe and assess those skills now? Evaluate any progress you made toward reaching the goal you set for yourself.

Entry 22

Submit this entry the last day of class in a sealed envelope with your name on the envelope. I will record 10 points upon receiving the envelope. I will read the contents after I have submitted final grades.

> Over the summer a friend e-mails that she has signed up for this class in the fall. She asks you what she needs to do in order to do well in the course. What would you tell her? Telling her to drop the course and get into another section is fine, so long as you tell her why. On the other hand, you might share with her what you would do differently if you were taking the course again. If you've done well in the course, to what would you attribute your success? What important things, if any, have you learned?

Handouts That Develop Learning Skills

The sample handouts in this appendix are useful in developing specific learning skills and learner self-awareness. Here are some brief suggestions for possible use:

"Successful Students: Guidelines and Thought for Academic Success": A positive and constructive handout that describes good learning behaviors, it might be attached to the course syllabus or distributed when students have demonstrated some less-than-successful behaviors.

"Ten Commandments for Effective Study Skills": The style captivates, and at the same time, its contents deliver constructive messages about studying.

"Discussion Guidelines for Students": The author includes these in his syllabus. They offer a detailed description of actions that improve discussion.

"Learning from the Research on Taking Lecture Notes": This handout highlights a research study and might be an effective prompt to get students to consider their own note-taking behaviors.

"Consider a Study Group": Here is a strategy that encourages students to form study groups. It offers an incentive for doing so and some help on group process issues.

"Notetaking Types and Characteristics to Help Students Succeed": This concise matrix can be used to make students aware of some of the different methods of taking notes.

Successful Students: Guidelines and Thoughts for Academic Success

Source: Steven J. Thien and Andy Bulleri, the *Teaching Professor,* 1996, *10*(9), 1–2. Reprinted with permission from Magna Publications.

Successful students exhibit a combination of successful attitudes and behaviors as well as intellectual capacity. Successful students. . .

1. *are responsible and active.* Successful students get involved in their studies, accept responsibility for their own education, and are active participants in it!
2. *have educational goals.* Successful students have legitimate goals and are motivated by what those goals represent in terms of career aspirations and life's desires.
3. *ask questions.* Successful students ask questions to provide the quickest route between ignorance and knowledge.
4. *learn that a student and a professor make a team.* Most instructors want exactly what you want: they would like for you to learn the material in their respective classes and earn a good grade.
5. *don't sit in the back.* Successful students minimize classroom distractions that interfere with learning.
6. *take good notes.* Successful students take notes that are understandable and organized, and they review them often.
7. *understand that actions affect learning.* Successful students know their personal behavior affects their feelings and emotions which in turn can affect learning. Act like you're disinterested and you'll become disinterested.
8. *talk about what they're learning.* Successful students get to know something well enough that they can put it into words.
9. *don't cram for exams.* Successful students know that divided periods of study are more effective than cram sessions, and they practice it.
10. *are good time managers.* Successful students do not procrastinate. They have learned that time control is life control and have consciously chosen to be in control of their lives.

Ten Commandments for Effective Study Skills

Source: By Larry M. Ludewig, the *Teaching Professor,* 1992, *6*(10), 3–4. Reprinted with permission from Magna Publications.

Thou Shalt Be Responsible and Thou Shalt Be Active—For There Be No Other Passage to Academic Success!

Responsibility means control. Your grade in a class is relatively free of any variables other than your own effort. Sure, you may have a lousy professor. It happens. But remember: you are the one who has to live with your grade. It goes on *your* grade report, not your *instructor's.*

If you are seeking a way of increasing learning and improving grades without increasing your study time, active classroom participation is your answer. Look at it this way: classroom time is something to which you are already committed. So, you can sit there, assume the "bored student position"—arms crossed, slumped in the chair, eyes at half-mast—and allow yourself an "out-of-body" experience. Or, you can maximize your classroom time by actively listening, thinking, questioning, taking notes, and participating totally in the learning experience.

Thou Shalt Know Where Thy "Hot Buttons" Are, and Thou Shalt Push Them Regularly!

The next time you seat yourself in class, ask yourself these questions:

- What am I doing here?
- Why have I chosen to be sitting here now?
- Is there some better place I could be?
- What does my presence here mean to me?

Your responses to these questions represent your educational goals. They are the "hot buttons," and they are, without a doubt, the most important factors in your success as a college student.

College is not easy. Believe it or not, there will be times when you tire of being a student. And that's when a press or two on the hot buttons can pull you through!

If Thou Hath Questions, Asketh Them. If Thou Hath No Questions, Maketh Some!

Just as a straight line usually indicates the shortest distance between two points, questions generally provide the quickest route between ignorance and knowledge.

In addition to securing knowledge that you seek, asking questions has at least two other extremely important benefits. The process helps you pay attention to your professor and helps your professor pay attention to you.

Thou Shalt Learn That Thou and Thy Professor Maketh a Team— and Thou Shalt Be a Team Player!

Most instructors want exactly what you want: they would like for you to learn the material in their respective classes and earn a good grade. After all, successful students reflect well on the efforts of any teaching; if you learned your stuff, the instructor takes some justifiable pride in teaching.

Thou Shalt Not Parketh Thy Butt in the Back!

Suppose you pay $50 to buy concert tickets for your favorite musical artist. Do you choose front row seats or the cheap seats at the rear of the auditorium? Why do some students who spend far more money on a college education than on concerts willingly place themselves in the last row of the classroom? In class, the back row gives invisibility and anonymity, both of which are antithetical to efficient and effective learning.

Thou Shalt Not Write in Thy Notes What Thou Faileth to Understand!

Avoid the "whatinthehellisthat" phenomenon experienced by most college students. This unique reaction occurs when students first review their notes for a major examination. Being unable to read, decipher, or comprehend the mess that passes for notes, students are likely to utter the expression that grants this particular phenomenon its name.

If Thine Interest in Class Be Gone, Faketh It!

If you are a good actor, you may even fool yourself into liking the lecture.

How do you fake interest? You simply assume the "interested student position"; lean forward, place your feet flat on the floor in front of you, maintain eye contact with your professor, smile or nod occasionally as though you understand and care about what your instructor is saying, take notes, and ask questions.

Thou Shalt Know That If Silence Be Golden—Recitation Shalt Be Platinum!

Recitation is not only good for checking whether or not you know something; it's perhaps the best method for learning it in the first place. Reciting unquestionably provides the most direct route between short-term and long-term memory.

Thou Shalt Knoweth That Cram Is a Four-Letter Word!

If there is one thing that study skills specialists agree on, it is that divided periods of study are more efficient and effective than a single period of condensed study. In other words, you will learn more, remember more, and earn a higher grade if you prepare for Friday's examination by studying one hour a night, Monday through Thursday, rather than studying for four hours straight on Thursday evening.

Thou Shalt Not Procrastinate—and Thou Shalt Beginneth Not Doing It Right Now!

An elemental truth: you will either control time or be controlled by it! There is no middle ground. It's your choice: you can lead or be led, establish control or relinquish control, steer your own course or have it dictated to you.

When I ask students which they prefer, choosing their own path or having it chosen for them, they almost uniformly select the first option. In spite of this response, however, failure to take control of their own time is probably the number one study skills problem of college students

So, these are the Ten Commandments for Effective Study Skills. They work, but don't take my word for it. Try them! Use them! Make them your own. What have you got to lose except poor grades and sleepless study nights?

Discussion Guidelines for Students

Source: By Howard Gabennesch, the *Teaching Professor,* 1992, 6(9), 6. Reprinted with permission from Magna Publications.

- Try to make comments that connect ideas from the course with phenomena outside the classroom, and between ideas in one part of the course and those in a different part.
- Avoid war stories, rambling speeches heavily punctuated with the word "I," and raw opinions that we could just as easily get from the average patron at the nearest tavern who has never heard of this course and its assigned reading.
- Realize that when our emotions are aroused our brain wants to take orders from them. It is essential, therefore, to be willing to disconnect one's brain from one's gut long enough to render due process to ideas, particularly those that are unpopular or personally distasteful. This is an unnatural act, and requires courage. You will probably find it easier to join lynch mobs from time to time.
- Understand that the right to have an opinion does not include the right to have it taken seriously by others. Nor is having an opinion necessarily laudable in itself. An opinion is only as good as the evidence, theory, and logic on which it is based.
- Be careful about basing your opinions uncritically on the testimony of experts. Experts are subject to error and bias. They often disagree with other experts. All of this applies to the authors of your texts and your professors.
- Beware of the tendency to view questions in dichotomous terms, such as either-or, all-or-none. The world is a complex, messy place where absolute answers are hard to find, gray is more common than black and white and contradictory things are often in the same package.
- Appreciate the importance of the distinction between "the truth" and "the truth, the whole truth, and nothing but the truth."
- Value tentativeness. It's OK to admit you're unsure. It's OK to change your mind.

Learning from the Research on Taking Lecture Notes

Source: Johnston, A. H., and Su, W. Y. "Lectures—A Learning Experience?" *Education in Chemistry,* May 1994, pp. 76–70. Article summary by Maryellen Weimer, the *Teaching Professor,* 1994, *8*(9), 2. Reprinted with permission from Magna Publications.

Get this: the average lectures contains about 5,000 spoken words. The average student ends up with about 500 of those words in his or her notes. Key question: How do students pick their 500 words?

To answer that question A. H. Johnston and W. Y. Su analyzed student notes and the lectures they listened to in a first year chemistry class across a three-year period. The total number of subjects in their study was small but the uniqueness and thoroughness of the analysis make the findings noteworthy. In addition to detailed reviews of the student notes, they also recorded faculty lectures, noted their board work and reviewed other visually presented material.

In brief, they found:

- On average, students recorded about 90 percent of the blackboard information in terms of both words and information units, defined as the smallest block of knowledge that could stand as a separate assertion. However, the conclusion does not imply that student notes were complete. Rather, it illustrates the commonplace student assumption that all they need is the written material.
- Inaccuracies in the notes occurred most frequently when students were copying diagrams, numerical figures, equations and items on transparencies. Rarely did any faculty corrections end up in student notes.
- What most often did not appear in students' notes was anything related to demonstrations, examples of applications, detailed sequences of arguments, and meanings of technical terms and symbols.

Four basic note-taking styles emerged from this research analysis:

- Students who write down only what appears on the board and have an incomplete record of that.
- Students who write down what appears on the board and have all that material.
- Students who have the board material and other material.
- Students with "elaborated notes" which contained extra or connective material not explicitly given in the lecture.

The researchers found a correlation between note-taking style and test performance. On average 45 percentage points separated students with notes from the first category listed from those in the final category.

As for an overall finding, the researchers concluded, "Only about one third of the students in the sample were leaving the lecture with most of the information units recorded and with substantially complete notes."

Consider a Study Group

Sources: Study group guidelines adapted from H. J. Robinson, the *Teaching Professor,* 1991, 5(7), 7, and study group bill of rights ideas adapted from D. G. Longman, the *Teaching Professor,* 1992, 6(7), 5. Both reprinted with permission from Magna Publications.

Study groups give students the opportunity to discuss problems raised in the course, to read and comment on the written work of others, to help and tutor each other by working jointly on course materials, to test each other's knowledge, to share the cost of expensive and optional course texts and to learn how to work cooperatively with peers. Consider organizing one with a group of your colleagues!

If you do decide to form a study group, the following guidelines outline how those groups will work in this class.

- Groups of 4 to 6 students are formed by the mutual agreement of the members.
- To be considered a study group for the class, groups must register with the instructor, providing group member names and student ID numbers.

- Groups may expel a member (say one who is using the group as opposed to contributing to it) by unanimous vote.
- If group membership falls below 4, the group is automatically disbanded unless they vote in a replacement.
- No students may belong to more than one study group and no student is required to belong to any study group.
- Groups organize their own activities, deciding what to do at their meetings. The instructor would be happy to meet with groups to suggest activities and/or to review proposed study plans. This meeting is optional for the groups.
- Registered groups receive bonus points on all assignments according to the following formula. The bonus is based on the average of all individual grades received by the group members. If the group average is A, all members receive three percentage points; if it's B, two percentage points, and if it's a C one percentage point. If an individual member receives an A but the group average is C, the member still receives the one percentage point bonus.

If you would like to participate in a study group, but don't know students in the class well enough to organize one, please let the instructor know. The instructor will be happy to help students organize groups.

Study groups, indeed all groups, are successful if members agree to work together constructively. Groups should spend time at the beginning discussing how they would like the group to work together. They might profitably discuss, revise and agree to accept the "bill of rights" that follows.

Study Groups Bill of Rights for Individual Members

- You have the right and responsibility to select study sites and times that are convenient for all members.
- You have the right to contribute to the formation of group goals that have measurable outcomes and deadlines.
- You have the responsibility to be an active participant, not a passive receiver, in the group process. In addition, you have the right to expect active participation from other group members.

- You have the right to have meetings begin and end promptly and to participation in study sessions without needless interruptions.
- You have the right to participation in a group that works cooperatively and handles disagreements constructively.
- You have the right to expect that the group will stay on task and you have the responsibility for helping the group to do so.
- You have the right to ask group members to limit socialization or discussion of extraneous topics before and after study sessions.
- You have the right to closure. This includes feelings of accomplishment (1) at the end of each study session, by evaluating if the group has met its goals, (2) after each exam and assignment, by debriefing with members to evaluate performances, and (3) at the end of the class by assessing the value of the group experience to you.

Notetaking Types and Characteristics to Help Students Succeed

Source: Lisa Shibley, the *Teaching Professor,* 1999, *13*(9), 3. Reprinted with permission from Magna Publications.

See table on opposite page.

Types of Notes	Conventional	Two-Column	Outline	Concept Map	Matrix
Uses	Traditional method.	Summarize key ideas in far left column.	Students use to review and find relationships among topics and subtopics.	Helps define key ideas and relationships.	Helps define key ideas and relationships.
Benefits	Convenient for students.	Helps with factual details. Room for re-organization after class. Good for multiple choice exams.	Students include more key ideas, more details and examples. Great for preparing for multiple choice and short answer exams.	Students discover more relationships. Leads to higher-order thinking. Great for preparing for essay exams.	Students discover more relationships. Leads to higher-order thinking. Great for studying for essay exams.
Attentiveness	Lose valuable information because try to write as much down as possible.	Students may still lose valuable information as write down too much information.	Focus on ideas and relationships during lecture, then writing down notes.	Focus on ideas and relationships during lecture, then writing down notes.	Focus on ideas and relationships during lecture, then writing down notes.
Lecture Rate	Difficult for students to keep up. Ideas get lost.	Summarization in left column during lecture so ideas lost.	Students capture more ideas.	Students capture more ideas.	Students capture more ideas.
Process	Involves listening, large short term memory, writing down information.	Involves listening, large short term memory, writing down information.	Students write down key ideas and indent under topics to add related materials.	Students write down key ideas and connect them.	Write topics across the top row and general characteristics down the first column.
Format	Verbatim notes. No indentations. Full sentences.	Far left column for topics and summaries. Right for details, etc.	Indented topics. Roman numerals, numbers or bullets used.	Key ideas with circles around them connected by lines.	Table, similar to this one.

Appendix C

| **Reading Lists**

The four reading lists in this appendix—good books on active learning, successful small group dynamics, personal reports of experiences with learner-centered teaching, and an eclectic reading list on learning—are included for different reasons. The first two contain resources on topics not addressed in the book. As important as active learning and small group dynamics are to the successful implementation of learner-centered teaching, there is not time or reason to spell out the how-to's when many good sources already exist on both topics.

The second two lists highlight and otherwise promote some of the literature on learning that is relevant to and supportive of the approaches set out by this book. Faculty learn from colleagues, and so there is a reading list that identifies first-person accounts of attempts to make teaching more learner-centered. Another reading list identifies various sources that relate to the specific areas of empirical and theoretical work on learning. It relates particularly to Chapter One, where I highlight some of the lessons on learning derived from the literature.

None of these lists is comprehensive. I have not read everything, and my intent was not to create lists that impress by virtue of their inclusiveness. Many important sources and much good work does not appear on these lists. With the reading list on learning, not all the sources are equally well written or accessible to readers not well versed in this literature. All the reading lists include sources that influenced, directed, and shaped my thinking about learning and how we might better promote it. They changed how I teach.

I hope the material referenced in the book and contained in these reading lists will motivate faculty to read more widely and deeply. There is much to be learned about how students learn and about how our teaching has an impact on that learning.

Good Books on Active Learning

Interest in active learning is old enough to have spawned some excellent sources. Articles proliferate; there are so many that one or even a collection of them fails to capture the comprehensiveness of our knowledge and experience in this area. I identify books here because they treat the topic broadly. This reading list is directed more for faculty who, despite a commitment to active learning, have read little about it. These sources include many generic techniques and strategies, but they also do well with the theory and research that support active learning, explaining why and how it works so effectively to engage and involve students with content and learning.

Bean, J. C. *Engaging Ideas: The Professor's Guide to Integrating Writing, Critical Thinking and Active Learning in the Classroom.* San Francisco: Jossey-Bass, 1996. Superb collection of strategies applicable to many disciplines.

Bonwell, C., and Eison, J. *Active Learning: Creating Excitement in the Classroom.* Washington, D.C.: ERIC Clearinghouse on Higher Education and the Association for the Study of Higher Education, 1991. Considered by many to be the definitive source on active learning; especially good summary of the research.

McNeal, A. P., and D'Avanzo, C. (eds.). *Student-Active Science: Models of Innovation in College Science Teaching.* Fort Worth, Tex.: Saunders College Publishing, 1997. Some programmatic descriptions but lots of good chapters written by science faculty who are working with active learning strategies in science courses.

Meyers, C., and Jones, T. B. *Promoting Active Learning: Strategies for the College Classroom.* San Francisco: Jossey-Bass, 1993. Very well written, with lots of strategies and excellent background information.

Millis, B. J., and Cottell, P. G. *Cooperative Learning for Higher Education Faculty.* Phoenix, Ariz.: ACE/Oryx Press, 1998. A wonderfully comprehensive collection of strategies and information on cooperative learning.

Successful Small Group Dynamics

Groups do not work well automatically, on their own (consider most faculty committees). Those who design and then use group activities must attend to the logistical details that make groups function well. This reading list identifies sources particularly good on the organizational and functional details of effective group work. It is for faculty who use group work (or think they might) and want those groups to function in ways that promote, not inhibit, learning.

Bacon, D. R., Stewart, K. A., and Silver, W. S. "Lessons from the Best and Worst Student Team Experiences: How a Teacher Can Make a Difference." *Journal of Management Education,* 1999, *23*(5), 467–488. A unique study that extrapolates from student reports a series of recommendations for the design and execution of group projects.

Lerner, L. D. "Making Student Groups Work." *Journal of Management Education,* 1995, *19*(1), 123–125. Sanguine, sensible advice on the design and use of group work.

Millis, B. J., and Cottell, P. G. *Cooperative Learning for Higher Education Faculty.* Phoenix, Ariz.: ACE/Oryx Press, 1998. A great book on cooperative learning that includes much group dynamics information.

Tiberius, R. G. *Small Group Teaching: A Trouble-Shooting Guide.* Toronto: Ontario Institute for Studies in Education, 1989. Identifies what can go wrong, how to prevent it, and how to take care of it if it happens.

Woodberry, R. D., and Aldrich, H. W. "Planning and Running Effective Classroom-Based Exercises." *Teaching Sociology,* 2000, *28*(3), 241–248. Advice applicable in many different disciplinary contexts and with many different kinds of in-class activities.

Personal Reports of Experiences with Learner-Centered Teaching

All the sources listed here were written by faculty members who report on experiences related to their efforts to make teaching more learner-centered. Many of these authors are quoted (some at length) in this book. They are reflective and remarkedly candid in the discussion of their teaching experiences. I would call them all learner-centered teachers, but their support is for these approaches generally, not necessarily the specifics laid out in this book. All are writings that have influenced my thinking and have inspired and encouraged me.

Black, K. A. "What to Do When You Stop Lecturing: Become a Guide and a Resource." *Journal of Chemical Education,* 1993, *70*(2), 140–144. A chemistry professor insightfully and reflectively recounts his experiences completely redesigning his chemistry courses.

Brookfield, S. D. *Becoming a Critically Reflective Teacher.* San Francisco: Jossey-Bass, 1995. In addition to introducing critical pedagogy ably, contains many personal experiences and reflections of Brookefield's own growth and development.

Clark, D. C. "High-Risk Teaching." *Teaching Professor,* 1994, *8*(8), 1–2. Reports on experiences of letting students become involved in the evaluation process.

Ditzier, M. A., and Ricci, R. W. "Discovery Chemistry: Balancing Creativity and Structure." *Journal of Chemical Education,* 1993, *71*(8), 685–688. Excellent on how many conclusions students can discover for themselves in a science course.

Felder, R. M., and Brent, R. "Navigating the Bumpy Road to Student-Centered Instruction." *College Teaching,* 1996, *44*(2), 43–47. The best piece I have read that deals with student resistance to learner-centered approaches.

Gallos, J. W. "On the Art of Teaching Management." *Journal of Management Education,* 1997, *21*(4), 445–447. Asks all the right questions about the rationale behind an instructor's approach.

Paulson, D. R. "Active Learning and Cooperative Learning in the Organic Chemistry Lecture Class." *Journal of Chemical Education,* 1999, *76*(8), 1136–1140. An especially good example of how the effects of learner-centered strategies can be assessed.

Tompkins, J. *A Life in School: What the Teacher Learned.* Reading, Mass.: Addison-Wesley, 1996. An amazing personal memoir that chronicles an English professor's growth and development as a teacher.

Walck, C. L. "A Teaching Life." *Journal of Management Education,* 1997, *21*(4), 473–482. Written at midcareer about the elemental aspects of teaching, those assumed or taken for granted

The Literature on Learning: An Eclectic Reading List

This collection of reading material ties closely to the contents of Chapter One. I have assembled a collection of sources that summarize, highlight, and otherwise report on the main areas of work that pertain to learning. I have opted for sources that can be read and understood with relative ease, although not all are easy to read. Literature on learning is like that in all other fields: written for the benefit of those working in the area. The language is not always clear or easily penetrable by those on the outside. The list is not comprehensive; some excellent and definitive sources do not appear. But this is the literature that got me started thinking about learning and the kind of instruction that might best promote it.

Autonomy and Self-Direction in Learning

Boud, D. (ed.). *Developing Student Autonomy in Learning.* London: Kogan Page, 1981. An early anthology that persuasively establishes how education makes students dependent learners; proposes a variety of ways to develop autonomy.

Candy, P. C. *Self-Direction for Lifelong Learning.* San Francisco: Jossey-Bass, 1991. A great source—thorough, well referenced, well organized, and easy to read.

Zimmerman, B. J. "Self-Regulated Learning and Academic Achievement: An Overview." *Educational Psychologist,* 1990, *25*(1),

3–17. Excellent short overview that does well with definitional issues.

Critical and Radical Pedagogy

Braye, S. "Radical Teaching: An Introduction." *Teaching Professor,* 1995, *9*(8), 1–2. A great single-page introduction to radical pedagogy.

Freire, P. *Pedagogy of the Oppressed.* (Rev. ed.) New York: Continuum, 1993. The work (first released in 1970) that some have said will be as significant at the end of the twentieth century as Dewey's *Thought and Action* was at the beginning of the century.

Horton, M., and Freire, P. *We Make the Road by Walking: Conversations on Education and Social Change.* Philadelphia: Temple University Press, 1990. A well-edited conversation between two important and innovative educational theorists.

Giroux, H. A. *Teachers as Intellectuals: Toward a Critical Pedagogy of Learning.* Westport, Conn.: Bergin and Garvey/Greenwood Press, 1988. Not easy reading but a good example of how critical pedagogy moved forward from Freire's first work.

Leistyna, P., Woodrum, A., and Sherblom, S. A. (eds.). *Breaking Free: The Transformative Power of Critical Pedagogy.* Cambridge, Mass.: Harvard Educational Review, 1996. Nice collection of pieces that taken together will enlarge understanding of critical pedagogy.

McLaren, P., and Leonard, P. *Paulo Freire: A Critical Encounter.* New York: Routledge, 1993. Thorough and informative exploration of Freire's work.

Shor, I. *Empowering Education: Critical Teaching for Social Change.* Chicago: University of Chicago Press, 1992. Another key scholar writing in this area; written about education generally, not just higher education.

Feminist Pedagogy

Ellsworth, W. "Why Doesn't This Feel Empowering? Working Through the Repressive Myths of Critical Pedagogy." *Harvard*

Educational Review, 1989, *59*(3), 297–324. A feminist critique of critical pedagogy.

Belenky, M. F., Clinchy, B. M., Goldberger, N. R., and Tarule, J. M. *Women's Ways of Knowing.* New York: Basic Books, 1986. Classic book that challenges long-standing assumptions about the nature of knowledge.

hooks, b. *Teaching to Transgress: Education as the Practice of Freedom.* New York: Routledge, 1994. Superb reflective and personal narrative that explores much of the theory and practice of feminist pedagogy.

Lewis, M. "Interrupting Patriarchy: Politics, Resistance, and Transformation in the Feminist Classroom." *Harvard Educational Review,* 1990, *60*(4), 467–488. Explores the application of feminist pedagogy in the classroom.

Maher, F., and Tetreault, K. T. "Inside Feminist Classrooms: An Enthnographic Approach." In L. Border and N. Chism (eds.), *Teaching for Diversity.* New Directions for Teaching and Learning, no. 49. San Francisco: Jossey-Bass, 1992. A pragmatic piece that addresses the conduct of feminist pedagogy in the classroom.

Constructivism

Fosnot, C. T. (ed.). *Constructivism: Theory, Perspectives and Practice.* New York: College Teachers Press, 1996. Covers a range of topics and issues, all readable and some including practical suggestions.

Jaworski, B. *Investigating Mathematics Teaching: A Constructivist Enquiry.* Bristol, Pa.: Falmer Press, 1994. Considers the application of constructivist theories in a discipline where content is tightly configured and not as geared to discussion.

Prawat, R. S., and Floden, R. E. "Philosophical Perspectives on Constructivist Views of Learning." *Educational Psychology,* 1994, *29*(1), 37–48. Excellent short overview of the philosophical origins and underpinnings of the theory.

Steff, L., and Gale, J. (eds.). *Constructivism in Education.* Hillsdale, N.J.: Erlbaum, 1995. Great collection providing a comprehensive overview of constructivism.

Cognitive and Educational Psychology

Biggs, J. *Teaching for Quality Learning at University: What the Student Does.* Bristol, Pa.: Open University Press, 1999. Excellent book that covers all aspects of instructional practice in terms of research on learning.

Biggs, J. "What the Student Does: Teaching for Enhanced Learning." *Higher Education Research and Development,* 1999, *18*(1), 57–75. An excellent condensation of the book in the previous entry.

Marton, F., Hounsell, D., and Entwistle, N. (eds.). *The Experience of Learning: Implications for Teaching and Studying in Higher Education.* (2nd ed.) Edinburgh: Scottish Academic Press, 1997. Looks at the work and findings precipitated by the classic study cited next.

Marton, F., and Saljo, R. "On Qualitative Differences in Learning— I: Outcome and Process." *British Journal of Educational Psychology,* 1976, *46*(1), 4–11. Classic study that identified deep and surface approaches to learning.

Ramsden, P. (ed.). *Improving Learning: New Perspectives.* London: Kogan Page, 1988. Another outstanding collection that integrates and explores research on learning.

Rawson, M. "Learning to Learn: More Than a Skill Set." *Studies in Higher Education,* 2000, *25*(2), 225–238. Makes a strong case for developing learner self-awareness.

Integrative Overviews

Gardiner, L. F. *Redesigning Higher Education: Producing Dramatic Gains in Student Learning.* Washington, D.C.: ERIC Clearinghouse on Higher Education and the Association for the Study of Higher Education, 1994. Brings together in one place an amazing collection of work on learning, an impressive overview of this vast literature, and sensible recommendations based on the literature

Stage, F. K., Muller, P. A., Kinzie, J., and Simmons, A. *Creating Learner Centered Classrooms: What Does Learning Theory Have to Say?* Washington, D.C.: ERIC Clearinghouse on Higher Education and the Association for the Study of Higher Education, 1998. Superb monograph that clearly and cogently writes about major educational theories; the best introduction and overview of radical pedagogy and constructivism that I have encountered.

References

Allen, J., Fuller, D., and Luckett, M. "Academic Integrity: Behaviors, Rates and Attitudes of Business Students Toward Cheating." *Journal of Marketing Education,* 1998, *20*(1), 41–52.

Amstutz, J. "In Defense of Telling Stories." *Teaching Professor,* 1988, *2*(4), 5.

Angelo, T. A., and Cross, K. P. *Classroom Assessment Techniques: A Handbook for College Teachers.* (2nd ed.) San Francisco: Jossey-Bass, 1993.

Appleby, D. C. "Faculty and Student Perceptions of Irritating Behaviors in the College Classroom." *Journal of Staff, Program, and Organizational Development,* 1990, *8*(1), 41–46.

Aronowitz, A. "Paulo Freire's Radical Democratic Humanism." In P. McLaren and P. Leonard (eds.), *Paulo Freire: A Critical Encounter.* New York: Routledge, 1993.

Astin, A. W. "The Changing American College Student: Thirty-Year Trends, 1966–1996." *Review of Higher Education,* 1998, *21*(2), 115–135.

Ayers, W. "Thinking About Teachers and the Curriculum." *Harvard Educational Review,* 1986, *56*(1), 49–51.

Baecker, D. L. "Uncovering the Rhetoric of the Syllabus." *College Teaching,* 1998, *46*(2), 58–62.

Barnes, C. P. "Questioning in College Classrooms." In C. L. Ellner and C. P. Barnes (eds.), *Studies of College Teaching.* Lexington, Mass.: D. C. Heath, 1983.

Barr, R. B., and Tagg, J. "From Teaching to Learning—A New Paradigm for Undergraduate Education." *Change,* Nov.-Dec. 1995, pp. 13–25.

Barrineau, N. W. "Time to Be a Student Again?" *Teaching Professor,* 2000, *14*(7), 6.

Barton, L. O. "Ten Advantages of a Student-Centered Test Design." *Teaching Professor,* 1994, *8*(1), 4.

Baxter Magolda, M. *Knowing and Reasoning in College: Gender-Related Patterns in Student Development.* San Francisco: Jossey-Bass, 1992.

Bean, J. C. *Engaging Ideas: The Professor's Guide to Integrating Writing, Critical Thinking and Active Learning in the Classroom.* San Francisco: Jossey-Bass, 1996.

Beaty, L. "Consultation Through Action Learning." In C. Knapper and S. Piccinin (eds.), *Using Consultants to Improve Teaching.* New Directions for Teaching and Learning, no. 79. San Francisco: Jossey-Bass, 1999.

Becker, A. H., and Calhoon, S. K. "What Introductory Psychology Students Attend to on a Course Syllabus." *Teaching of Psychology,* 1999, *26*(1), 6–11.

Belenky, M. F., Clinchy, B. M., Goldberger, N. R., and Tarule, J. M. *Women's Ways of Knowing.* New York: Basic Books, 1986.

Benvenuto, M. "Teaching Is Learning—Maximum Incentive, Minimum Discipline in Student Groups Teaching General Chemistry." *Journal of Chemical Education,* 2001, *78*(2), 194–197.

Biggs, J. *Teaching for Quality Learning at University: What the Student Does.* Bristol, Pa.: Open University Press, 1999a.

Biggs, J. "What the Student Does: Teaching for Enhanced Learning." *Higher Education Research and Development,* 1999b, *18*(1), 57–75.

Biggs, J., Kember, D., and Leung, D.Y.P. "The Revised Two-Factor Study Process Questionnaire: R-SPQ-2F." *British Journal of Educational Psychology,* 2001, *71*(Pt. 1), 133–149.

Black, K. A. "What to Do When You Stop Lecturing: Become a Guide and a Resource." *Journal of Chemical Education,* 1993, *70*(2), 140–44.

Boice, B. "Classroom Incivilities." *Research in Higher Education,* 1996, *37*(4), 453–486.

Boud, D. (ed.). *Developing Autonomy in Student Learning.* London: Kogan Page, 1981.

Braye, S. "Radical Teaching: An Introduction." *Teaching Professor,* 1995, *9*(8), 1–2.

Brookfield, S. D. *Becoming a Critically Reflective Teacher.* San Francisco: Jossey-Bass, 1995.

Bruffee, K. A. *Collaborative Learning: Higher Education, Interdependence, and the Authority of Knowledge.* Baltimore, Md.: Johns Hopkins University Press, 1993.

Calandra, A. "Angels on a Pin." *Saturday Review,* Dec. 21, 1968, p. 60.

Candy, P. C. *Self-Direction for Lifelong Learning.* San Francisco: Jossey-Bass, 1991.

Cassini, C. "Collaborative Testing, Grading." *Teaching Professor,* 1994, *8*(4), 5–6.

Chism, N.V.N. *Peer Review of Teaching: A Sourcebook.* Bolton, Mass.: Anker, 1999.

Church, M. A., Elliot, A. J., and Gable, S. L. "Perceptions of Classroom Environment, Achievement Goals and Achievement Outcomes." *Journal of Educational Psychology,* 2001, *93*(1), 43–54.

Clark, D. C. "High-Risk Teaching." *Teaching Professor*, 1994, *8*(8), 1–2.

Covington, M. V. "A Motivational Analysis of Academic Life in College." In R. P. Perry and J. C. Smart (eds.), *Effective Teaching in Higher Education: Research and Practice*. New York: Agathon Press, 1997.

Covington, M. V., and Omelich, C. L. "Controversies or Consistencies: A Reply to Brown and Weiner." *Journal of Educational Psychology*, 1984, *76*(1), 159–168.

Dansereau, D. F., and Newbern, D. "Using Knowledge Maps to Enhance Teaching." In W. E. Campbell and K. A. Smith (eds.), *New Paradigms for College Teaching*. Edina, Minn.: Interaction Book Company, 1997.

Deshler, D. "Metaphors and Values in Higher Education." *Academe*, Nov.-Dec. 1985, pp. 22–29.

Dunn, J. P. "The Winning Teacher: Metaphors from Coaching." *Teaching Professor*, 1992, *6*(9), 1–2.

Ege, S. N., Coppola, B. P., and Lawton, R. G. "The University of Michigan Undergraduate Chemistry Curriculum: 1. Philosophy, Curriculum and the Nature of Change." *Journal of Chemical Education*, 1996, *74*(1), 74–91.

Eisner, E. W. "The Art and Craft of Teaching." *Educational Leadership*, Jan. 1983, pp. 5–13.

Falchikov, N., and Boud, D. "Student Self-Assessment in Higher Education: A Meta-Analysis." *Review of Higher Education Research*, 1989, *59*(4), 395–430.

Fassinger, P. A. "Understanding Classroom Interaction: Students' and Professors' Contributions to Students' Silence." *Journal of Higher Education*, 1995, *66*(1), 82–96.

Fassinger, P. A. "Professors' and Students' Perception of Why Students Participate in Class." *Teaching Sociology*, 1996, *24*(1), 25–33.

Felder, R. M., and Brent, R. "Navigating the Bumpy Road to Student-Centered Instruction." *College Teaching*, 1996, *44*(2), 43–47.

Feldman, K. A. "Effective College Teaching from the Students' and Faculty's View: Matched or Mismatched Priorities?" *Research in Higher Education*, 1988, *28*(4), 291–344.

Finkel, D. L. *Teaching with Your Mouth Shut*. Portsmouth, N.H.: Boynton/Cook Publishers, 2000.

Flachmann, M. "Teaching in the Twenty-First Century." *Teaching Professor*, 1994, *8*(3), 1–2.

Fleming, N. D., and Mills, C. "Not Another Inventory: Rather a Catalyst for Reflection." In D. H. Wulff and J. D. Nyquist (eds.), *To Improve the Academy*. Stillwater, Okla.: New Forums Press, 1992.

Fosnot, C. T. (ed.). *Constructivism: Theory, Perspectives and Practice*. New York: College Teachers Press, 1996.

Fox, D. "Personal Theories of Teaching." *Studies in Higher Education*, 1983, *8*(2), 151–163.

Fraser, B. J. *Classroom Environment*. London: Croom Helm, 1986.

Fraser, B. J. "Twenty Years of Classroom Climate Work: Progress and Prospect." *Journal of Curriculum Studies*, 1989, *21*(4), 307–327.

Fraser, B. J., Giddings, J., and McRobbie, C. J. "Development and Cross-National Validation of a Laboratory Classroom Environment Instrument for Senior High School Science." *Science Education*, 1993, *77*(1), 1–24.

Fraser, B. J., Treagust, D. F., and Dennis, N. C. "Development of an Instrument for Assessing Classroom Psychosocial Environment at Universities and Colleges." *Studies in Higher Education*, 1986, *11*(1), 43–53.

Frederick, P. "The Dreaded Discussion: Ten Ways to Start." *Improving College and University Teaching*, 1981, *29*(3), 109–114.

Freire, P. *Pedagogy of the Oppressed*. New York: Herder and Herder, 1970.

Freire, P. *Pedagogy of the Oppressed*. (Rev. ed.) New York: Continuum, 1993.

Gallagher, T. J. "Embracing Student Evaluations of Teaching: A Case Study." *Teaching Sociology*, 2000, *28*(2), 140–147.

Gardiner, L. F. "Why We Must Change: The Research Evidence." *Thought and Action*, Spring 1998, pp. 71–87.

Garner, M., and Emery, R. A. "A 'Better Mousetrap' in the Quest to Evaluate Instruction." *Teaching Professor*, 1994, *8*(9), 6.

Gaultney, J. F., and Cann, A. "Grade Expectations." *Teaching of Psychology*, 2001, *28*(2), 84–87.

Genereux, R. L., and McLeod, B. A. "Circumstances Surrounding Cheating: A Questionnaire Study of College Students." *Research in Higher Education*, 1995, *36*(6), 687–704.

Gmelch, W. H. *Coping with Faculty Stress*. Thousand Oaks, Calif.: Sage, 1993.

Goza, B. K. "Graffiti Needs Assessment: Involving Students in the First Class Session." *Journal of Management Education*, 1993, *17*(1), 99–106.

Green, D. H. "Student-Generated Exams: Testing and Learning." *Journal of Marketing Education*, 1997, *19*(2), 43–53.

Grow, G. O. "Teaching Learners to Be Self-Directed." *Adult Education Quarterly*, 1991, *41*(3), 125–149.

Hebert, F., and Loy, M. "The Evolution of a Teacher-Professor: Applying Behavior Change Theory to Faculty Development." In D. Lieberman and C. Wehlburg (eds.), *To Improve the Academy, 20*. Bolton, Mass.: Anker Publishing, 2002.

Herreid, C. G. "Case Studies in Science—A Novel Method of Science Education." *Journal of College Science Teaching*, 1994, *23*(4), 221–229.

Herreid, C. G. "Dialogues as Case Studies—A Discussion on Human Cloning." *Journal of College Science Teaching*, 1999, *29*(2), 245–256.

Hill, N. K. "Scaling the Heights: The Teacher as Mountaineer." *Chronicle of Higher Education*, June 16, 1980, p. 48.

Hilsen, L. R. "A Helpful Handout: Establishing and Maintaining a Positive Classroom Climate." In K. H. Gillespie (ed.), *A Guide to Faculty Development: Practical Advice, Examples, and Resources*. Bolton, Mass.: Anker Publishing, 2002.

Hobson, S. M., and Talbot, D. M. "Understanding Student Evaluations: What All Faculty Should Know." *College Teaching*, 2001, *49*(1), 26–31.

Hogan, M. "Taking the Angst out of Returning Papers." *Teaching Professor*, 1994, *8*(10), 6.

hooks, b. *Teaching to Transgress: Education as the Practice of Freedom*. New York: Routledge, 1994.

Horton, M., and Freire, P. *We Make the Road by Walking: Conversations on Education and Social Change*. Philadelphia: Temple University Press, 1990.

Howard, J. R., Short, L. B., and Clark, S. M. "Students' Participation in the Mixed Age Classroom." *Teaching Sociology*, 1996, *24*(1), 8–24.

Hoyt, D., and Perera, S. "Teaching Approach, Instructional Objectives, and Learning." Manhattan, Kans.: IDEA Center, Kansas State University, 2000.

Jacobs, L. C., and Chase, C. I. *Developing and Using Tests Effectively: A Guide for Faculty*. San Francisco: Jossey-Bass, 1992.

Janick, J. "Crib Sheets." *Teaching Professor*, 1990, *4*(6), 2.

Jarvis, P., Holford, J., and Griffin, C. *The Theory and Practice of Learning*. London: Kogan Page, 1998.

Johnson, P. E. "Getting Students to Read the Syllabus: Another Approach." *Teaching Professor*, 2000, *14*(3), 1–2.

Kagan, S. "Group Grades Miss the Mark." *Cooperative Learning and College Teaching*, 1995, *6*(1), 6–8.

Karabenick, S. A. "When Students Need Help." *Journal of Professional Studies*, 1990, *13*(3), 41–56.

Karabenick, S. A. (ed.). *Strategic Help Seeking: Implications for Learning and Teaching*. Hillsdale, N.J.: Erlbaum, 1998.

Karabenick, S. A., and Knapp, J. R. "Help Seeking and the Need for Academic Assistance." *Journal of Educational Psychology*, 1988, *80*(3), 406–408.

Karabenick, S. A., and Knapp, J. R. "Relationship of Academic Help Seeking to the Use of Learning Strategies and Other Instrumental Achievement Behavior in College Students." *Journal of Educational Psychology*, 1991, *83*(2), 221–230.

Kardash, C. M. "Evaluation of an Undergraduate Research Experience: Perceptions of Interns and Their Faculty Mentors." *Journal of Educational Psychology,* 2000, *92*(1), 191–201.

Katz, R. N., and others. *Dancing with the Devil: Information Technology and the New Competition in Higher Education.* San Francisco: Jossey-Bass, 1999.

Kearney, P., and Plax, T. G. "Student Resistance to Control." In V. P. Richmond and J. C. McCroskey (eds.), *Power in the Classroom: Communication, Control, and Concern.* Hillsdale, N.J.: Erlbaum, 1992.

Keeley, S. M., Shemberg, K. M., Cowell, B. S., and Zinnbauer, B. J. "Coping with Student Resistance to Critical Thinking: What the Psychotherapy Literature Can Tell Us." *College Teaching,* 1995, *43*(4), 140–145.

Kember, D., and Gow, L. "Orientations to Teaching and Their Effect on the Quality of Student Learning." *Journal of Higher Education,* 1994, *65*(1), 58–74.

Kiewra, K. A., and others. "Fish Giver or Fishing Teacher? The Lure of Strategy Instruction." *Teaching Professor,* 2001, *15*(2), 4.

King, A. "From Sage on the Stage to Guide on the Side." *College Teaching,* 1993, *41*(1), 30–35.

Kinsella, K., and Sherak, K. "Classroom Work Style Survey." *Teaching Professor,* 1995, *9*(8), 3–4.

Kloss, R. J. "A Nudge Is Best: Helping Students Through the Perry Scheme of Intellectual Development." *College Teaching,* 1994, *42*(4), 151–158.

Knapp, M. L., and Hall, J. A. *Nonverbal Communication in Human Interaction.* (3rd ed.) New York: Holt, Rinehart and Winston, 1992.

Knapper, C. K., and Cropley, A. J. *Lifelong Learning and Higher Education.* London: Croom Helm, 1985.

Knapper, C. K., and Cropley, A. J. *Lifelong Learning in Higher Education.* (3rd ed.) London: Kogan Page, 2000.

Kohn, A. *No Contest: The Case Against Competition.* Boston: Houghton Mifflin, 1986.

Longman, D. G. "Bill of Rights Promotes Study Groups." *Teaching Professor,* 1992, *6*(7), 5–6.

Lyons, P. R. "Assessing Classroom Participation." *College Teaching,* 1989, *37*(1), 36–38.

MacGregor, J. (ed.). *Student Self-Evaluation: Fostering Reflective Learning.* New Directions for Teaching and Learning, no. 56. San Francisco: Jossey-Bass, 1993.

McBrayer, D. J. "Tutoring Helps Improve Test Scores." *Teaching Professor,* 2001, *15*(4), 3.

McCabe, D. L., and Trevino, L. K. "What We Know About Cheating: Longitudinal Trends and Recent Development." *Change,* Jan.-Feb. 1996, *28*(1), 29–33.

Maharaj, S., and Banta, L. "Using Log Assignments to Foster Learning: Revisiting Writing Across the Curriculum." *Journal of Engineering Education,* 2000, *89*(1), 73–77.

Mallinger, M. "Maintaining Control in the Classroom by Giving Up Control." *Journal of Management Education,* 1998, *22*(4), 472–483.

Marini, Z. A. "The Teacher as a Sherpa Guide." *Teaching Professor,* 2000, *14*(4), 5.

Marsh, H. W. "Students' Evaluations of University Teaching: Dimensionality, Reliability, Validity, Potential Biases, and Utility." *Journal of Educational Psychology,* 1984, *76*(5), 707–754.

Marton, F., Hounsell, D., and Entwistle, N. (eds.). *The Experience of Learning: Implications for Teaching and Studying in Higher Education.* (2nd ed.) Edinburgh: Scottish Academic Press, 1997.

Marton, F., and Saljo, R. "On Qualitative Differences in Learning—I: Outcome and Process." *British Journal of Educational Psychology,* 1976, *46*(1), 4–11.

Mealey, D. L., and Host, T. R. "Coping with Test Anxiety." *College Teaching,* 1992, *40*(4), 147–150.

Menges, R. J. "Improving Your Teaching." In W. J. McKeachie, *Teaching Tips: Strategies, Research, and Theory for College and University Teachers.* (9th ed.) Lexington, Mass.: D. C. Heath, 1994.

Mentkowski, M., and others. *Learning That Lasts: Integrating Learning, Development and Performance in College and Beyond.* San Francisco: Jossey-Bass, 2000.

Moulds, R. "An Interactive Annotations Assignment." *Teaching Professor,* 1997, *11*(4), 6.

Mourtos, N. J. "The Nuts and Bolts of Cooperative Learning in Engineering." *Journal of Engineering Education,* 1997, *86*(1), 35–37.

Murray, H. G. "Low-Inference Classroom Teaching Behaviors and Student Ratings of College Teaching Effectiveness." *Journal of Educational Psychology,* 1983, *75*(1), 138–149.

Norcross, J. C., Dooley, H. S., and Stevenson, J. F. "Faculty Use and Justification of Extra Credit: No Middle Ground?" *Teaching of Psychology,* 1993, *20*(4), 240–242.

Norcross, J. C., Horrocks, L. J., and Stevenson, J. F. "Of Barfights and Gadflies: Attitudes and Practices Concerning Extra Credit in College Courses." *Teaching of Psychology,* 1989, *16*(4), 199–203.

Nunn, C. E. "Discussion in the College Classroom: Triangulating Observational and Survey Results." *Journal of Higher Education,* 1996, *67*(3), 243–66.

O'Banion, T. *Creating More Learning-Centered Community Colleges.* Mission Viejo, Calif.: League for Innovation in the Community College, 1997.

O'Neill, K. L., and Todd-Mancillas, W. R. "An Investigation into the Types of Turning Point Events Affecting Relational Change in Student-Faculty Interactions." *Innovative Higher Education,* 1992, *16*(4), 277–290.

Oddi, L. S. "Development and Validation of an Instrument to Identify Self-Directed Continuing Learners." *Adult Education Quarterly,* 1986, *36*(2), 97–107.

Pascarella, E. T., and Terenzini, P. T. *How College Affects Students.* San Francisco: Jossey-Bass, 1991.

Perry, R. P. "Perceived Control in College Students: Implications for Instruction in Higher Education." In R. P. Perry and J. C. Smart (eds.), *Effective Teaching in Higher Education: Research and Practice.* New York: Agathon Press, 1997.

Perry, R. P., and Magnusson, J.-L. "Effective Instruction and Students' Perceptions of Control in the College Classroom: Multiple-Lectures Effects." *Journal of Educational Psychology,* 1987, *79*(4), 453–460.

Perry, Jr., W. G. *Forms of Intellectual and Ethical Development in the College Years: A Scheme.* New York: Holt, Rinehart, and Winston, 1968.

Perry, Jr., W. G. *Forms of Intellectual and Ethical Development in the College Years: A Scheme.* San Francisco: Jossey-Bass, 1999.

Pollio, H. R., and Beck, H. P. "When the Tail Wags the Dog: Perceptions of Learning and Grade Orientation in and by Contemporary College Students and Faculty." *Journal of Higher Education,* 2000, *71*(1), 84–102.

Pollio, H. R., and Humphreys, W. W. "Grading Students." In J. H. McMillan (ed.), *Assessing Students' Learning.* New Directions for Teaching and Learning, no. 34. San Francisco: Jossey-Bass, 1988.

Qin, Z., Johnson, D. W., and Johnson, R. T. "Cooperative versus Competitive Efforts and Problem Solving." *Review of Research,* 1995, *65*(2), 129–143.

Ramsden, P. "Studying Learning: Improving Teaching." In P. Ramsden (ed.), *Improving Learning: New Perspectives.* London: Kogan Page, 1988.

Rawson, M. "Learning to Learn: More Than a Skill Set." *Studies in Higher Education,* 2000, *25*(2), 225–238.

Rusth, D. B. "Two-Try Testing." *Teaching Professor,* 1996, *10*(6), 6.

Sahadeo, D., and Davis, W. E. "Review—Don't Repeat." *College Teaching,* 1988, *36*(3), 111–113.

Sarros, J. C., and Densten, I. L. "Undergraduate Student Stress and Coping Strategies." *Higher Education Research and Development,* 1989, *8*(1), 1–13.

Sessoms, J. L. "Letting Students Select Paper Due Dates." *Teaching Professor,* 2001, *15*(4), 2.

Shrock, A. A. "The Sign at the Side of the Door." *Teaching Professor,* 1992, *6*(6), 8.

Siegel, R. " 'This Is You:' Writing Well and the Case Method." *Teaching Professor,* 1993, *7*(8), 5.

Silverman, R., and Welty, W. M. *Case Studies for Faculty Development.* White Plains, N.Y.: Pace University, 1992.

Springer, L., Stanne, M. E., and Donovan, S. "Effects of Small Group Learning on Undergraduates in Science, Mathematics, Engineering and Technology: A Meta-Analysis." Paper presented at the annual meeting of the Association for Higher Education, Albuquerque, N.M., 1997.

St. Clair, K. L. "A Case Against Compulsory Class Attendance Policies in Higher Education." *Innovative Higher Education,* 1999, *23*(3), 171–180.

Stage, F. K., Muller, P. A., Kinzie, J., and Simmons, A. *Creating Learner Centered Classrooms: What Does Learning Theory Have to Say?* Washington, D.C.: ERIC Clearinghouse on Higher Education and the Association for the Study of Higher Education, 1998.

Starling, R. "Professor as Student: The View from the Other Side." *College Teaching,* 1987, *35*(1), 3–7.

Strommer, D. W., and Erickson, B. E. *Teaching College Freshmen.* San Francisco: Jossey-Bass, 1991.

Tichenor, L. L. "Student-Designed Physiology Labs." *Journal of College Science Teaching,* Dec. 1996-Jan. 1997, *20*(3), 175–181.

Tompkins, J. "Teaching Like It Matters." *Lingua Franca,* Aug. 1991, pp. 24–27.

Upcraft, M. L. "Teaching and Today's College Students." In R. J. Menges, M. Weimer, and others, *Teaching on Solid Ground: Using Scholarship to Improve Practice.* San Francisco: Jossey-Bass, 1996.

VanderStoep, S. W., Fagerlin, A., and Feenstra, J. S. "What Do Students Remember from Introductory Psychology?" *Teaching of Psychology,* 2000, *27*(2), 89–92.

Vella, J. *Taking Learning to Task.* San Francisco: Jossey-Bass, 2000.

Weimer, M. "Cost-Benefit Testing." *Teaching Professor,* 1988a, *2*(5), 5.

Weimer, M. "What Should Future Teaching Be Like?" *Teaching Professor,* 1988b, *2*(2), 1.

Weimer, M. "Exams: Alternative Ideas and Approaches." *Teaching Professor,* 1989, *3*(8), 3–4

Weimer, M. *Improving College Teaching.* San Francisco: Jossey-Bass, 1990.

Weimer, M. "Extra Credit: Taking Sides and Offering Advice." *Teaching Professor,* 1991, *5*(3), 5–6.

Weimer, M. "Participation: Verifying and Refining What We Know." *Teaching Professor,* 1996, *10*(7), 1–5.

Weinstein, C. E., Palmer, D. R., and Hanson, G. R. *Perceptions, Expectations, Emotions and Knowledge About College.* Clearwater, Fla.: H and H Publishing, 1995.

Weinstein, C. E., Schulte, A. C., and Palmer, D. R. *Learning and Study Strategies Inventory.* Clearwater, Fla.: H and H Publishing, 1987.

Wingspread Group on Higher Education. *An American Imperative: Higher Expectations for Higher Education.* Racine, Wis.: Johnson Foundation, 1993.

Winston Jr., R. B., and others. "A Measure of College Classroom Climate: The College Classroom Environment Scales." *Journal of College Student Development,* 1994, *35*(1), 11–35.

Woods, D. R. "How Might I Teach Problem Solving?" In J. E. Stice (ed.), *Developing Critical Thinking and Problem-Solving Abilities.* New Directions for Teaching and Learning, no. 30. San Francisco: Jossey-Bass, 1987.

Woods, D. R. "Participation Is More Than Attendance." *Journal of Engineering Education,* 1996, *85*(3), 177–181.

Zimmerman, B. J. "Self-Regulated Learning and Academic Achievement: An Overview." *Educational Psychologist,* 1990, *25*(1), 3–17.

Index

Teaching: authoritarian, 9, 23–28, 96, 97–99; changes required in, 8–17; orientations to, 14. *See also* Learner-centered teaching

Teaching College Freshmen (Stommer and Erickson), 167

Teaching Goals Inventory, 195–196

Teaching Professor, 214, 215, 218, 219, 220, 222

Techniques: appeal of, 185–186, 190–191; thinking beyond, 185–186

Telling, doing less, 83–85

"Ten Commandments for Effective Study Skills," 213, 215–217

Tenure decisions: faculty resistance and, 163; instructional assessment and, 197

Terenzini, P. T., 177

Test and exam questions: cost-benefit approach to, 136–137; extra credit, 136; student challenges of, 138; student development of, 38, 62, 134–135, 136, 137, 142–143

Test and exam results: debriefing, 137–138; poor, responsibility for, 111–112; using, to promote self-awareness, 65–66, 111–112

Tests and exams: answer-changing on, 65–66; construction principles for, 129; group, 88–90, 135, 142–143; hidden agenda in, 127–129; in learning-centered evaluation, 16–17, 133–138; review for, 38, 126, 133–135; stress reduction for, 126–127; using, to promote learning, 133–138; using, to promote self-awareness, 65–66. *See also* Evaluation

Textbook discussion skills, self-awareness development and, 64

Textbook selection, 29

Theory: on balance of power, 8–10; on content, 10–13; on evaluation, 16–17; overview of, 8–17; on responsibility for learning, 15–16; on teacher role, 13–15

Thien, S. J., 214

Threatened, feeling: as source of faculty resistance, 162; as source of student resistance, 151–152, 159–160

Tichenor, L. L., 39

Time on task, 31

Tinkering with teaching, 188–190

Todd-Mancillas, W. R., 171

Tompkins, J., 9

Transformation. *See* Improvement, instructional

Treagust, D. F., 100, 101, 109

Trevino, L. K., 121

Turning points, 171

Two-try testing, 136

U

Upcraft, M. L., 96

V

VanderStoep, S. W., 165

Vella, J., 71

Volunteering *versus* being called on, 36

von Glaserfeld, E., 12

Vulnerability, teacher, 26–28, 193–194

Vygotsky, L., 12

W

Weimer, M., 4–5, 36, 49, 127, 136–137, 185, 187, 219

Weinstein, C. E., 59

"What-most-irritates-you" question, 110–111

Wingspread Group on Higher Education, 18

Winston, Jr., R. B., 100

Women's psychology, 7, 13, 176. *See also* Feminist pedagogy

Women's Ways of Knowing (Belenky et. al), 13

Woods, D. R., 37, 50, 140

Writing Across the Curriculum movement, 141

www.active-learning-site.com, 59, 196